D0891739

*A Provincial Elite
in Early Modern Tuscany*

✦

The Johns Hopkins University
Studies in Historical and Political Science
114TH SERIES (1996)

A Provincial Elite in Early Modern Tuscany

✦

Family and Power in the Creation of the State

GIOVANNA BENADUSI

THE JOHNS HOPKINS UNIVERSITY PRESS

BALTIMORE AND LONDON

© 1996 The Johns Hopkins University Press
All rights reserved. Published 1996
Printed in the United States of America on acid-free paper

05 04 03 02 01 00 99 98 97 96   5 4 3 2 1

The Johns Hopkins University Press
2715 North Charles Street
Baltimore, Maryland 21218-4319
The Johns Hopkins Press Ltd., London

ISBN 0-8018-5248-X

Library of Congress Cataloging in Publication Data
will be found at the end of this book.
A catalog record for this book is available from the British Library.

To MARIA GRAZIA NICCOLAI BENADUSI
and GIANCARLO BENADUSI

Contents

Figures and Tables

Figures

Tables

Acknowledgments

During the years in which this book took shape I received help, support, and advice from many institutions, scholars, mentors, and friends. Each encouraged me to rethink issues, explore different questions, and broaden my conceptual boundaries. They all made me aware that although writing a book is an intensely lonely and private experience, it is also a public and collaborative effort.

Research for this book was funded by a number of institutions and made possible by the professional help of several people. I am pleased to acknowledge the financial support of the American Council of Learned Societies, the National Endowment for the Humanities, Syracuse University, and the University of South Florida. I am also most grateful for their special assistance to the staff and personnel of the Archivio di Stato in Florence and the Inter-Library Loan Office at the University of South Florida. I wish to thank Alka Indurkhya for her invaluable help in producing the graphs and tables in this book. In particular I would like to express my gratitude and friendship to Alessandro Brezzi for facilitating my research in the Poppi archives.

At different stages and in various settings I presented my research findings to a number of friends and scholars and greatly benefited from their incisive suggestions. In Italy I owe a special mention to Renzo Pecchioli and Giovanni Cherubini, who first encouraged me to study provincial society in early modern Tuscany. Paolo Pirillo, Isabelle Chabot, Michael Rocke, Daniela Lombardi, and Riccardo Spinelli shared with me ideas about research and history and offered hospitality to an uprooted scholar. I owe an immeasurable debt to Ann Fraser Ottanelli for the continuous assistance that considerably improved the style and the substance of the book. For many years Giancarlo Benadusi carried out the arduous responsibilities of an unpaid research assistant. In the United States a number of scholars and friends contributed to enrich my project and improve the book, particularly Cissie Fairchilds, Dennis Romano, Carol Manning, Laurie Nussdorfer, and Jules Kirshner. For reading the manuscript in its entirety and providing useful suggestions I wish to thank Thomas Cohen and Samuel K. Cohn Jr.

Colleagues and friends at the University of South Florida created a supportive and friendly environment. Peggy Cornett, Sylvia Wood, and Gail Smith contributed precious daily assistance. William Murray helped me save essential data when my computer crashed. Robert Ingalls provided release time from teaching and service so that I could write the manuscript. Nancy Hewitt (now at Duke University) read my dissertation; Kathleen Paul and Louis A. Perez Jr. (now at the University of North Carolina, Chapel Hill) read portions of the manuscript and offered intellectual stimulation and companionship. I am especially indebted to them for their sharp comments and heartening counsel and for doing their best to simplify and clarify my prose. Laurel Graham, Laura Edwards, Ward Stavig, and Ella Schmidt provided moral support and welcome distractions. I wish to thank Jennifer Friedman for always being there when I needed commiseration and reassurance, and Deborah Weissman for her affection. Marco Orrù has been a friend and an intellectual companion. He was always ready to share his time with me and hear out my ideas, read extensive portions of the manuscript, provided insightful comments, and offered advice on statistical matters. Most of all, his logical rigor helped me rethink and reorganize many early drafts of my research.

During the last ten years I have benefited from an ongoing dialogue with a group of friends and mentors who supported this project since it was a dissertation topic. Their interest in and enthusiasm for my work have been and are an inspiration. Anthony Molho encouraged intellectual rigor and stimulation from the moment I set foot in the Florentine archives. Judith Brown offered extensive comments, constant encouragement, and supportive criticisms throughout her numerous readings of my work, always gracefully compelling me to rethink and clarify my argument. Edward Muir first directed my interests toward social history. Throughout the years he provided help in many different ways. Most of all, he always reminded me to look at the larger purpose in our endeavor to understand past societies and cultures.

Finally, my family helped create a reassuring and encouraging environment. I am grateful to Ann Fraser Ottanelli and Vittorio Ottanelli for their help and warmth. Fraser Ottanelli has lived with this book as long as I have and did his best to maintain my belief in the strength of this project. He contributed to it in more ways than I can name. Since their births, Carlo and Vittorio Benadusi Ottanelli shared with me my worries and struggles while providing the every-day love and humor much needed to keep me sane. I am indebted to my parents, who have always given me confidence and support. This book is dedicated to them.

Abbreviations and Dates

Abbreviations

ACA   Archivio Comunale di Arezzo
ASF   Archivio di Stato di Firenze
ASP   Archivio di Stato di Pisa
AVA   Archivio Vescovile di Arezzo
AVP   Archivio Vicariale di Poppi
BCP   Biblioteca Comunale di Poppi
BNF   Biblioteca Nazionale di Firenze

Dates

Since the Florentine year began on March 25, all the dates between January 1 and March 24 have been converted to the Gregorian calendar.

A Provincial Elite
in Early Modern Tuscany

✦

✦

Introduction

This book examines the lives of provincial elites, the women and men who lived at the edge of power but who contributed to the creation of new regional states. It is also about the Florentine territorial state as it developed into a more complex and unified regional system. Attention is given to the collective experiences of Tuscan provincial families and the ways that power and resistance operated at the everyday level of social relations, both in the private sphere and in the public space. Through these experiences we are able to understand the processes by which class, gender constructs, and relations of authority were created and reinforced in early modern Tuscany.

The evolution of the state is a central theme of late Renaissance and early modern historiography. One of the principal issues in the debate involves the transformation of fragmented and divided territorial units into more unified and centralized political entities. Between the fifteenth and seventeenth centuries, European rulers steadily expanded state institutions and strengthened their authority over local powers. During this same period, the Italian territorial states and the republican city-states were replaced by more centralized regional political entities. Florence stands out among the new Italian regional states.

The Florentine polity underwent significant changes over three centuries. By the 1440s nearly all towns, fiefs, and territories surrounding Florence had lost their independence and passed under Florentine political control.[1] The Florentine territorial state became fully established and organized as a confederation of city-states which, although dominated by Florence, preserved their laws and territories (*contadi*). Between the 1490s and the 1520s foreign invasions, domestic turmoil, plagues, and business failures hastened the consolidation of central authority as the administrative and judicial prerogatives previously granted to provincial communities were lessened.

During the second half of the sixteenth century, however, after the Medici reasserted their rule over Florence and enlarged their dominion with the conquest of Siena and its territories, the old structures of the republic were consolidated and adapted to the new political, economic, and social environment of a regional system. An expanded peripheral bureaucracy and a centralized legal system backed by a permanent military structure linked all parts of the dominion to the capital city and unified the Medici authority.[2] Examples of the centralizing reforms introduced by the Florentine grand dukes include Cosimo I's creation of the new magistracy of the Nove Conservatori della Giurisdizione e del Dominio and the unification of the juridical system by Ferdinand I. The Medici policy of undermining the political autonomy of local governments and creating new provincial elites employed in the state bureaucracy and loyal to the ruling house also contributed to the consolidation of a more centralized regional state.

The historiography of the state derives its interpretative orientation from a variety of sources. Between the 1850s and the 1950s the classic works of Jacob Burckhardt, who conceived of the state as a work of art, and Max Weber, who emphasized the creation of impersonal bureaucracies, dominated the image of the early modern state. They identified the state with the policies and personalities of central rulers and the activities of new bureaucracies. Their research stressed centralization and absolutism as the main characteristics of early modern European political systems.[3] This interpretation strongly influenced the scholarship dealing with the formation of the Italian regional state.

A historiographical tradition embracing Francesco Guicciardini in the sixteenth century to Benedetto Croce in the 1920s and 1930s depicted the sixteenth and seventeenth centuries as a period of political crisis in Italy, characterized by the collapse of republican governments, the loss of Italian independence, and foreign domination.[4] The political and moral decline of Italian society and polity was further emphasized when placed against a European background, where centralization and absolutism triumphed. These conditions thus became the reasons why Italy had failed to develop the territorial nation-state like other European powers. Consequently, historians dealing with the formation of the Italian states consistently minimized the importance of this period and directed their attention to what appeared as the more glorious centuries in Italian history: the Renaissance, or the early nineteenth century, the Risorgimento.[5]

At the beginning of the twentieth century, Antonio Anzilotti and Federigo Chabod began to reconsider the political developments of the sixteenth century in relation to the emergence of the Italian regional state.[6] First Anzilotti in 1910 with Tuscany, and later Chabod in the 1930s with Milan, pointed to the sixteenth century as the time when Italian regional rulers, like monarchs in other European countries, consolidated their power. Anzilotti detailed the absolutism of the Medici ruler Duke Cosimo I, and Chabod explored the development of the Milanese state bureaucracy. Anzilotti considered the personality of Duke Cosimo as the central force behind reforms intended to guarantee public order and equality among all subjects. These themes were further explored by Danilo Marrara in 1965.[7] He focused, however, on the centralization of power by examining the institutional reforms of the first Medici ruler. Marrara stressed the traditional idea that Cosimo de' Medici established in Florence the basis for a modern principate in the form of a "monarchic-absolutist" state like the ones in the rest of Europe.[8]

Thus from Anzilotti to Marrara developments in Tuscan scholarship followed a European-wide interpretative tradition central to which was the proposition that the state was linked to the person and policies of Duke Cosimo. This interpretation also advanced a linear model of state formation. In this unilateral vision of state building, the perspective was limited to the role of the dominant city and reductively fixed the formative years of the regional state to the first half of the sixteenth century.

In recent decades historians have challenged the traditional approach by going beyond central institutions to incorporate peripheral areas. During the 1970s, European scholarship on state formation began to redefine the meaning of political centralization and absolutism as the political system of sixteenth- and seventeenth-century Europe. Historians of France followed the pioneer works of Pierre Goubert. They discovered weaknesses in the absolutist institutions of Louis XIV and identified resistance within provincial societies.[9] Italian historians worked along similar lines. Their studies argued that the reforms of the rulers coexisted with persistent local autonomy in the provinces of Italian regional states.[10] Elena Fasano

Guarini found evidence of this persistent duality of power in the Medicean state. She established continuity between republican institutions and the Medicean state structure. In the sixteenth century, Fasano Guarini argued, Cosimo and his successors consolidated governmental structures without changing institutions established earlier in the fifteenth century. She thus presented the evolution of the Tuscan regional state as a continuous process from the fifteenth to the eighteenth century, when Tuscany began to be administered by the rulers from the house of Lorraine.[11]

The new research has broadened our understanding of the institutional foundations of central powers. But it still has retained much of the traditional narrow scope in which emphasis is given to measuring the strength of central authority rather than appreciating the role of the periphery in state building. The assumption that a new geographical dimension should be added to the debate on state building has been particularly congenial to a new generation of institutional historians who have seized the suggestion. They have transcended the old institutional approach and by accentuating the role of provincial elites and class interests have presented the process of state formation as a socially embedded one.[12] In the past ten years, scholars have analyzed the dynamics of state building either in terms of alliances between the state and provincial notables—as William Beik argues about French absolutism—or, as in the case of historians of Italy, in terms of shifting interests of local elites from provincial politics to the larger context of the state through bureaucratic careers.[13]

A substantial amount of literature now exists on the socioeconomic and political changes surrounding the consolidation of the state and their effects on the subject communities. Historians have, to be sure, opened new methodological possibilities with important implications for understanding the internal dynamics of state formation, but they have also maintained conservative traits by embracing a selective process and a unilateral interpretation of the early modern state. Most important, scholarship has not dealt with the active role of peripheral towns in shaping the process of state consolidation. The periphery has instead often been addressed as a passive party in an otherwise complex process, as simply a context acted upon from above by the institutional and political reforms enacted by early modern rulers in the process of centralization.

In accordance with this position, historians of early modern Tuscany have examined provincial elites as two separate and distinct

groups. The elites who remained in provincial towns have been analyzed as representative of local ruling groups who through a monopoly of local power and resources influenced their immediate society. The second group of elites, those who moved to the capital and
filled the high-ranking positions in the state administration, have
been singled out as the new regional elites that contributed to state
consolidation.[14] However, not all leading provincial families were
aristocrats, wealthy merchants, businessmen, large landowners, and
major officeholders. Not all were granted the high honors usually
conferred on wealthier provincial notables, such as Florentine citizenship, professional advancement to high-ranking positions in the
bureaucracy and in courtly services, and membership in the prestigious Order of Santo Stefano, created by Duke Cosimo in 1562.[15] Finally, many did not move from their municipal context into the
wider setting of the regional state.

The traditional emphasis on professional achievements in a centralized state bureaucracy has led historians to emphasize flight from
the municipal world as the principal means by which provincial notables transformed themselves from a local to a regional elite and became the privileged vehicles for the consolidation of the state.[16] This
approach views state formation as a process that compares and separates one source of power (central) with the other (local), without
fully considering the complexity of the relations between the numerous constituencies of the state. Furthermore, the division between
local and regional elites suggests the existence of two distinct contexts in which two substantially different groups acted independently. Control of central structures is thus achieved only at the expense of peripheral powers, thereby precluding the possibility of
their interaction on common ground. This assumption puts institutions above society. It encourages the premise that the capital city
played a more important role than did the periphery and that the
wealthiest, most prominent political elites were the dominant historical subjects in state consolidation.

The significance attached to bureaucratic careers has also emphasized politics as the dominant means through which to examine the
formation of the state. Emphasis on professional achievements has
come at the expense of local female notables and lesser elite men
who did not gain access to high positions in the state administration
and who, consequently, are relegated to a passive role in the dynamics of state building.[17]

The historical reality studied in the present volume suggests a different contextual perspective with multiple social dimensions. I argue that the history of the early modern state cannot be comprehended independent of its communities' specific contributions and without grasping the different spheres of social interaction that shaped people's lives and everyday experiences.[18] For this reason I have studied the families of shopkeepers, wool producers, landholders, notaries, and military officers who lived in Poppi, in northeastern Tuscany, between 1440 and the early 1700s.

The actions and choices of provincial notables were by and large unexceptional. In contrast with what occurred in other Tuscan towns such as Pistoia and Pisa, the Poppi families did not provoke tumultuous struggles by asking for more autonomy from the Florentine government. Consequently they did not directly influence the political actions of central rulers. Poppi families did not make a dramatic and direct impact on the larger political reality of the Tuscan state. But their collective stories are nevertheless significant. Familial and communal relations in Poppi reveal what the state looked like "in the village," in the municipal environment as well as in the day-to-day relations with the larger society and polity.[19] The ordinary lives of the women and men of the Poppi provincial elite reveal the political nature of human experience and show the private dimensions of political life. They thus suggest a way to understand the fragile and evasive implications of power relations in connection with both public and private life and the pressures produced by broader Italian and European events.

The study of family strategies of the lesser elites of Poppi provides a way to explore the multitude of experiences that framed the process of state consolidation. Despite Tamara Hareven's stress on the family as an active participant in the larger historical process, the family has not been sufficiently regarded as playing a definitive role in the consolidation of the state.[20] Family and state have instead been treated as two separate historiographical issues. Historians of the family have analyzed family patterns in relation to socioeconomic and demographic trends but have rarely related them to state politics. The family has often been seen as affected by the institutional and political reforms of early modern European rulers in centralizing and strengthening their power but unable to affect the dynamics of state formation.[21]

Lesser provincial elites were not passive players in a larger socioeconomic and political drama. On the contrary, they were important historical subjects participating in the complex dynamics of domination and subjugation in which the process of state building was enmeshed. Provincial elite families forged marriage alliances, strategized professional and financial decisions, and articulated distinct patrimonial practices. They made decisions, they fashioned choices, they selected lines of action, always as part of larger strategies in an intelligible social system that gave order to their world. In turn, this social system helped them endure changes and served to fashion their lives and the society in which they lived.

Concentration on the politics of provincial families adds a crucial dimension to the complex dynamics of state formation by bringing together social history, gender, economic development, and political history. Methodologically I combined different approaches. From social history I borrowed the statistical approach, which, by showing long-term collective trends, liberates the previously silent endeavors of ordinary people.[22] I also employed the microhistorical approach, which underscores the importance of individual experiences and the contextualization of social representation. By favoring the narrative of the sources this method gives full voice to the historical subjects and thus allows diverse forms of participation and expression to emerge.[23] At the same time, however, diversity notwithstanding, the communities of the state and their people collectively shared the constraints and the commitments of the state as a whole. Finally, the insights of both historical sociology and anthropology suggested a variety of analytical approaches to conceive of politics and power. I have considered them not as autonomous spheres but as mediated by a web of diverse social and personal interactions that shape and reproduce all areas of society.[24]

The first three chapters in Part I set the context in which relations occurred and introduce the players of the story: the community and the central government, the local ruling families and the Florentine rulers and functionaries. In 1444 Poppi was incorporated into the Florentine state. Over the next 150 years families of wool manufacturers, shopkeepers, petty landowners, and notaries emerged at the leadership of the political life of the community and created an oligarchic form of government. They established a monopoly over the highest political and administrative offices in the community and concentrated the greater part of local wealth in their own hands. During the same time, the Florentine government began to systematize its authority. The tendency to lessen the administrative and judicial autonomy of local institutions combined with the emergence of the local ruling class. This section concludes with an examination of the changing dynamics of power and authority in provincial society. Local ruling families consolidated their control over the local government at the same time that the Tuscan territorial state was transformed into a complex and unified regional system.

Part II analyzes the familial strategies of the Poppi elite between the sixteenth and the early seventeenth centuries. It identifies the mechanisms through which the local ruling class maintained a hold on the municipal government and society at the time the Medici rulers sought to centralize power. The leading Poppi families distinguished themselves by wealth, family tradition, service in the professions, participation and office holding in the municipal government, and successful intermarriage with other families. In this period they reevaluated their financial interests, family traditions, and professional goals in the context of broader conjunctures and political circumstances. The redefinition of familial and communal relations and interests allowed the leading families of Poppi to preserve their preeminent position within the town and in time elaborate new family strategies and thus refashion their social identity.

Part III shows the consolidation of provincial elites. The leading families abandoned their traditional artisanal activities to become large property owners. Many changed their career strategies from notarial activity to pursue opportunities in law, medicine, the church, and especially the military. By the end of the seventeenth century, new professions and broadened matrimonial exchanges had contributed to the creation of a strong social group bound together by common economic interest, a shared commitment to the new state, and common family ties. The changes in the family politics of the Poppi elite were a result of its growing sense as a new regional patriciate. The Poppi elite also played a major role in the shaping of a new relationship between provincial communities and the central government. Shifting familial and communal politics contributed to the formation of the regional state by promoting a unified and homogeneous definition of what it meant to be a regional elite.

Local notables and the provincial societies to which they belonged played an important role in the process of state growth. This book shows first that the impulse for the formation of a regional elite came from the diverse and often divergent family strategies devised by provincial notables within their local societies. Impetus for the emergence of a regional elite came further from participation in the administration of the state. Provincial elites followed different paths to achieve success as members of both their communities and the regional state. These paths varied according to changes that occurred in the social, cultural, and economic world of provincial Tuscany. No less important in forging strategies to redefine the family were changes in the process of state consolidation in the periphery.

By addressing the history of the state and its connection with the history of provincial families, I have reexamined some of the central issues of the historiography on state building. This approach goes beyond traditional interpretations of the state which use urban, patrilineal, hierarchical, and male-defined categories of analysis to redraw the conceptual uniformity that precludes space for class, gender, and contextual diversity. Clearly the political and economic relationship between peripheral societies and the Florentine government was often one of subordination and dominance. But if provincial society and its elites were restrained, they still acted. The women and men of provincial Tuscany developed strategies to influence the very system that dominated them and in the process redefined concepts of power and domination and influenced state building in decisive ways.

I

✦

The Structures of Power

Throughout the early modern time, in Tuscany, local and central structures of power were in constant fluctuation. During the fifteenth century the formation of the state was reflected in the organization of new political and administrative units, as vicariates and *podesterie* were established. These developments suggest changes in the territorial configuration of the state as towns, cities, and rural villages were grouped together. They also reveal the unfolding of new forms of authority between the fifteenth century and the rise of the Medicean grand duchy in the sixteenth century.

The creation of peripheral and local administrative structures was part of a broader scheme conceived and sustained by Florence to consolidate its authority. The republican government encouraged rural districts and towns to draft new statutes and to practice self-government. Municipal councils and local magistracies were intended to maintain social order in the dominion and to provide an intermediary support system for the transmission of directives from central administration to peripheral bureaucracies. The new provincial administrative structures thus were the privileged channel through which the Florentine government exercised its control over the dominion. By using this policy the central government created more uniform and stable state structures. It also fostered the creative energy of peripheral communes aimed at establishing their own politico-administrative tradition.[1]

Between the last decades of the fifteenth century and the middle of the sixteenth, international and domestic turmoil and recurring epidemics led the Florentine government to increase its control over the dominion and to strengthen central authority. Rising European and Italian powers selected the Italian peninsula as the ground on which to unfold the drama of international and national rivalries. In 1494 the Medici were expelled from Florence. The republican regime that followed ended in 1512. Over the next twenty years Florence saw one last attempt at republicanism, between 1527 and 1530, and the return of the Medici first in 1512 and again, for good, in 1530. These years of factionalism, political turmoil, plague, and ruin resulted in the restriction of provincial autonomy and the suppression of local privileges.

When the Medici returned to Florence in 1530, they began ruling as dukes. In 1559 they further acquired the title of grand dukes of Tuscany. From this date they became the principal holders of power in the city and in the dominion, and their authority remained unchallenged until the extinction of their line with the death of Gian Gastone in 1737.[2] The new princely rule of the Medici established a state based on a court nobility and privileged networks of patronage. They centralized the institutions of the state and made them instruments of their personal rule. In particular, during the rule of Cosimo I, control over local administration tightened as municipal autonomies were weakened. Fasano Guarini has seen evidence of this change in the increased participation of central functionaries in drafting the new statutes. The reduction of vital aspects of local administration, which now fell under the control of new magistrature such as the Nove Conservatori, created by Cosimo in 1560, also testified to the changing politics of the first Medici grand dukes. By the end of the sixteenth century, the development of new institutions and the decline in provincial autonomy led to a more centralized and authoritarian state organization.

The Florentine government developed new administrative institutions that undermined the political and economic independence of provincial towns. At the same time, however, local ruling families elaborated new political strategies in order to preserve their political control over the town. These families successfully located and manipulated local areas of power which the centralizing efforts had not invaded by relying on family relationships, friendship loyalties, and collective interests. The relationship that unfolded between local rulers and central power led to a state with more unified and authoritarian structures and a provincial society with more elitist forms of social and political organizations.

The next three chapters provide an analysis of the political changes in provincial society and the mechanisms through which local families shaped the municipal government and maintained a hold on the town politics. Central rulers and local powers underwent a process of redefinition of their political rights. They grew together, forged parallel strategies aimed at consolidating their authorities, and strove to maintain social and political stability in their community and in the state. Ultimately, their relationship involved a constant renegotiation of power and redefinition of political dynamics.

ONE

♦

The Local Setting
Poppi and the Casentino

The traveler who goes to Poppi from Florence follows the course of the Arno east as far as Pontassieve. Just past the town one turns off the main highway and starts up the Flaminia Minor, an ancient Roman road that climbs northeast in the midst of evergreen forests to the Consuma Pass at the top. From here the road descends in a series of sharp turns, and after a few kilometers the Casentino Valley appears in a splendid view, its hills crowned by villages and castles and the whole encircled by the wooded chain of the Apennines. Poppi stands at a height of 427 meters on one of these hills, which is surmounted at its highest point by the crenelated castle of the Counts Guidi, feudal overlords of the Casentino until 1440, when the area was annexed to Florence.

Since the tenth century the Guidi were probably among the most powerful feudal families in Tuscany, lords of vast holdings that extended from the Casentino to the Romagna and to the Pistoiese.[1] In the twelfth century, the upper Casentino officially became a feudal province under the *signoria* of the Counts Guidi by the privilege granted them by Emperor Frederick I Barbarossa. The earliest documents about the Guidi of Poppi date from 1150, when the town became one of the political centers of the family. Initially, the Counts Guidi of Poppi lived in a tower of which a ruin remains today. Only later, in the mid-thirteenth century, were the town walls and the castle itself built as evidence of the transformation of Poppi from a strategic center to a socioeconomic and residential community.[2] During the early 1300s the Guidi fell into decline. Following a series of fratricidal wars, the numerous branches of the family lost their former unity and fragmented their patrimony. This fragmentation has been seen in the family's inheritance policy, which did not follow the principle of primogeniture. During the first half of the fourteenth century, patrimonial divisions among the many offspring of Guido Guerra III occasioned resentments and differences that degenerated into the destruction of the Guidi family.[3]

Between the 1340s and 1440 the Guidi territories in the upper Casentino and Bibbiena in the lower Casentino were annexed by and subjected in successive stages to the government of the Florentine state during the republic's second phase of expansion. In 1359 Bibbiena, since the tenth century a fief of the bishop of Arezzo, passed under the rule of the Florentine republic, which made it the center of a podesteria.[4] In 1343 Pratovecchio surrendered spontaneously to Florence, and in 1348 the inhabitants of Castel San Niccolò rebelled against the tyrannical behavior of their count, "taking from him the castle with its treasure and equipment." In the following year they formally asked for annexation to the Florentine republic. In 1402 Stia also asked to join the Florentine state, after the Counts Guidi of the branch of Palagio had been driven out of town.[5] By then, only Poppi remained under the control of the Guidi of Battifolle.

The Casentino Valley, in the upper reaches of the Arno to the east of the Via Cassia Vetus, which joins Arezzo to Florence, is elliptical in shape and extends for 38 kilometers in length and 33 in width. Except on its southern end, where it opens toward Arezzo, the Casentino is closed in on all sides by the natural borders of the Apennines. To the northeast, the Serra Alps of the Falterona chain divide the area from Romagna. To the south and southeast, the mountains of La Verna and the Catenaia Alps mark the borders of the Val Tiberina; to the southwest and west, Pratomagno and the Consuma provide boundaries with the Valdarno di Sopra and the Val di Sieve.[6]

In the sixteenth century the Casentino consisted of the area called Upper Casentino, subdivided into the two podesterie of Pratovecchio and Castel San Niccolò and the vicariate of Poppi, and Lower Casentino, which included only the podesteria of Bibbiena.[7] All together these four administrative units of the Florentine state extended for 467 square kilometers, equivalent to 2.1 percent of the grand-ducal territory and to 3.4 percent of the state's rural land.[8] In 1552, 15 percent of the population of the Florentine state lived in the larger cities; the remaining 85 percent was distributed among the smaller towns and rural areas.[9] The Casentino, with 21,273 inhabitants, comprised 3.6 percent of the population of the Tuscan state.[10]

In the more peripheral mountainous valleys of Tuscany such as

the Casentino, the Mugello, Val Tiberina, Lunigiana, and Garfag-
nana, the many villages and towns, capped by their medieval castles,
were strategically placed on hills above the hazards of rivers, un-
healthy marshlands, and attacks from unfriendly forces.[11] The towns
were surrounded by mountains and cut across by rivers and streams.
So was and is Poppi. Only 65 kilometers from Florence and less than
40 kilometers from Arezzo, Poppi stands on an isolated hill almost
at the center of the Casentino. According to the census ordered by
Cosimo I in 1552, 1,450 people constituting 323 households lived in
Poppi. In the following century, as in the rest of the valley and other
rural areas, the population progressively declined until the 1632 census, when only 704 inhabitants were registered.[12] By 1642 a considerable increase was evident, and in 1745 Poppi's population ap-
proached the mid-sixteenth-century level with 254 households and
1,329 mouths.[13]

Throughout the sixteenth and seventeenth centuries, Poppi and its
rural communes registered the lowest population among the other
podesterie of the Casentino: 742 households and 3,473 people in
1552, and 674 households and 3,066 people in 1642. In the same years
the podesteria of Bibbiena was not considerably larger than that of
Poppi, but the other two in the Upper Casentino were twice as popu-
lated. The podesteria of Castel San Niccolò had 1,541 households
and 7,097 people in 1552 and 1,451 households and 6,291 people in
1642.[14] Despite its small size, Poppi consistently filled an important
political and administrative role throughout the centuries, first as a
strategic center of the feudal Guidi counts and later as the center of
the vicariate of the Casentino under Florentine domination.

I

Poppi has changed little since the local chronicler Ser Bernardo Lapini described it in the mid-seventeenth century. Then, as today, the
traveler headed to Poppi on foot crossed the bridge which "banked
and channeled" the Arno River as it flowed on the eastern side "at
the foot of the steep side of the hill on which Poppi is situated."[15]
Past the bridge, the traveler began climbing the ancient paved road
which ended at the Porta a Badia. The gate, placed to the north of the
town, was once the main one, "since it was directly accessible to traffic from Florence, Arezzo, Romagna, and Umbria."[16] The mile-long

wall that girded the town and is in part still standing was built in the mid-thirteenth century, when construction for the castle began. Along the wall there were three other gates. First, to the east was the Ancherona Gate, which did "not serve the town so much as it serve[d] those who [had] vineyards on the slopes below and fields on the plain."[17] Continuing to the south along the wall, one came to the Porta a Fronzola, next to which a row of buildings curving back to the west was incorporated in the walls. To the west, the Porta a Porrena had been the main gate in the Middle Ages, but by the seventeenth century it was useful only to the "mountaineers from Cetica, from Montemignaio and from all other parts of Castel San Niccolò."[18]

From the Porta a Badia the town's main street, paved in large, irregular blocks of stone, followed, then as now, the route from the Church of San Fedele to the central square, where it forked in two directions. One part curved up to the castle, and the other continued in a straight line between ancient houses to the Fronzola Gate. On the highest point of the hill the imposing castle still stands, until recently the political heart of the town. First residence of the Counts Guidi, it later became the seat of both the vicar of Florence and the municipal government, a situation that lasted until recently, when the castle became the depository of the local archives and the modern library. Opposite the castle, on the north side of town, stands the Vallombrosian Monastery, constructed in 1262. The monastery was originally built before 992 by Count Tegrimo II at Strumi, about one kilometer outside Poppi, and given to Vallombrosa around 1089. When the Guidi moved their residence into Poppi during the second half of the twelfth century, they also rebuilt the monastery inside the town walls.[19]

The town was divided into three parishes. The oldest church was San Marco, built in 1242; the parish comprised the central area of the town around the main square and the streets leading to the castle. The parish of San Fedele was probably the most socially mixed. It was attached to the Vallombrosian Monastery and included the main street, which ran from the monastery to the central square. Here one could find the main palaces and the wealthiest shops belonging to the emerging leading families. The parish also comprised the *chiassi*, the dark and narrow alleys which, departing from the main street, ran down along the western and southern sides of the slope. These were mostly inhabited by small artisans and workers. Lastly came the parish of San Lorenzo. Placed in the south side of the town, this church served the most populous neighborhood, which extended along the narrow Borgo dei Cenci, from which branched off even narrower and darker alleys. Although the parish of San Lorenzo was the poorest and San Marco later would serve the greatest number of patrician residences, no precise line of social demarcation divided the parishes. Often different branches of the same families lived in all three, as was the case of the three branches of the Crudeli and Rilli families, who lived in different parishes.[20]

For almost its entire length, the main street is flanked by low porticoes, then as today the heart of the social and commercial life of the town. Here were the numerous retail shops and workshops for the production and sale of local products and foodstuffs. Prior to the 1590s, the town enjoyed a lively commercial activity. The main street housed at least nine grocery stores, two bakeries, two butcher shops, three drugstores, one haberdasher, one barber, one tailor, and one cobbler.[21] The main local industries centered around wool, leather, iron, and kilns. The two kilns that produced bricks, tiles, and vases were placed near the Arno, as were the workshops involved in dying wool.

The shops were situated at street level below the residence of their owners and renters. This architectural pattern, as had been the case in fourteenth-century Florence, indicated the blending together of the private and public worlds, of domestic space with busy economic activity.[22] The Poppi youths strolled along the porticoes, visited the tavern, or stood by the entrance of shops, working, talking with friends, and looking at passersby.[23] This dense interaction promoted social as well as commercial activity and provided the foundation for urban growth and consolidation. It also reflected the socioeconomic identity of the urban environment and of the people that controlled it. Such an environment was fundamentally commercial and artisanal. The people that helped produce it were shopkeepers and small wool producers.

II

The porticoes and the private and public spaces in town constituted the most distinguished features of the Poppi urban skyline. The mountains, the river, and the narrow and irregular fields on the terraced slopes of the hills and on the plain defined the landscape around the town and represented its ecological features. The beauty of the natural landscape surrounding Poppi, today a center of tourism for its green hills, temperate climate, and suggestive ruins, had been acclaimed by poets, chroniclers, and travelers of the past. In his history of Florence Gino Capponi praised the Casentino for being "small but blessed for the freshness of its setting."[24] Dante was also familiar with the valley both as a participant in 1289 in the Battle of Campaldino and later as an honored guest of the feudal overlords after his exile from Florence. In the *Inferno* he remembered the Casentino for its "ruscelletti che dai verdi colli . . . discendon giuso in Arno, facendo i lor canali freddi e molli."[25] In the sixteenth century the local landscape continued to captivate the attention of voyagers such as the Venetian Leonardo Alberti, who described the sloped and terraced fields on the sides of the hills as "abounding in grain, wine and other things."[26]

In the sixteenth and seventeenth centuries, Poppi agriculture was characterized by small and irregular fields under a system of multiple-crop farming based predominantly on vineyards, grains, fodder, and vegetables. The Poppi territory possessed more land under cultivation than the surrounding mountainous territory of the rural communes. In 1588 the *estimi* (tax surveys on all landed property) of Poppi covered 1,177 hectares of fields, most of them in the terraced slopes of Poppi and in the valley along the river. These slopes, which remain today despite recent abandonment, speak to the arduous labor of a prevalently rural population that had brought most of the more fertile land, both hilly and level, under cultivation. The seventeenth-century notary Lapini confirmed that all around the town, "on the slopes the earth [was] fertile and produce[d] every sort of crop [where] already the ancients had planted vineyards in every direction well beyond the slopes adjacent to the town."[27] Along the fields in the countryside a number of narrow (only recently paved) roads ran between the town's gates and the rural villages. They formed a web of lines between town and country, indicating at the same time a sense of coexistence and domination between Poppi and its surrounding countryside.

If the town's wall delimited the physical boundaries of Poppi, its natural outline was formed by the encircling mountains, which benefited the local inhabitants with their products. In the last century the woods and forests covered approximately 40 percent of the whole territory of the Casentino. The mountaintops, which reach elevations averaging between 1,200 and 1,300 meters (the highest peak is 1,658 meters), provided, then as now, a natural border encircling the valley and delimiting the sense of space of the viewer standing in the center of town. From the tops, where forests abound with beech and pine, the land descends gradually, first through groves of chestnut and oak, then over the foothills, and finally to the long and narrow valley floor, which widens out only in the proximity of Poppi and neighboring Bibbiena.

From the mountains came products that supported the local economy. The high forests offered wood for local artisans and for commerce, in particular for the production of wine barrels. The territory at midmountain, testifying to a consciously organized mountain economy aimed at mastering a fundamentally poor and dry soil, produced chestnuts, which were the mainstay of the diet of the rural population, and oaks, which sustained pig breeding. Chestnuts provided a fundamental reserve especially in times of famine and bad harvests, when a limited agricultural production failed to sustain the population. Writing in the 1630s, the local notary, Bernardo Lapini, had no doubt that chestnuts "were the most important product" for the town.[28]

The Arno River, enlivened by numerous streams along its course from Monte Falterona in the northwest to the plain of Arezzo, can be seen running along the fields touching the lower slopes. Today the river is channeled by artificially made banks that contain and channel its direction, but formerly it was considerably more irregular and broader, and several small islands interrupted its path, producing a number of narrower branches.[29] For Poppi and the other communities of the valley, the river generated devastation and ruin, but it also aided the precarious nature of the local agriculture.

The Arno periodically overflowed, damaging crops in the surrounding plains despite the precautions taken by local landowners, who built banks along the river. The local estimi recorded the impact of the river by describing fields formerly cultivated which had been "eaten up by the Arno," "covered by the Arno," or become *padule* (swamp). The numerous floods caused by the Arno and its affluents often required intervention by the Captains of Parte Guelfa, the office in charge of supervising the preservation of state properties such as fortresses, roads, rivers, and bridges, whose maintenance was of vital importance for the commercial prosperity of the state.[30] During the sixteenth century, this office intervened numerous times to re-store flood-damaged bridges that connected traffic routes considered commercially important.[31]

Although a reason for concern to the local landowners, the Arno offered, even in the swamps, a source of profit. A part of the land was permanently covered by shallow marshes, in some of which one could fish for eels, to this day a celebrated dish from the area. In general, the river was an important source of food. Fish was a significant staple in the diet of the local population, especially during religious celebrations, when river fish was traditionally served. Moreover, from the riverbed were extracted pebbles for construction materials. No less important, the river was a vital source for both the local wool and the leather industries, which, in the various stages of production, required large amounts of water.

The Arno also served for transporting lumber from the mountains, in particular Falterona, destined for the markets in Arezzo. But the hazards of the river as a means of transportation and communication are well known, and in the Casentino, merchants preferred to use the main road. Cutting across the fields in the valley, this road linked Poppi with Florence and Arezzo and connected it with the commercial centers and markets of the region.[32] It also linked Florence and Arezzo with the western areas in Romagna and with the Romagna Fiorentina. The office of the Captains of Parte Guelfa periodically allocated substantial funds for the restoration of this route, suggesting not only that traffic was intense but also that the route was a priority for the central government.[33]

III

Between the sixteenth and the seventeenth centuries, the socioeconomic and political position of Poppi and the organization of the Florentine state changed. In 1440 the Florentine army marched on Poppi and took the town by force. Thereafter, from the residence of the Counts Guidi Poppi became a subject town of the Florentine state.

The success of the Battifolle branch of the Guidi family in holding on to their territories of Poppi, Fronzola, and Quota depended largely on their political alliance with the Florentine government, first begun in the mid-thirteenth century. The breakup in the Guidi family led them into a dependent relation with their powerful neighbor. The alliance with Florence was formalized in the second half of the four-teenth century by a pact of "*accomandigia*," which stipulated that, in return for assistance and military protection, the Guidi agreed to make an offering "yearly for the feast of San Giovanni of the palio, equivalent to a symbolic act of submission and loyalty."[34] In 1439, however, Count Francesco Guidi lost the centuries-old signoria of the family by allying himself with the troops of Filippo Maria Vis-conti, ruler of Milan, led by Niccolò Piccinino against the Florenti-nes. After the defeat of the troops of Piccinino near Anghiari, the Florentine army drew Francesco and his family out of Poppi, and in July 1440 the "Articles of Submission of Poppi, Quota and Fronzola to the Florentine Republic" were drawn up.[35]

On the basis of these articles Poppi became the seat of the vicar, the official representative of the central power, and the center of its podesteria. Together, the three podesterie of Bibbiena, Castel San Niccolò, and Pratovecchio and the vicariate of Poppi constituted the new administrative structure of the Casentino Valley.[36] This political organization of the Casentino was retained until the Leopoldine re-forms of the second half of the eighteenth century. Although not the largest, the most populous, or the most prominent commune in the valley, Poppi became the capital of the Casentino, a position that the Medici grand dukes further strengthened.[37]

During the fifteenth century the Florentine government curbed the prerogatives of larger provincial cities and towns over their sur-roundings by extending central control over rural districts through the creation of vicariates and podesterie directly subjected to the au-thority of the Florentine government.[38] This trend, in part, was re-versed at the beginning of the following century, when provincial cities and towns regained a certain degree of control over their hin-terlands.[39] The new territorial configuration of the state reflected new forms of social and political interactions between rural villages and towns merged in the same podesteria or vicariate.

By the middle of the fifteenth century, the Florentine territorial state was organized into vicariates, podesterie, and *capitanati* in which the single communities maintained their laws and territories as a confederation of city-states.[40] At the head of each of these units was a state-appointed functionary who served as a local judge—a vicar, a captain, or a *podestà*—and represented the central govern-ment at the local level. Under each functionary were lesser officials,

such as judges, notaries, and men-at-arms.[41] During the sixteenth
century, major officeholders were selected according to the importance of the post, either by lot (the usual method of selection for Florentine office holding) or by direct appointment of the grand duke,
from among eligible citizens of Florence and from members of the
provincial elite who had been granted Florentine citizenship. Minor
officials, however, were chosen from the ranks of provincial elites,
nominated by the superior officials and chosen by lot. Both higher
and lesser officials of provincial administration remained in office for
six months.[42]

Vicars, podestà, and captains, aided by their staff of notaries, performed a number of functions. The orders issued by the central administration were communicated to the provinces through the state
functionaries, who also assured the smooth functioning of local institutions and presided over government meetings.[43] Since the beginning of the fifteenth century, the role of vicariates in the peripheral
administration of the state had become more prominent, as vicars
became the penal and ordinary justices in the dominion.[44] This new
title, combined with the supervision of large territorial units that often comprised a number of podesterie, conferred on vicars a prominent role in provincial administration. They became key officials
linking the central government to its dominion.[45]

The political units of provincial administration had civil and
criminal jurisdiction, but, whereas capitanati and vicariates presided
over both civil and criminal cases, podesterie were limited to civil
actions.[46] The latter, in particular during the first half of the sixteenth century, were sometimes given authority in criminal cases,
except in violent offenses of public disorder or crime carrying the
death penalty. This was the case of the three podesterie of the Casentino, where the difficulty of the means of communication imposed
a certain decentralization of penal justice.[47]

In 1525 the vicariate of Poppi was invested with broader compe-
tence on criminal matters. The Florentine magistrates of the Consig-
lio dei Cento, realizing that crimes remained largely unpunished in
the area and that successful control depended on local officers, declared that the vicar of Poppi "be invested with full authority in
criminal matters in the same form and manner as other vicars under
Florentine jurisdiction."[48] This new provision affected also the rec-
tors of the other three podesterie, who, although they would continue to exercise the same authority over criminals, were now super-

vised by the vicar of Poppi. He had the power to intervene whenever the other podestà did not demonstrate sufficient care in inflicting punishment.[49]

During the second half of the sixteenth century, in conjunction with the consolidation of the Medicean government, the autonomy of the individual podesterie was reduced as they became unified in the vicariate of the Casentino with Poppi as its administrative center.[50] In 1580 a new reform in jurisdictional matters increased the administrative unification of the valley by expanding the authority of the vicar.[51] To create a more consistent and centralized distribution of justice, Francesco I concentrated criminal jurisdiction solely in the hands of the vicar of Poppi and imposed a unified legislation upon the entire territory of the Casentino.[52]

The unification of the valley under the administrative and juridical leadership of the vicar reflected the growth in the consolidation of Medicean authority over the dominion. No less important, it placed Poppi at the hearth of Florentine administration in the Casentino.[53] During the same period Poppi also became the political center of a podesteria that comprised six communes, each with its own administration: Poppi Dentro, Poppi Fuora, Fronzola, Ragginopoli-Lierna, Riosecco-Lucciano, and Quota.

Each of the communes in the podesteria had its own council and elected a mayor (sindaco) as its representative to the podesteria. As the largest commune, Poppi had two mayors, whereas Riosecco-Lucciano and Quota alternated a mayor between them every six months. The mayors, who met periodically to elect a chancellor and the district doctor, also had the task of sounding the large bell in the tower of Poppi to warn of bad weather and to signal the opening of the market on Saturday morning. They also authorized ordinary and extraordinary expenses in the podesteria, such as the doctor's salary and funds for roads and public building repairs.[54]

During the early sixteenth century, like other larger towns, Poppi created a new political-administrative tradition. In the process it increased its influence over the rural villages of its hinterland. It did so by centralizing its own administrative authority. In 1516 the Poppi riformatori—qualified men in charge of drawing up the statutes of the community—passed a statutory reform that strengthened Poppi's control over the rural districts. The reform decreed that the Poppi camarlingo had jurisdiction over the whole podesteria.[55] A camarlingo, usually a man of property, was responsible for local finances.

He was in charge of collecting and disbursing payments for the local administration and had the authority to denounce tax delinquents.[56] Obviously, a *camarlingo* from Poppi was in a better position to protect the interests of the townspeople, especially when some were expanding their landholding in the countryside.

In 1521 the Poppi government further strengthened its leadership over the rural villages. It was customary to appoint a *soprasindaco* from among the mayors of the six communes as the representative to the vicar.[57] Poppi officials, on the assumption that the administration of the podesteria was better performed by men coming from Poppi, since they were both more "expert and wise," changed the procedure. The reform established that whoever filled the position as standard-bearer of Poppi was automatically appointed as soprasindaco of the podesteria. With such a measure the municipal government asserted its prerogative to regulate access to central authority and placed Poppi at the head of its rural districts.[58]

During the sixteenth century, the development of central structures and the growth of Florentine authority took away some of the autonomy of the municipal government. It also contributed to the newfound centrality of Poppi in the politico-administrative life of the valley. This new position, in time, bestowed on the Poppi ruling families the awareness of a political and professional superiority not only over their rural districts but also toward the other towns of the valley. Thus, in 1556, for example, because of the inconvenience of having to travel to Poppi for every meeting with the vicar, the soprasindaci of the other three podesterie established that a notary from Poppi be chosen to act as their chancellor, "since Poppi notaries [were] more informed and practiced in matters involving the Vicariate."[59]

The position that Poppi came to fill within the new political system as depository of central authority influenced the process of formation of local ruling families. It compelled them to examine their identity beyond their municipal world and in a wider regional context.

IV

The transformations connected with the evolution of the Tuscan regional state influenced socioeconomic and political developments in Poppi. They affected the way the people of Poppi looked at themselves, both in relation to the municipal world and within the setting of the larger regional state. In this context, the mountains that encircle Poppi symbolized the ecological metaphor of two socioeconomic and political systems.

In 1501 the Poppi municipal council decreed universal immunity from debt on market days, "for the good and benefit and maintenance of the town of Poppi considering its location on a dry hill and in need of being frequented and visited by other men and people."[60] Later in the sixteenth century the local notary, Ser Mariano Catani, despite the elliptical shape of the valley, had no doubt that in relation to the surrounding mountains, the Casentino was round, "an almost perfect spherical circle of forty miles to which inhospitable and forbidding mountains in the form of a great wall form a proud and irregular crown and strong defense."[61] By the middle of the seventeenth century, Ser Bernardo Lapini, echoing the Greek model employed by Leonardo Bruni in his description of Florence written more than two centuries before, evoked the image of concentric rings circumscribing a central point.[62] Perhaps overstressing his civic pride, the local notary described Poppi as "among the most, and perhaps, the most prominent of all other towns in the State of Tuscany" and located the town "in the middle of the Casentino whose mountains surround it in a circle."[63]

The spatial representation of the local scene portrayed by both the municipal officers and the two notaries mirrored profound transformations in Poppi society as the town changed from isolated "hilltop" in the Casentino Valley to administrative and military center of the Tuscan state. At the beginning of the sixteenth century the local people perceived the mountains that surrounded Poppi as barriers isolating the valley from the world on the other side. In the course of the sixteenth and seventeenth centuries the outside world had ceased to be hostile and unfamiliar terrain and had instead become part of a beneficial relationship. The mountains helped glorify the success of local ruling families by highlighting both their confidence and the new position the town had acquired as an administrative and military center of the Tuscan state. They shaped the perception of these families of living in the middle of the valley and of fulfilling a central role in the state.

The ways that local people defined their town in relation to the mountains and to the new regional environment reveal the affirmation of a dominant provincial elite. As central authority consolidated, a group of local families placed itself in a position of domination in the social and political life of the town. In the decades between 1556 and 1632 these families represented 14 percent of the town's households but controlled 86 percent of its landed wealth and 70 percent of local industries. In this same period they monopolized 93 percent of the major political offices in the municipal government.[64] They were the former shopkeepers who first became notaries and later large landowners and military officers of the grand-ducal army.

These transformations also influenced the way that local leading families defined themselves and fashioned to their needs the public and private spheres of provincial life. In the literature of earlier centuries the poverty and ignorance of the people of the mountains had been common traits. Dante characterized the local counts as "filthy hogs, fitter for acorns than for any food made for human use."[65] Pievano Arlotto, writing a century later, called the local inhabitants "malicious men." Other Florentine authors writing between the thirteenth and fifteenth centuries classified them as "turbulent," "bold," and "violent," much as the population that lived in the countryside was commonly depicted by those who lived in the cities.[66]

During the sixteenth century, however, the way that some among the local people represented themselves and the manner in which they were characterized by outsiders changed. While the former often adapted a terminology and an attitude toward the lower classes which conformed to the earlier city writers, the latter modified their way of conceiving of provincial people. Contrary to their "violent" and "turbulent" predecessors, local notables portrayed themselves as "expert and wise men" and called themselves "peoples of means." Outsiders, reinforcing these traits, emphasized a split in the social composition of the town. State functionaries who periodically surveyed the territory of the Casentino stressed the poverty of the people and described many of them as peasants who regularly left to do seasonal work in Maremma.[67] In the 1580s a militia captain stationed in Poppi writing to his superior officer characterized local people as either "diggers and farmers" or *persone facultose*," emphasizing the disenfranchised status of the former and the economic well-being of the latter.[68]

Not much is known of the Poppi families prior to the late fourteenth century, but many of them had close ties with the surrounding rural society. Many came originally from the countryside and moved into town as it developed into a commercial and political center during the thirteenth and fourteenth centuries. Around the middle of the fourteenth century, according to the chronicler Mannucci, the Grifoni, who became a powerful ruling family, moved from Pagliericcio—a rural locality outside the wall—to Poppi, where they practiced the trade of blacksmith.[69] About the Rilli family, later one of the most distinguished in town and the only one to acquire the title of nobility, more is known because of its ties with the Counts Guidi. Francesca, wife of Matteo Rilli, when a resident of Sova, a rural locality outside the town's walls, had been a wet nurse to the last count of Poppi, Francesco. Before leaving town the count asked Florentine permission to give her his property at Bramasole outside the castle walls, a house in town, and the stables of the counts as a sign of gratitude. In the estimo of 1489, her son Niccolò owned approximately three and a half hectares of arable land and less than half a hectare of vegetable garden at Bramasole valued at 614 lire.[70]

As the Poppi families became urbanized, they began investing in commerce and industry, still retaining their interest in the land as well as the human and social contacts. Once these financial ventures were secured, this new urban bourgeoisie enlarged its possessions in the countryside, exploiting its people and its fields. During the sixteenth century, following a pattern common to other Tuscan and Italian urban elites, the Poppi families increased concentration of land at the expense of the lower and middle classes.

During the sixteenth century, land reclamation increased the agricultural profits of the wealthier local families, who next proceeded to expropriate the lands of the small peasant owners and then to exploit their labor. Between 1517 and 1701, the general trend of land distribution was toward increasing inequality and greater concentration of agricultural wealth. The total amount of land held by small proprietors, owning under three hectares, and by the medium-small ones, owning between four and ten hectares, shrank considerably. Conversely, during the same period, although the number of large property owners remained stable, the amount of land they held increased, in particular through the expansion of holdings in the rural communes of the podesteria.[71] For example, by 1536, residents of Poppi, all from the leading families, owned 41.7 percent of the land value in the commune of Fronzola, which then increased to 48.6 percent in 1592–93. The expansion of the rural possessions of the urban ruling families strengthened their control over the economy of rural communes in the podesteria and sustained their authority in Poppi.

The commercial and industrial activities that formerly characterized the urban economy of the town had also been considerably reduced following a trend that reflected not only the general economic conjuncture of the 1590s but also the transformation in the lifestyle of a rising local elite. By the 1630s the leather industry disappeared altogether, and wool production declined to the point that only half of the shops had remained open. The kiln industry survived the crisis of the late sixteenth century. It remained important throughout the following century as evidence of an expanded building activity undertaken by the new ruling families.

Between the sixteenth and the seventeenth centuries, the medieval heritage of Poppi blended with new features. The building of new two- and three-story palaces above the medieval porticoes and low buildings transformed the main street from an industrial and commercial center into a more residential area. Changing architectural features revealed the development of new lifestyles and changed patterns of power. They also showed the degree to which the Poppi elite conformed to the already established Florentine style of patrician residences. Many of the new leading families felt the need to enlarge and remodel their old and humble residences, "comfortable—Lapini wrote—but not suitable to the wealth" they now enjoyed.[72] The local elite families encouraged a separation between the public and private space and created along the main street a more exclusive residential area.

The erection of new public buildings also revealed the socioeconomic transformations of local leading families. In 1565 the convent of the Augustinian nuns, today the Camaldolese, was built with the donation of Dianora Pauolozzi, from a local ruling family, to shelter unmarried daughters of the town's elite. A few years later, in 1568, Francesco Grifoni, who lived in Rome but came from an ancient and honorable local family, donated the largest sum of money to build the collegiate church of San Marco in an act intended to stress his religious and civic commitment to his hometown. Finally, in 1657 the chapel dedicated to the Madonna del Morbo was built thanks to the donations from private citizens grateful for having survived the ravages of the numerous plagues that struck between the fourteenth and the seventeenth centuries. The small baroque church that now stands in the main square represented the assertion of the collective prestige of a self-assured elite and epitomized the elite's consolidated position as benefactor and protector of Poppi.

In the years following the annexation of Poppi to the Florentine state, the local families strove to strengthen their control of local society and to assert themselves as the town's ruling class by monopolizing office holding. The emergence to a position of control of a group of local families was reflected in the process that shaped the local magistrature.

TWO

◆

The Emergence of Ruling Families
Patterns of Office Holding

The articles of submission drawn up between Florence and its subject cities and towns established the right of municipal governments
either to retain their communal laws or to draw up new statutes
upon the approval of Florentine magistrature. Since the early decades
of the 1400s, the Florentine government had removed smaller towns
from the direct control of larger cities such as Pistoia, Pisa, and
Arezzo. These towns were further encouraged to write their own
laws and regulations to fashion a local political tradition and thus
support both local and central political practices.[1] Thus, despite the
presence of representatives of central authority, local officials carried
on their own administration through elected councils and municipal
magistracies that regulated ordinary communal activities.

The administrative structures in Poppi reveal the ingenuity that
characterized local political life during the sixteenth century. The
local autonomy furthered by Florence did more than simply produce a support system that strengthened central authority. Those
municipal governments which, like Poppi, lacked a communal legacy used the space left open by the Florentine administration first
to strengthen a new self-governing tradition and later to adapt the
newly established system of government to the interests and aspirations of the emerging ruling families.

I

During the early years of Florentine domination, the creative vitality of Poppi was reflected in an active political life, which nonethe-

less advanced by experiment. Over the course of fifty years after the annexation to Florence, officeholders charted new rules and drafted new reforms intended to give shape to the municipal councils. At this time, the still-fluid political system that emerged reflected the search for general and organizational principles upon which to found the municipal government.

Between 1441 and the end of the century, the riformatori met seventeen times to formulate additions and corrections and to give shape to the local governing body.[2] The reforms changed the territorial boundaries of the administrative jurisdiction and established the constitution of the town's council. In 1441 the jurisdiction of the commune of Poppi extended to include both the town and its contado. By 1449 the territory of the commune was divided into Poppi Dentro (comprising the town and its immediate surroundings) and Poppi Fuora (contado).[3] Ten years later, these two units were separated both geographically and administratively into the communes of Poppi Dentro and Poppi Fuora.[4] In 1441 jurisdictional transformations were followed by changes in the composition and organization of the local magistrature, including a council formed by one standard-bearer, four priors, and ten councilors, for a total of fifteen officers. By 1451, except for the standard-bearer, who always came from the town, the selection of the other officials reflected the division of the territorial units: four priors and three councilors came from Poppi, and the other four priors and three councilors were selected from among citizens of the contado (table 2.1).[5] By the 1450s, in line with the separation between Poppi Dentro and Poppi Fuora, the officials of the Poppi council decreased to ten officers— one standard-bearer, four priors, and five councilors, all from Poppi.[6] In 1476 a further reduction in the numerical composition of the council, made necessary by recurring epidemics and the consequent demographic decline in the community, lowered the number of councilors to two and the total number of officers to seven members.[7]

By 1501 the number of council members rose to its highest point in the history of the local government. With the 1501 reform, the city governing body expanded and a second council was formed. The First Council (called Ordinary Council after 1521) comprised thirteen members who, together with thirteen additional councilors called *arroti*, formed the Second, or General, Council. The First Council was now composed of the standard-bearer, two select priors (*priori scelti*), two general priors (*priori generali*), four councilors, and four

TABLE 2.1
Composition of the Ordinary and General Councils between 1440 and 1633

Year	Standard-bearer	Priors	Select Priors	General Priors	Councilors	Super-numerary	Total Ord. Council	Arroti	Total Gen. Council
1440s	1	4			10		15		
1451	1	4 + ∠			3 + 3		15		
1460s	1		2	2	5		10		
1476	1		2	2	2		7		
1501	1		2	2	4	4	13	13	26
1516	1		2	2	4	3	12	12	24
1526	1		2	2	4		9	12	21
1544	1		4	2			7	7	14
1633	1		4				5	4	9

supernumerary councilors (*aggiunti*).[8] The Second Council, however, was not yet a permanent body, and the arroti were thus nominated orally by each member of the other council each time the Second Council had to be called into session. The reform of 1501 ended the first phase in the shaping of a local political tradition. At this time, the composition of local offices was aimed at broadening political participation to a wider number of people. It reflected the numerical increase and socioeconomic development of an emerging group of artisans, shopkeepers, notaries, and small landowners. Like the mainland notables of the Venetian towns, they wanted more representation and direct political involvement in the administration of the local government.[9]

The statutory reform of 1501 also inaugurated more systematic political practices, thereby giving governance a more efficient public image. The procedures to call the council into session were spelled out, with great concern that the correct form be followed. Thus, meetings began with "all the others remaining silent [while] the first prior put forth with sweet words and elegant phrases" the issues to be discussed.[10] It was further established that the council could convene only in its official room in the castle. This new rule replaced a common practice of meeting in private places, such as the shops of local artisans or homes. In 1451, for example, the standard-bearer and the priors had met at the house of Carlo Niccoletti, druggist, and a few years later, in 1456, the schoolteacher was selected by the council convened in the shop of Santi Niccoletti called Matarazza.[11] Finally, for the first time, the local statutes made a reference to the external appearance of the officers, who were encouraged to wear their best outfit during the council sessions rather than the familiar work apron, the *pannuccia*.[12]

During the first half of the sixteenth century, the profile of the local magistrature remained basically the same. But changes in the composition of the local magistrature mirrored the beginning of an elitist direction in local politics and society. Contrary to the situation in the earlier period, the administrative reforms reflected a clear strategy of making office holding the exclusive domain of a limited group of people.

In the decades following 1501, the trend toward broadening the composition of the councils ended. With the 1526 reform, the supernumerary councilors disappeared from the political scene, and the council's membership decreased from thirteen to nine members. The

General Council became a permanent body, and the arroti were regularly elected and remained in office for six months, as did the members of the other council.[13] In 1544 even the councilors disappeared from the First Council, whereas the number of select priors grew from two to four, making a total of seven officials. With this reform, membership in the General Council also decreased from twelve to seven.[14] By 1544 the two governing bodies had little more than one-half the members of 1501 (table 2.1). The reform of 1594 did not change the numerical composition of the two councils, which declined again in 1633 after the plague took a heavy toll on the Poppi population.[15]

Between 1526 and 1544 the decline in membership of the two governing bodies was partially dictated by devastating epidemics in the 1520s and 1530s. The riformatori, however, justified the reduction in the number of seats of the two councils not simply by a lack of people but rather by a "shortage of men with the right requisites" to govern.[16] The changes in the composition of the Poppi government reveal the consolidation of Poppi ruling families. As their socioeconomic position stabilized, these families showed an increased confidence in their ability to control local politics. In the process they began to shape more hierarchical forms of local organization.

During the early sixteenth century, the elitist direction manifested in the composition and modes of governance was strengthened by changes in the functions of the local magistrature. Until 1501 a single council legislated on every political and administrative question concerning both ordinary and extraordinary matters and approved new articles and statutes. In 1501 and subsequent years, even if the composition of the governing body shrunk, the functions of the Ordinary Councils strengthened considerably. The Ordinary Council discussed expenses and ordinary administration and distributed salaries and sums for charity. It also allocated the taxes to be paid to the central government and determined the direct tax to be collected from individuals. Moreover, the nine officials could pardon the community's debtors wholly or in part and nominated *incantatori* of the gabelles and tax collectors. Lastly, the council appointed all salaried officeholders who were not selected by lot, such as the chancellor, the usher of the councils, the *donzello*, the employee responsible for the proper functioning of the town clock, and the annually chosen schoolteacher. The council also approved the calling of special elections.[17] The group of nine officials was joined by the supernumerary councilors for special matters such as the appointment of ambassadors and the determination of their salaries.[18]

It had been general practice since the fifteenth century that motions could be presented only by the *proposto*, the mediator and spokesman for both councils. During the fifteenth century, the proposto had been chosen from among council members at each session.[19] The reform of 1501 strengthened the role of the proposto. He now remained in office for eight days. Moreover, only the standard-bearer and the priors were eligible for this position.[20] After motions were presented, only these five officials had the right to vote. Their approval was needed before any motion could be submitted to the other councilors for discussion and a vote.[21] In practice, therefore, the standard-bearer and the four priors had complete legislative authority. The other councilors only ratified the approved motions. According to the 1501 reform, the General Council convened only to nominate the riformatori, the officers charged with drawing up new statutes; to establish the eligibility of citizens for public office; and to supervise the election of a new council every six months. Only this broader council approved new reforms.[22]

In the decades after 1501, the political role of the General Council increased while its membership diminished. Between 1516 and 1526, functions heretofore performed by the restricted group of nine officials were given over to the supervision of the two councils, which, at this same time, had lowered their membership from thirteen to nine and from twenty-six to twenty-one respectively (table 2.1). The General Council acquired control over the nomination of the majority of salaried officials, except the *donzello* and the person in charge of the town clock, and over the approval of special business and expenses, which had previously been the allotted task of the larger Ordinary Council.

The 1594 reform definitively established the respective responsibilities of Poppi's two governing bodies. The new statutory articles clarified the separation of functions between the Ordinary and General Councils. The General Council controlled the nomination of all salaried officials, including ambassadors, attorneys, and lawyers who represented the community to the central government. Moreover, it was the business of this council to decide special funding that exceeded fourteen lire, although such measures also had to be approved by the representative of the central government, the Chancellor of the Nine.[23] The Ordinary Council retained control of routine disbursements of revenue and could allocate regular funds under five lire and special funds under fourteen lire without approval of the chancellor. It also had responsibility for matters related to the collective life of the community—the nomination of masters of ceremony, the setting of dates for the grape harvest, the approval of the town miller. The Ordinary Council, as keeper of the city seal, could also legalize documents and authorize access to the administration's ledgers.[24] This last function conferred on the Ordinary Council the symbolic status of center of local power.

Overall, the reform of 1594 strengthened the autonomy of the Ordinary Council as the supervisor of local matters and the main arena for the political activities of local ruling families. Here important decisions were made and elaborated before being introduced in the General Council. Popular representation, on the other hand, was wider in the General Council. On it the ruling families bestowed the position of official representative of the community. The General Council was in charge of overseeing the electoral process, although by 1594 this process was already performed by the selected group of four riformatori. Because the General Council was the political body in which popular representation was wider, the Poppi ruling families also used it as the platform for expressing resistance to the central government.

These were the most dynamic and formative years in the social and political life of Poppi, when a new ruling class emerged. These local families created and consolidated the institutions of the Poppi government and gained control of local politics. The changes in the organization of the municipal government originated during a period of demographic crisis. These changes, however, also reflected the tendency to concentrate authority within a restricted ruling group. The two municipal councils became the depository of local political tradition as well as centers of elitist power.

II

The reforms of the local magistrature and of the governing bodies reflected the development of a tighter hierarchical structure of local politics and society. An analysis of the frequency of office holding shows the degree to which power was concentrated and indicates who in the community could aspire to political leadership.[25]

From the mid-fifteenth century until 1556, forty-seven families filled 591 of the 700 appointments of standard-bearer, select prior, and general prior.[26] Among these forty-seven families, seven accounted for 248 appointments, assuming office more than thirty times. Another seven obtained between 20 and 29 appointments each, for a total of 170 seats. A third group of six families held between 10 and 19 appointments each, for a total of 76 seats. Altogether, twenty of the forty-seven leading families, or 43 percent, occupied 496 of the 591 positions, or 84 percent of the total appointments (table 2.2).[27] The remaining 97 appointments were divided among twenty-seven other families.

Among the forty-seven families that occupied most high government offices, twenty-two did not appear on the Poppi political scene in the later period. Seven disappeared before the end of the fifteenth

TABLE 2.2

Frequency and Percentage of Office Holding
among Twenty Families, 1448–1556

Names	Frequency	Percentage
Grifoni	42	7.1
Rilli	41	6.9
Pauolozzi	36	6.1
Cascesi	35	5.9
Niccoletti	33	5.6
Crudeli	31	5.2
Fontanini	30	5.1
Fatucchi	28	4.7
Bonilli	27	4.6
Beccai	26	4.4
Buondi	25	4.2
Lapucci	23	3.9
Martini	21	3.6
Battistoni	20	3.4
Rastrellini	15	2.5
Sociani	15	2.5
Cresciuti	13	2.2
Lapini	13	2.2
Soldani	11	1.9
Manfidi	11	1.9
Total	496	83.9

Note: Frequency and percentage based on 591
positions.

century, eight during the early decades of the sixteenth century, and seven during the government of Cosimo I. The fate of most of these families is unknown because they disappeared without a trace. We do know, however, since they were of ancient and distinguished families, that seven of these—the Bardi, Bonilli, Burchi, Migli, Manfidi, Turriani, and Vannucci—died out because of lack of male descendants.

If some families disappeared from local politics, others emerged anew. As in other provincial towns, the local magistrature provided opportunities for political and social advancement, especially for those families that distinguished themselves by both professional qualification and wealth.[28] Of the twenty families awarded the greatest number of offices in this period, eighteen were local and only two were outsiders. Ten new families achieved major administrative positions at this time. Six families entered the stage at the beginning of the sixteenth century and four during the rule of Cosimo.[29] Five among these newcomers filled the top office of standard-bearer.[30]

Between 1574 and 1632, forty families occupied the office of standard-bearer (116 positions), select prior (457 positions), and general prior (233 positions), for a total of 806 times altogether.[31] Fifteen families held major office for the first time. During the rule of Francesco I (1574–87), eleven new families entered the council; the remaining four appeared in the first decades of the seventeenth century Of those fifteen families, eleven had fleeting political careers and never held the office of standard-bearer. Of the other four, which in the course of the seventeenth century were to become among the town's most prominent, only members of two of them were standard-bearer in this period.[32]

Nine of the aforementioned forty families (22.5 percent) occupied 40 or more appointments, for a total of 446, or 55.3 percent of the positions available. Six families filled between 29 and 39 appointments, for a total of 191, and seven families obtained between 10 and 19 appointments. Altogether, therefore, twenty-two families (55 percent) filled 750 out of 806 top appointments, or 93.1 percent of the total (table 2.3). The remaining 45 percent of the families filled only 6.9 percent of these offices.[33] Of the remaining six families, four were originally from Poppi and, although already council members in the previous century, had only now reached political prominence in the community; the other two were outsiders.[34] For these latter families antiquity was not by itself a sufficient prerequisite for office holding. Neither was wealth. By now a number of prerequisites were neces-

TABLE 2.3
Frequency and Percentage of Office Holding
among Twenty-two Families, 1574–1632

Names	Frequency	Percentage
Cascesi	61	7.6
Lapucci	60	7.4
Rilli	56	6.9
Soldani	52	6.5
Niccoletti	49	6.1
Grifoni	43	5.3
Martini	43	5.3
Sociani	42	5.2
Catani	40	5.0
Lapini	35	4.3
Pauolozzi	34	4.2
Tommasini	33	4.1
Fatucchi	30	3.7
Rastrellini	30	3.7
Baldacci	29	3.6
Crudeli	19	2.4
Buonfanti	18	2.2
Beccai	17	2.1
Battistoni	16	2.0
Mannucci	15	1.9
Folli	14	1.7
Fontanini	14	1.7
Total	750	93.1

Note: Frequency and percentage based on 806 positions.

sary to bolster one's family's political career in the community and enter the ranks of the governing families.

Concentration of power can be further shown by an analysis of office-holding frequency during three periods: 1448–81, 1507–36, and 1537–56. Twenty surname groups that filled the most number of offices held respectively 64, 85, and 89 percent of the available seats. During the decades between 1574 and 1609 and between 1610 and 1633, in contrast, the frequency of the same surname groups went from 94 to 92 percent of the total. These numbers indicate an overall progressive concentration that first became noticeable in the early decades of the Cinquecento and consolidated at the end of the century. In this same period, however, there were still significant fluctuations among officeholder families. The Lapucci, Sociani, and

Soldani, for example, increased their frequency from twenty-three, fifteen, and eleven designations, respectively, to sixty, forty-two, and fifty-two. The concentration of public office among a group of families who defined themselves according to political rights, ancient origins, family ties, profession, and wealth thus coexisted with relative political mobility. As in the case of Prato and other larger cities, mobility allowed for some rotation of major offices among local families.[35]

In the century after the 1631 plague, the ruling group became even smaller and power further concentrated, reflecting the evolution of increasingly hierarchical social and political structures. Between 1633 and 1715, twenty-nine families shared 617 positions.[36] Of these, ten held important office for the first time, but only three supplied standard-bearers.[37] Five obtained 40 or more appointments and filled 311 of the 617 positions. Two families occupied between 29 and 39 positions each, whereas six families held between 10 and 19 positions each. Overall, thirteen families held 505 appointments, or 81.8 percent of possible offices (table 2.4). The remaining sixteen families held 112 appointments, or 18.2 percent of the total.

Between 1448 and 1715, of the seventy-seven families holding major public office, thirty-seven represented the actual ruling elite

TABLE 2.4

Frequency and Percentage of Office Holding among Thirteen Families, 1633–1715

Names	Frequency	Percentage
Crudeli	71	11.5
Sociani	65	10.5
Rilli	63	10.2
Barboni	58	9.4
Soldani	54	8.8
Martini	36	5.8
Folli	34	5.5
Baldacci	27	4.4
Ducci	27	4.4
Giorgi	20	3.2
Durazzi	18	2.9
Tommasini	18	2.9
Bassi	14	2.3
Total	505	81.8

Note: Frequency and percentage based on 617 positions.

charged with political and economic administration. Six of the thirty-one families who contributed standard-bearers were too small in numerical composition to be listed among the top officeholders. Twenty of the thirty-one families were at the head of municipal government from 1448 until 1632. Of these, four had disappeared in the early decades of the sixteenth century and five more by the end of the century. Of the sixteen surnames that remained at the apex of local government for more than two centuries, only five families survived the demographic crisis of the seventeenth century. With the crisis four more families disappeared, and by the 1650s an additional five died out. Among the remaining eleven families, six emerged during the middle of the sixteenth century, and of these, three were local families already present in the lower positions since the latter part of the fifteenth century.[38] In the course of the two centuries, the eight newcomer families had sons who married into old local families and thereby, as shown later, acquired the status and privileges of the families of their wives. These families established themselves as the town's ruling class and exercised their power by firmly seizing and controlling the local political system.

Of the families that most frequently provided standard-bearers and priors, thirty-one kin groups predominated, even if with a relative degree of fluidity. These thirty-one families constituted the Poppi ruling class, whose composition changed as old families died out and new ones emerged within the inner circle of local government. By concentrating power in their hands, these thirty-one families were able to manipulate the levers of power to their own advantage, shaping a new common identity. The Poppi elite used the local institutions to advance its political influence, to create new sources of authority, and to elaborate a new elitist definition of political participation. Office holding became the foundation upon which professionally qualified and politically confident families created an oligarchic regime, defended their collective interests, and retaliated against any challenge to their newly emerging power. Above all, to dominate office holding and perpetuate an oligarchic form of government, these families had to control the eligibility process.

III

During the Cinquecento, the elaboration of new theories of self-government was reflected in the frequent modifications of the requirements for office holding. The debates over eligibility revealed the efforts toward defining authority as well as the principles upon which authority rested. Who had the right to exercise authority and to participate in self-government? This issue was resolved in favor of a group of local families who sought to adjust the popular character of the new political tradition to suit its own interests and aspirations. By the end of the sixteenth century, it became clear that the government belonged to these families, who legitimized themselves by their political rights. Changes concerning both the electoral process and eligibility for office holding show evidence of the growing influence in local politics of one group of families.

The procedure involving the dual processes of *squittinio* (scrutiny) and *imborsazione* (the candidate's names were placed in pouches from which the winners were drawn) reveals the growing exclusiveness of political participation. These procedures were supervised by the riformatori and formed perhaps the most delicate phase in the political life of the community. By controlling these processes the ruling class controlled access to local government and in turn reinforced the power of the institutions.

The important role played by the riformatori in local governments and their influence and control over local administration in other Tuscan cities and in Florence itself have often been underscored.[39] In Poppi the General Council elected the riformatori every five years; eight riformatori were elected in 1448, six in 1476, and four in 1501. After the last date the number remained unchanged.[40] Until 1501 the General Council nominated and approved the riformatori, but restrictions and controls on the mechanism of nomination increased in later years. In the reforms of 1511 and 1546, three of the four riformatori were nominated directly by the standard-bearer and the priors, and one was nominated by the councilors.[41] The reform of 1594 legalized a procedure that had long been in force: it was now the exclusive prerogative of the vicar, the standard-bearer, the proposto, and the first select prior to nominate the riformatori, although final approval rested with the General Council.[42] Poppi did not go to the extremes of Arezzo, where only a few families had the right to be elected as riformatori.[43] But like Pescia and Santa Croce sull'Arno, where only certain, more prominent families had the prerogative of nominating the riformatori, Poppi kept that office under the direct control of those families who held the principal government offices.[44] Contrary to practices in other Tuscan cities, such as Prato and Pisa, however, the local, rather than the central, government kept control of the nomination of the riformatori until the later decades of the seventeenth century, when the grand duke nominated them. This practice was short lived, and by 1700 the local government regained its prerogative on the nomination of the riformatori, even if final approval had to be given by the Nove Conservatori.[45]

The growing exclusiveness of this office is also reflected in the restricted pool of candidates from which the riformatori were chosen and by the narrow criteria adopted to determine suitability for election. Until 1501 the riformatori were chosen from among all those held suitable for office, provided they were *"prudenti homeni"* of the community.[46] From 1552 on, the choice was to be made from among only ten candidates.[47] Unfortunately, the mechanism involved in selecting these ten remained unknown until 1594. This new statutory reform set down precise rules. Candidates were now to be "four local men of good reputation, known to be God-fearing and zealous in matters of public good and well-being concerning each and all, knowledgeable or at least practiced and expert for their age in the administration of such office."[48] Between 1507 and 1594, of the sixty-three total available positions for the office of riformatore, fifty-nine were shared by twenty-four families.[49] These same families also monopolized the highest government offices and filled the position of standard-bearer 122 out of 127 times.

The duty of the riformatori was "to reform, increase or diminish each and every reform and new provision in order to govern and maintain the commonwealth of the community."[50] Whatever they established had to be approved first by the General Council and subsequently by the Florentine magistrature. Another duty of the riformatori was to conduct the scrutiny and *imborsazione* for local offices, which took place in secret. The four riformatori, in the presence of the vicar, a priest, and the chancellor, placed the name of each citizen judged eligible in pouches bearing the names of the offices in question.[51] The four riformatori had ample freedom "to put and include in said pouches whomever they please[d] on the condition that they [were] men qualified and capable of filling such office."[52] Together with the General Council, they judged the eligibility for office of Poppi citizens according to the specific requirements they had previously formulated in the statutes.

By controlling eligibility, the riformatori controlled access to local government and supervised the elaboration of new articles for the local statutes. Between the 1540s and 1594, the articles concerning eligibility indicated the altered interests and directions of local society. In particular they emphasized the parameters for defining who had the right to participate in government and thus exercise authority. Revisions of eligibility requirements reflected the need to adapt and reinterpret office holding in light of changing demographic and socioeconomic circumstances. They also indicated the trend toward protecting the interests and goals of a more defined group of families which was emerging at the leadership of local society.

The major part of the reform of 1501 covered the mechanisms regulating eligibility requirements of Poppi citizens for public office.[53] As in the majority of Tuscan cities and towns, citizenship, together with age and tax requirements for office, was essential for admission to public office.[54] In Poppi, anyone who was a town resident and taxpayer for twenty-five years was eligible for public office.[55] Within the confines of this general regulation there were further limits regarding age, which varied according to the office in question. In 1501 the standard-bearer, for example, was the senior member of the council and had to be at least thirty-three years old. Priors and councilors of the Ordinary Council had to be at least twenty-five years old.[56] In addition, in order to aspire to the highest positions, certain financial conditions were required: the standard-bearer must have paid taxes totaling at least one soldo and four denari, the priors eight denari, and the councilors six.[57]

In 1544 the reforming committee increased both age and tax requirements of councilors (arroti) of the General Council to the level of more prestigious offices. Initially, anyone who had been a citizen for at least five years and was twenty-five years of age could be elected. Making participation in this less influential office more selective, the riformatori limited the eligibility of the councilors to twenty-eight years of age and to the same tax requirements as the priors.[58] But in 1594, a new article again lowered age requirements for admission to both councils. On the whole the changes were minimal. The standard-bearer was now required to be thirty years old instead of the customary thirty-three years of age. The requirements for select and general priors changed respectively from twenty-five to twenty-four and twenty-one. A notable exception was in the case of the councilors, whose age was lowered from twenty-five years to eighteen.[59]

The changes in age requirements may be attributed to the increased mortality rate of the time, which exacerbated fears of family decline and extinction. The new age prerequisite for the councilors, however, reflected the desire of the ruling families to accelerate and facilitate the political participation of their younger sons. By allowing a wider participation of their sons, the Poppi families restricted office holding only to those who enjoyed financial status as well as professional prerequisites and family connections. At the same time they controlled access to political participation of those families who might have had financial status but lacked the other required qualifications to be part of the ruling group.

The Ferruzzi family, wealthy farmers from the Sova district outside the Poppi walls, is of particular interest. Between the end of the fifteenth century and the beginning of the sixteenth, brothers Giovanni and Antonio moved into Poppi.[60] In 1535 the three sons of Giovanni possessed eighteen hectares, Antonio's heir twenty. Together the Ferruzzi households held thirty-eight hectares, thus numbering among the fifteen largest landowners in town. Regardless of their relatively elevated economic position, the Ferruzzi made no breach in the ruling circle. In 1510 Antonio held a position of select prior. During the following years his son, Fabiano, and grandson, Luca, were elected a total of three times to the post of general prior. Giovanni's descendants held offices of any importance only twice—that of general prior in 1531 and 1554.[61] After this date, family members no longer held any significant positions.

The Ferruzzi were wealthy farmers, but despite the accumulation of a large landed patrimony they did not overcome their humble social extraction. The family did not include notaries, teachers, and doctors, the professions so important not only to political participation but also to social mobility in Poppi society. Lacking professional status, the Ferruzzi were excluded from the ranks of the local ruling class. Thus, economic well-being did not suffice as a qualification for civic office. At the beginning of the sixteenth century, two families who owned considerable amounts of land—the Rampini and Ferruzzi—were not included in the ranks of the ruling class.

Although economic status did not, by itself, suffice as a qualification for civic office, wealth remained an important prerequisite throughout the early part of the sixteenth century. In particular, wealth was not an important condition for individual households as long as the extended kin enjoyed financial stability. Differences in the size of property held among the members of a single family, as Chojnacki has shown for fourteenth-century Venice, were often caused by "temporary generation gaps" that arose during the period necessary to execute a will.[62]

In the case of the Crudeli, the disparity in the amount of property held by uncle and nephew did not affect the degree of the political participation of the family. At the beginning of the sixteenth century, the two Crudeli branches combined owned almost fifty-four hectares, only two of which belonged to Francesco of Jacopo and the remainder to his uncle Bernardo. In the same period Francesco held major civic office eight times; Bernardo, seven.[63] A similar case was that of the Rilli brothers. Between 1508 and 1538 Ser Agnolo served three times as general prior, four times as select prior, and four times as standard-bearer. His younger brother, Ser Giovanni, began his local administrative career in 1521 and ended it in 1545, having served five times as general and select prior and standard-bearer.[64] Since the family's patrimony had not yet been divided, Agnolo held only seven hectares he must have bought on his own. Ser Giovanni owned the greater part of the land, calculated at forty-nine hectares.

Economic well-being, however, was particularly important for newcomer families who aspired to enter into the ruling group. Ser Francesco di Stefano, a notary from Soci, five kilometers from Poppi, moved there at the beginning of the sixteenth century; Soldano di Niccolò Soldani came to Poppi from Florence in the 1450s and became a citizen of the town sometime during the 1470s.[65] Ser Francesco Sociani and his three sons, Francesco, Ser Stefano, and Giovanbattista, were notaries and landowners. As soon as their residency requirements in Poppi were met, they began an active political life in the municipal government, holding fifteen of the highest positions between 1523 and 1556.[66]

In the 1520s Giovanbattista di Niccolò Soldani still did not have the financial prerequisite to fill the office of the standard-bearer.[67] In the first decades of the sixteenth century, however, the Soldani intermarried with the Bardi, an ancient and notable Poppi family that was in the process of becoming extinct and whose patrimony the Soldani subsequently inherited. The improvement in the social and financial status of the family led to a sudden increase in its involvement in the political life of the community, and in 1539 Giovanbattista was elected standard-bearer.[68] In the following seventeen years, Giovanbattista, his three sons, Vincentio, Lorenzo, and Niccolò, and his brother Francesco held a total of eleven major offices.[69]

In the second part of the century, while many of the Poppi ruling families were becoming economically more stable, financial qualifications declined in importance among the criteria for office holding. In 1568, in view of the continued lack of qualified candidates, tax requirements for the offices of standard-bearer and prior were waived for any citizen of Poppi bearing the degree of doctor. The reform of 1568 stated:

> Communities and lands are well led and governed when their offices are held by intelligent and experienced people, . . . and to encourage everyone to aspire to an education and because from this will follow the good and honorable administration of our community, we desire and resolve that . . . every member in the community who shall achieve the title of Doctor shall be eligible for and may occupy any government office even that of standard-bearer whether or not he owns any land or that which he owns is sufficient to qualify now or in the future. . . . Nor shall he be obliged . . . to pay any differences in taxes or to purchase land . . . against his will and convenience.[70]

The impetus behind this article was the recent return to Poppi of Doctor Vincenzo Amerighi. Vincenzo was born to Elisabetta Rilli from Poppi, one of the town's most prominent families. During the first half of the sixteenth century, Elisabetta married a man from nearby Pratovecchio. Upon the death of her husband, she returned to her paternal home with her three young children. After completing his education at the University of Pisa, Vincenzo settled in Poppi, but his absence and his mother's original departure had left the Amerighi with little property and no opportunity for local political participation.[71] The perpetuation of power within a contained group was a prime motive behind the suspension of wealth as a criterion for office holding. It was this incentive that allowed Vincenzo to join the local ruling group.

Although political office ceased to be wedded to wealth, family tradition and professional qualifications became ever more important conditions. The office-holding career of the Catani reflected the changes concerning eligibility. They began participating in the political life of Poppi in the 1540s. The claim of the family to be among the most ancient in town did not, by itself, facilitate its inclusion in the local ruling group. The small family patrimony, which at its height did not reach eighteen hectares, did not help either. Rather, their entrance into the oligarchy coincided with a change in professional qualifications.

In the fifteenth century the Catani, tailors of no great wealth, were known as *"cornacchia"* (a noisy bird). In the 1450s a certain Mariano *"cornacchia"* was offered the position of operating the town's clock.[72] By the beginning of the Cinquecento, the surname Catani was commonly used in preference to *cornacchia* to address the members of the family. At this time, Mariano Catani had accumulated a small patrimony of eleven hectares and had seen to the education of his son, Piero, who in 1537 began his career as a notary. From 1537 to 1594, Ser Piero was very active in his notarial practice, as was his son, Ser Mariano, who succeeded him in the profession. At the same time, the Catani also had a brilliant political career, frequently filling the offices of prior and standard-bearer.[73] Between 1548 and 1592, Ser Piero was general prior four times, select prior six times, and standard-bearer twice.[74] At the end of the century, both of Ser Piero's sons, Ser Mariano, notary, and Maestro Giovanbattista, a druggist (*cerusico*), became social and political leaders of the community. Ser Mariano and Maestro Giovanbattista were elected respectively twice and four times as general prior, eight and ten times as select prior, and twice and once as standard-bearer.[75] Thanks to their notarial career, practiced in both the private and public spheres, the Catani accrued political, social, and also economic advantages.

The lack of considerable wealth did not constitute a barrier to political advancement, as long as the ruling families ultimately controlled those who were employed in the professions. In 1579 the government asked and obtained permission from Florence to oversee the entrance of doctors, notaries, and teachers from other towns who wanted to practice their profession in Poppi. Only the staff of the vicar was not included in this reform. The local government thus had the right to supervise the practice of these professions in town.[76] In 1594, when the economic depression threatened the social position and economic situation of the oligarchy, the riformatori protected the political supremacy of their families by taking advantage of their control over the professions. They thus extended the right to hold high public office to notaries and schoolteachers, "it being reputed by the Community that a wise and educated poor man [was] better able to govern and administer the community than a rich and prosperous illiterate."[77] With this strategy the Poppi families preserved the cohesion of the ruling group during a period of declining prosperity.

By the end of the century, it became increasingly apparent that office holding was based on a tight network of family connections and interpersonal loyalties. In 1555 the lack of "men fit to govern" had justified the drawing up of a new article intended to make office holding the exclusive domain of a restricted group.[78] This article decreed that the names of all the candidates for the office of standard-bearer could be placed in the pouches for the other offices as well, thus increasing the probability of office holding by certain people. Furthermore, without reaching the extremes of other towns, such as Siena, where political offices had become hereditary, the 1594 reform gave officeholders the right to transfer their position to a relative at least as long as they themselves were in office.[79] It was decreed that in case of justified absence, a relative *"in secondo grado"* could substitute for the standard-bearer, and the priors and councilors could be replaced by relatives *"fino al quarto grado."*[80] Political participation and family ties reinforced each other. Together they legitimized and sustained the claim to power by the Poppi ruling group. They also furthered mutual support upon which a new class solidarity was forged.

The statutory reforms of the end of the sixteenth century reflected the economic downturn that threatened the socioeconomic and political position of the ruling group. They were thus elaborated to maintain and strengthen the social supremacy of an oligarchy. The reforms concerning eligibility were intended to protect the monopoly of public office by those families who numbered notaries, schoolteachers, and doctors among them. With the new reforms the ruling group safeguarded its dominance by supervising the political participation of new families, such as the Ferruzzi, coming from the countryside who had the wealth but neither the family tradition nor professional qualifications. But they were also intended to supervise the access to office holding of outside families that came into Poppi either through marriage or at the service of the state.

The 1594 reform did not draw up precise regulations for eligibility for public office except in the case of military officers. To limit the prerogatives of the military officers who came from other towns but resided in Poppi at the service of grand-ducal troops, it was decreed that all officers, in order to be considered as candidates for the office of standard-bearer, had to give proof of "having themselves, their fathers or their ancestors enjoyed and exercised such office one or more times."[81] Although limiting office holding for some, the new reforms facilitated the admittance of others into the ruling group. In particular, they benefited new families who had entered local society by taking part in the provincial bureaucracy and, most important, by marrying local men and women. Some of these newcomers, though lacking taxable wealth in the community, had professional qualifications fitting the new eligibility requirements.

For families such as the Mannucci and the Baldacci, wealth was never a prerequisite for participating in the political life of the community because they enjoyed professional standing. At the end of the sixteenth century, the Mannucci appeared for the first time among the community's political elite. The family counted notaries and teachers among its members but possessed less than one hectare of land. The Baldacci family was listed as possessing nothing whatsoever. Professional qualifications and matrimonial ties with notable local families guaranteed the political and economic advancement of the two families.

Ser Mariotto Baldacci, a notary, had moved from Anghiari to Poppi in the 1550s.[82] Some years later he married Bartolomea, the only heir of Torello Manfidi, from an old and established Poppi family.[83] In the ensuing years the Baldacci, although they had no patrimony, filled numerous civic offices, and as early as 1597 the son of Mariotto and Bartolomea, Messer Assuero, was elected to the highest municipal position, that of standard-bearer.[84] During the first three decades of the seventeenth century, four of the Baldacci held the position of general prior ten times, that of select prior eleven times, and standard-bearer twice.[85] Only during the seventeenth century did the Baldacci accrue considerable wealth, and in the estimo of 1701 the family owned about twenty-two hectares of land.

Similarly, Giovanbattista Folli, a notary, had moved to Poppi from Pisa during the same period as the Baldacci.[86] Professional qualifications and matrimonial ties with one of the oldest families in town were at the core of the advancement of Giovanbattista and, most important, of other Folli in the Poppi ruling class. By 1583 Giovanbattista was married to Bartolomea Pauolozzi, only heir, together with her sister, of Giovanni.[87] Following the example of Giovanbattista, Girolamo di Antonio Folli, a druggist, also moved to Poppi and married a local woman who, however, was not part of the ruling families.[88] The branch of Giovanbattista Folli ended with Caterina, his and Bartolomea's only child.[89] Moreover, given his career in the provincial lesser bureaucracy, Giovanbattista occupied only one position as general prior of the municipal council in 1597.[90] By the 1580s, after a careful policy of land investment, the Folli of Girolamo owned about eighteen hectares of land. In this same period, the political activity of the family increased as it entered the ranks of the local ruling class.[91] Economic success and the network of family ties which Giovanbattista established with his marriage to Bartolomea were fundamental to the political and social ascent of the Folli in Poppi society.

During the sixteenth century, the development of the local magistrature mirrored the rise of a group of families. These families took control of the politics and administration of the community and had established themselves as the town's rulers. Their success in monopolizing the local government depended on their ability to manipulate eligibility requirements for office holding. The ruling families shaped a political system that was instrumental in creating, extending, and maintaining their social and political supremacy within the community as well as out in the contado. They also used their monopoly of local government to shape new political practices founded on new forms of authority.

Over the long run, control of the mechanisms of power helped Poppi's ruling families refigure the nature of their relationship with the central government and establish political continuity and stability in the community. Over the short term, however, it led to conflicts with central authorities.

THREE

✦

Dynamics of Power and Authority
Poppi and Florence

Studies of the consolidation of the regional state have traditionally emphasized the coexistence of centralizing reforms and local autonomies in fifteenth- and sixteenth-century Tuscany. According to this scholarship, during the fifteenth century the central government, in the process of reorganizing the Florentine state, used peripheral institutions to effect state building and expand its control. In authoritarian grand-ducal Tuscany, state consolidation ensued directly from the Medici in their efforts at increasing their authority and contracting local autonomy.[1] In both cases, however, the politics of central government led to the emergence of two layers of power, the local and the central. This interpretation is based on the assumption that the evolution of the state as characterized by the emergence of a duality of power originated from a political scheme formulated from above, conceived and supervised first by the Florentine republic and later by the Medici grand duchy.

An analysis of local politics suggests that there are additional perspectives to be considered when studying state building. The reforms of local statutes and their enactment reveal the persistence of autonomy in local politics and its coexistence with growing levels of control from the central government. Layers of state control and areas of local autonomy, however, gave shape to two forms of power which not only coexisted with but also mutually sustained the structures and practices of state building, leading to a relationship between central and local rulers which was interconnected and ultimately interdependent.

During the fifteenth century, officeholders utilized the margins of autonomy granted by the central government to create a political structure that strengthened their control over local politics. Consequently, the ruling families used office holding and the political rights associated with it as privileged vehicles to assert their legitimacy and establish an oligarchic regime. By the early 1500s, however, Poppi, like other provincial towns, experienced a steady encroachment of central authority in local affairs. The leading families did not openly revolt, but they resisted central interference in local matters. The General Council became the forum for political protest and the riformatori its leaders. The conflict lasted until the 1530s. Over the next two centuries, the Poppi leading families secured for themselves new forms of authority by shaping ingenious practices through which they strengthened their hold on the town government and society. They also fashioned creative ways of relating and interacting with central powers. The changes in local society thus both revealed and conditioned broader transformations in the political system of republican Florence and in the rise of the grand duchy of Tuscany.

I

Fifteenth-century Florentine state consolidation was aimed at organizing and regrouping the recent territorial conquests. It also favored the growth of local governance and the elaboration of local bodies of law. During this time smaller towns identified Florence as their emancipator from the control of larger provincial cities. Rural statutes such as that of the communes in the Pistoia hinterland often portrayed an image of Florence as impartial arbiter and supporter of local rights and self-government.[2] Florence had also been instrumental in freeing Poppi from a feudal past and in establishing a communal tradition.

In the early government minutes and in the first statutory drafts, Poppi municipal officials referred to Florence using a paternalistic metaphor that echoed fifteenth-century humanist writers who portrayed Cosimo de' Medici as defender of Florentine liberty and *"Pater-Patriae,"* father of the homeland.[3] Combining a filial and subservient attitude, the Poppi officials expressed their devotion and gratitude to the Florentines. In 1454 they portrayed themselves not only as "veri et perfecti filij" but also as "servitores Maggiori et potentissimi populi florentini."[4] Over the next fifty years the municipal councilors never failed to respect and acknowledge Florentine authority. Thus they drew statutory reforms "ad magnificentiam et exaltationem Maggiori et Potentissimi populi florentini et ad exaltationem serenissime partis guelforum." Only in a second instance were new statutes drafted "ad pacem et tranquillitatem populorum et hominum ac Villarum curie puppij."[5] Government minutes emphasized that the vicar always occupied a central position. The council, the Poppi officers wrote, convened only by order, "*comandamento*," of the vicar, who supervised the council meeting.[6]

In everyday social interaction the political father-son metaphor was transformed into a patron-client relationship.[7] The council saw the vicar as the intercessor between Florence and Poppi. In 1480 the councilors sent the former vicar, Piero Corsini, some wine, "the kind he like[d] the best[,] . . . for having supported the commune of Poppi." The motive for the gift was a loan from the vicar to repair the clock of the castle.[8] In the following year local ambassadors went to visit Corsini in Florence, pleading with him to intercede in favor of the town concerning the postponement of tax payments to the Florentine government. In June 1481, when Piero's wife delivered a baby, the council sent another gift of two chickens.[9]

During the fifty years after annexation, Poppi enjoyed relative political and administrative autonomy from Florence. The central government regularly approved without substantial modification or interference local reforms drawn up by the municipal government. At this time, the town established new institutions and gave shape to a local system of government to manage ordinary communal activities. The central government resorted to the local self-governing structures to exercise its control over the dominion. For instance, the local *camarlinghi* collected taxes for both the municipal and central governments. The commune of Poppi saw to the collection of rates due for taxes to the office of the Monte Comune from the other communes in the podesteria. In addition, the officers in charge of supervising local public properties supported the task of the vicar by reporting transgressors to his office.[10] The Florentine government endorsed a combination of forms of control and autonomy to build a support system to its authority and enforce public order.

The coexistence of central and local spheres of power, however, could lead to conflicting models of governance, especially in the larger Tuscan cities (such as Pistoia and Pisa), which had a strong communal tradition of self-government. But Florence had already imposed short-term restrictions in their margins of autonomy and self-government.[11] Indeed, Pistoia and Pisa prerogatives over vast hinterlands prompted the Florentine territorial reorganization begun in the early 1400s. In smaller rural towns that had been more recently enfranchised, Florentine rulers allowed for larger margins of independence. Here autonomy was granted in return for devoted subservience. As in Poppi, conciliation and harmony were framed within the father-son imagery which, at least initially, sustained their relationship. This paternalistic domination bolstered the authority of the central government without suppressing the much needed creative vitality of local society.

II

During the early sixteenth century the submissive and appeasing terms of the earlier period disappeared. The tone of the opening statement of council meetings changed. The loyal and deferential child revolted against the "magnificent" father. In 1501 the preamble written by the local chancellor for the government minutes made no reference to the role of the vicar. On the contrary, it stated that the council could only be called into session by the proposto or by the standard-bearer. Only in an emergency could the vicar call the council into session.[12] The change reflected a deterioration in the relations between the central government and local officers as Florence tightened its control by restricting the administrative autonomy of the municipal government.[13] As Florence intervened more directly in local politics and undermined local legislative initiatives, the emerging ruling families fought back to protect their own interests.

   Between 1512 and the 1530s Florentine officials curtailed initiatives drafted by the local oligarchy to safeguard its own interests. In 1501 the riformatori tried to shield Poppi notaries from the competition of their Florentine colleagues who had arrived in the wake of the vicar. The new article decreed that Florentine notaries could not write up local contracts, "per commodo delli huomini della terra di poppi et del paese."[14] Initially Florentine functionaries passed the reform, only to reverse it a few years later. In 1516 the riformatori tried again to discourage Florentine notaries from practicing in Poppi by requiring that out-of-town notaries file a copy of all contracts with the office of the priors without receiving any fee. But again they were unsuccessful.[15] In 1521 Florence nullified another attempt to protect the community, a refusal to admit poverty-stricken outsiders to the hospital within the town walls.[16] Finally, in 1526, Florence vetoed an increase in salary for the standard-bearer, the priors, and the councilors of Poppi and a proposal to tax foreign wine sold at fairs.[17]

The reforms advanced by the oligarchy did not benefit the larger community. The articles on salary increase for officeholders and the taxes on foreign wine promoted both the political and financial interests of the ruling families. Conversely, they were of no avail for those consumers and taxpayers who did not practice the profession and did not participate in government. An increase in salaries would have boosted public expenses and thus raised local taxes. A decline in competition, moreover, would have raised the price of wine and thus favored producers at the expense of consumers.

As for the reform that sought to limit the actions of foreign notaries, the implications transcended the municipal boundaries and interfered with the domain of central authority. Local notaries would have gained control over their profession and thus bolstered their own prestige in town. At the same time, the request to limit the practice of foreign notaries would have restricted some of the activities of Florentine notaries who came to Poppi as assistants to the vicar. By regulating foreign notaries the local council sought to challenge the authority they embodied as officers of the state. On its part, Florence interpreted the resolution of the Poppi government as a threat to its authority regarding the confines of local autonomy. The contrast between central rulers and peripheral notables, thus, was particularly intense over issues concerning the boundaries of power and the spheres of authority of local governments.

The municipal government repeatedly continued to be at odds with Florence. In 1521 Florentine officials undermined the local exercise of judicial authority. The council gave the two officers in charge of roads, rivers, and bridges the power to denounce and punish transgressors. Again, Florentine officials responded that only the vicar had the power to prosecute and punish those who evaded the law and to "jail anybody of whatever status, grade or condition."[18] The only power local officials had was to report violations of the law.

In the same year, local officeholders tried to offset the interference of the central government by augmenting the sphere of authority of the General Council. The riformatori, who were the organizers of political protest, counterbalanced the incursion of the central government into the field of local administration. They placed greater autonomy and responsibility within the General Council as the seat of legislative power with wider representation. They presented their political strategy in these terms:

> [The twenty-four men convened together] have and must have as much authority, power, and procedural rights as has the Commune of Poppi and having won a majority have sufficient power to have their decisions observed as would those of our Magnificent and Excellent Lords [of Florence]; and the majority of sixteen votes can eliminate or add in all or in part, whether debated or not, any of the three reforms made from 1501 to the present and decide on new sources of income and increase or diminish those existing as they please and never at any time can this majority be opposed in matters that concern the government of our lands, but their decisions must always be observed.[19]

Even if the statute further admitted that the vicar had to consent to all decisions taken by the council, Florentine officials were prompt in ordering that the new article be entirely suppressed.[20]

The struggle over authority and control reached its apex in 1526. Dismissing the reaction of the Florentines to the 1521 statute, the riformatori wrote defiantly that the two councils had "such authority as they had [in the past] and all measures that [were to] be decided by them [were] to be respected."[21] This time, the central government was even more intransigent; it specifically deleted "that part which authorize[d] the 9 councilors and 12 supernumeraries to do whatever they please[d]" and responded, "Everything that is decided upon by the aforementioned 9 councilors and 12 supernumeraries is to be approved in Florence according to the law and in no other way."[22] This resolution was short lived. In 1532 the Florentine magistrates justified a modification of the article because of the difficulties inherent in carrying out the reform, since it was "very inconvenient to bother those men to send to Florence for approval of every minimal thing and to give them so much trouble. Therefore, wanting to eliminate the damage and the inconvenience caused these men," the Florentine functionaries decided that only those decisions that were to remain in effect for more than one year were to secure the vicar's approval.[23] All resolutions relating to local administration, particularly the management of public income, which lasted for less than one year, remained under the jurisdiction of local authorities.[24]

Several factors combined to produce the clashes between Poppi and Florence. Italian and European economic downturns and political conflicts and changes in local society strained the relationship between local and central governments. Between the 1490s and the early 1530s, Florence experienced financial and political instability as a result of foreign invasions, domestic turmoil, and epidemics. The international conflict of the Italian wars combined with rapidly changing political systems in Florence. Within thirty years, Florence twice alternated a republican government with Medici rule. During these years important reforms affected the larger provincial cities, where participation of central functionaries in local politics increased, even if for brief periods. In Pistoia a new magistracy was established with the creation of *commissari*, functionaries directly nominated by and accountable only to the central government. In 1502 the Florentines directly nominated the priors in Arezzo. In 1510 Pisa faced similar actions.[25]

The conjunctural economic circumstances and political events of the early 1500s hastened the encroachment of the central government on local politics. Threatened by general economic hardship and political instability the central government devised new and more direct ways of governance. Broader external events also affected Poppi.

Between 1517 and 1530, the financial burdens of war and natural calamities worsened an already precarious economic situation caused by debts Poppi contracted with Florence for defaulted payment of taxes since 1511.[26] Over these years, war loans, taxes, and plague-connected subsidies followed one another at a constant pace.[27] Central authorities required Poppi to feed and house troops stationed in the area and also to maintain its own troops sent to the field in the service of Florence.[28] During the 1520s the situation degenerated further because of a series of plagues that raged throughout the Casentino, as in the rest of Tuscany, requiring local and central government subsidies to provide for the needy.[29] The weight of war-related expenses levied on the citizens was increased by plague-connected subsidies not only for the needs of the community but also for those of other towns in the vicariate. The burden placed upon the community often required additional funds, which were usually collected in the form of private loans. The local government thus became heavily indebted both to central authorities and to those Poppi families wealthy enough to provide loans of money or grain.

The early decades of the sixteenth century, however, were a dynamic period in the social and political life of Poppi. During this time a group of local families sought to create and mold the structures of the municipal government with the aim of dominating the political life of the community. Seeking to define local magistrature, defend autonomy, and assert their political supremacy, the riformatori presented an alternative ideal of governance, supported by a terminology that departed from the earlier filial tradition. During the second half of the fifteenth century, public documents conveyed deference, gratitude, and loyalty. Now, local functionaries appropriated words such as *power, authority*, and *rights*. They thus embraced the same terminology that the Florentines used to define the prerogatives of their authority over the dominion. This wording legitimized the Poppi officials to claim control of the municipal council and defy the authority of the central government.

By emulating the central government's conceptual patterns of power and authority, local ruling families came into competition with Florence. The emergence of these families and their claim to power over local society were viewed by Florence as a threat to its authority and a departure from its traditional ideals of governance. Prior to 1500, the interests of the municipal government had been one and the same with those of the people of Poppi. As the Poppi leading families became more self-assured and protective of their interests, the Florentine government felt challenged in its authority. As the families responded with resistance and opposition, Florence pursued a defensive policy. It reacted by curtailing the political and legislative functions of the local government. Most of all Florence, still retaining the traditional father-son imagery, responded by restricting the margins of autonomy of the leading families while, at the same time, protecting the interests of the larger community.

During the early sixteenth century, the actions undertaken by the central government to limit the political autonomy and economic prerogatives of Poppi were aimed at consolidating central rule and maintaining social order. But the strategies of the central government were not part of a defined, broader political scheme. The short-term duration of much of the Florentine legislation demonstrated the uncertainty of Florentine policy. Florence responded to local conditions and adopted new resolutions according to conjunctural circumstances and to critical developments within local environments. Its aim was to maintain control and protect its rule over the dominion. The reforms legislated under the Medici principate retained the same goal. They sought to maintain social order and strengthen central control over dynamic provincial towns. They further promoted notions of paternalistic domination. The ways the Medici accomplished their objective, however, differed as they chose a strategy of privilege toward local ruling groups.

III

The Medicean principate strengthened its supremacy over the dominion and restricted the economic advantages enjoyed by provincial towns. It also established centralized institutions that bypassed local offices. Cosimo I and his successors used the new administrative structures to enforce a new system centered on personal power and to curtail the margins of autonomy previously granted provincial towns.[30]

By the early 1530s the Medici had reasserted their rule over Florence. In the 1550s the consolidation of the Medici regime was enhanced further with the annexation of Siena and its territories. In 1559 Cosimo became the first grand duke of Tuscany. These developments lead to a period of peace and political stability in the state which facilitated new reforms aimed at consolidating central authority. The old structures of the republic were strengthened and adapted to the new political, economic, and social characteristics of a larger and more complex regional system at the expense of local independence.

In the middle of the sixteenth century, Duke Cosimo I began a systematic centralization of authority and unification of state institutions by limiting the degree of independence of local towns and broadening Florentine control. Between 1560 and the 1590s the jurisdictional and legislative uniformity in the dominion increased as vicars and other government representatives were given additional authority. Grand-ducal policies, designed to control the economy of the communities and to create more uniform jurisdictional practices throughout the dominion, resulted in the consolidation of state structures. In the 1560s, economic matters within the local communities were subordinated to the new office of the Chancellors of the Nine. In the 1580s, as discussed in Chapter 1, criminal matters were placed under the direct control of the vicar.

In 1560 the merging of the two bodies of the Cinque Conservatori and the Otto di Pratica into the single office of the Nove Conservatori della Giurisdizione e del Dominio represented an important step taken by Cosimo I to reinforce ties between the central and peripheral governments and render government control over local economic administration more efficient.[31] In the following years, the Chancellors of the Nine were scattered throughout the centers of the state. These functionaries were charged with ratifying the budgets of local governments and officers, supervising the updating of the account books and tax rolls of the communities, and ensuring that laws were carried out.[32]

In 1564, in another step toward the consolidation of Medici authority, Poppi was made the seat of the Chancellor of the Nine with supervision over the administration of the commune.[33] Prior to the reform of 1560, the municipal *camarlingo* had the task of presenting the budget to the Cinque Conservatori. The difficulty of carrying out this task because of transportation problems resulted in the setting up of the chancellor.[34] In 1595, in conformity with centralizing reforms, Ferdinand I established that the vicar of the Casentino, rather than being chosen by lot, was to be nominated directly by the grand duke. This was a practice reserved only for the most important communities of the state and performed by the Medici as direct manifestation of their personal power.[35]

Despite these structural changes, the Medicean government still sought the support of local administration. In fact, a centralization of the institutions often coexisted with the inefficiency of other political practices. Financial considerations were important reasons behind the limitations of the new system. A lack of sufficient provincial functionaries and of cooperation from local institutions and people did not facilitate the smooth operation of the new political machinery.[36] Municipal institutions remained the preferential channel employed by central authority to secure order and impose its control over the state. Sixteenth-century Medici rulers thus preserved some margins of autonomy in the peripheral towns, still essential to legitimate the power of the new principate and to appease local ruling groups.

Elena Fasano Guarini pointed to an increase in the elaboration and revision of local statutes after the 1550s.[37] Contrary to the earlier period, however, Fasano Guarini argued that the creative activity of peripheral towns did not reflect an increase in their sovereignty.

The new princely government removed local rulers from any substantial political decisions and limited their action to the sphere of prestige and remuneration connected with office holding.[38] What the local elites lost in power they gained in prestige. These transformations underscored the maturation of an aristocratic and authoritarian princely political system and reconfirmed the endurance of a duality of power.

In Poppi the Medicean principate opened a new phase when the central government curtailed the privileged economic position the town had enjoyed since the time of its submission to Florence. In the articles of submission of 1440 the Florentine government decreed that Poppi would be exempted *in perpetuo* from gabelles, both ordinary and extraordinary, and from customs duties, with the exception of those owed to the gate of Florence. Poppi merchants, artisans, and notaries were also exempted from paying registration fees to Florentine guilds. Furthermore, it was stipulated that Poppi could appropriate all legal fines of less than twenty-five lire, whereas those above this amount would be divided between Poppi and Florence.[39] In addition, Poppi enjoyed special fiscal privileges. The local government was granted the right of determining how the tax burden was to be distributed among the population. This system was similar to that of other towns, such as Prato, San Miniato, Civitella, and other communes in the vicariate of Firenzuola, but differed from towns that were taxed on the basis of their *massa d'estimo*, or taxable income of the land.[40]

Since 1463, as established by the articles of submission, Poppi, together with the communes of Quota and Fronzola in the podesteria, was obliged to pay 100 lire for the lighting of a wax candle for the feast of San Giovanni, the Florentine patron saint, a symbolic act all towns of the dominion were required to perform.[41] Twenty-five years after annexation, in 1469, the articles of submission also required that the community pay a semiannual tax to the Monte Comune of Florence in the amount of 125 lire. This sum did not vary throughout the sixteenth century.[42] Furthermore, the local government was to provide the vicar, headquartered in Poppi, with a salary that amounted to 150 lire every six months in 1440 and by the early 1500s stabilized at 187 lire.[43] Above these ordinary expenses, Florence required the communal government to disburse funds to pay for the maintenance of soldiers in time of war, for the repair of roads and bridges, and for emergencies resulting from bad harvests and epidemic diseases. From 1580 to 1599 Florentine authorities revoked the exemptions from customs duties and cereal and meat taxes. However, in order to protect the interests of the notaries and landowners, the central government continued to allow exemptions on stamp taxes for Poppi notaries and on direct taxes for its landowners. These stayed on the books until the eighteenth century.[44]

Florentine rulers reconsidered their strategy in dealing with the local ruling class. The new direction in the policies of the central government was reflected in the articles ratified by the community between 1532 and 1594. The riformatori convened eleven times to draft new articles and renew old ones, in addition to numerous meetings solely concerned with the *danno dato*, rules concerning the use of property and collective behavior. Contrary to the earlier period, Florentine functionaries regularly approved the actions of local officials with only minor corrections.

Just as in the earlier period, local authorities drafted new articles aimed at benefiting and empowering the local ruling families. The similarity to the issues covered by the riformatori at the beginning of the century is striking. This time, however, the central government did not perceive them as a challenge to its authority. In 1568 a request similar to that presented in 1526 aimed at protecting local wine from foreign imports was accepted by Florentine officials, who declared that only innkeepers could sell imported wine.[45] Similarly, the new article ratified in 1579 concerning local notaries and other professions paralleled the one rejected by the Florentines in 1501 and 1516. Now the riformatori went as far as to ask that the council be granted the power to supervise the entrance into town of notaries, doctors, and teachers. The only correction made by the Florentine officials regarded the notaries who came in the wake of the vicar, who could not be included in the new procedures.[46] Finally, in 1594 the local government introduced without opposition from Florence a salary increase for its functionaries. The salary of the standard-bearer increased from four lire to nineteen lire. Similarly, the priors quadrupled their pay, from two lire and ten soldi to nine lire and ten soldi. In contrast, the salary of the councilors only doubled, from one lira to two lire and eight soldi.[47]

During the first part of the sixteenth century, the Florentine government pursued a policy directed at restricting the privileges of the local ruling class. Later in the century, the Medicean principate tended to protect the interests of those same ruling families. As in the case of other larger towns of the Florentine district, the Medici arranged particular strategies with Poppi ruling families.[48] The changes in the approach of central authority toward local powers reflected important developments both in the Medici's conception of the state and in how local rulers conceived their power.

The imagery of the Medici regime retained a paternalistic slant. The early historians of the principate portrayed Duke Cosimo as the protector of the rights of his subjects.[49] Rather than being the defender of liberty, however, as in the case of the older Cosimo, he was the supporter of peace and public order. Cosimo and his successors strengthened their authority, legislated, gratified local oligarchies, and granted them privileges in the name of peace and order and in support of a new princely system.[50]

The combination of authoritarian tendencies and appeasement endorsed by the Medici in their new political practices reflected the evolution of the new princely state. The new forms of organization were more hierarchical and authoritarian. They were also more concerned with protecting and reinforcing the interests of provincial ruling families and thus with emphasizing privilege over ideals of equality of the subjects.[51] As Litchfield noted, "the myth of Florence became its absolute prince."[52] While strengthening their control, the Florentine rulers learned how to relate to changing local contexts. The Medicean government refashioned its relationship with municipal councils and with the ruling families of smaller towns. As these families consolidated their power in local society, created oligarchic regimes, and demonstrated their capacity to provide stability, they also became the preferential partners of the duke. In the long run local ruling families also became loyal supporters of the state by sustaining decentralized forms of political organizations such as the local militia.[53]

The expansion of authority of the new ducal regime and its institution of a policy of privilege corresponded with a change in the way Poppi rulers interacted with spheres of control and layers of autonomy in local society. Poppi ruling families forged new political strategies in light of the new centralizing procedures, in turn shaping their social, economic, and political environment. As in Pistoia a century earlier, the ruling families successfully secured for themselves relative autonomy in the management of municipal affairs and in their control of local society and polity.[54] They did this not by obtaining for themselves wider margins of autonomy but by enacting new political practices. By the 1530s Poppi ruling families replaced their opposition to centralization with the elaboration of new political strategies of alliance. Through these new policies they successfully established and expanded their privileged status and consolidated their control in Poppi. They also guaranteed the perpetuation of peace and stability in local society and in the state.

IV

During the second half of the sixteenth century municipal governments did not draft new statutory reforms; rather, they reorganized, stylistically embellished, and repackaged old statutes. The new reforms revealed the continuing vitality of local governments and also reflected the need of provincial towns to integrate their laws into the more authoritarian Medicean political structure.[55] Doubtless, the politics of control by the Florentine government was one of assertion of its political superiority counterbalanced by the formal submission of local ruling families. By reducing the political autonomy and economic prerogatives of the community, the central government intended to defend and assert its own central authority. But the lack of direct confrontation from the 1530s onward did not indicate passive acceptance of a subordinate role. The riformatori had no intention of giving up the control and privilege they fashioned and defended during the early decades of the century. Rather, the ruling oligarchy identified different ways of exercising its authority by redirecting its energies toward alternative spheres of power. Florence curtailed the legislative and executive power of local institutions and the economic privileges of the community, but the Poppi ruling class was able to conceive new forms of control. In particular it enacted new symbolic roles that at the same time fostered prestige and authority. Ultimately, the local ruling families retained a considerable hold over local society.

The earlier analysis of office holding has shown that during the sixteenth century several families took control of the politics and administration of the community and established themselves as the town's rulers. Office holding was an essential prerequisite for defining the social and political position of the ruling families. By concentrating power in their hands, the thirty-one families who supplied the highest functionaries to the municipality were able to manipulate further the levers of power to their own advantage and to shape the elaboration of a new political tradition. Contrary to the reform of 1501, which concentrated more on eligibility for office and on the electorial process, the reform of 1594 gave more attention to the rights and privileges connected with the holding of public office, to the creation of new offices, and to the external appearance of government officials.

On June 12, 1594, the officials of the General Council approved the draft of a new general reform of the community:

> Considering that everything to be found among mortals under the Heavens is subject to variation and change, in particular, governments, customs, and practices which are primarily concerned with place, time, and people and that for various reasons they are changing from one state to another, there is, thus, need of new methods, rules, orders, precepts, traditions, reforms, Statutes and provisions which will conform and be convenient to those of good standing and blessed life. . . . Inasmuch as in the past one Hundred Years people, modes of living and of conducting business have altered, new forms of government are made necessary with a consequent need of new provisions, reforms and orders to better maintain and, with prudence govern and direct the business at hand.[56]

The changes to which the councilors were alluding did not include new government procedures, since the 1594 reform in most cases reconfirmed resolutions that had been taken in the previous decades. Rather, they included the elaboration of new political strategies based on the reinterpretation of the image the ruling class had of itself and on the development of a new relationship between central authority and local powers.

Once in control of local offices, the Poppi ruling families used their position to advance their collective interests and authority and to elaborate a new public concept of themselves. Reforms introduced in 1569 and 1594 increased the social status and economic privilege of the highest officeholders. The reform of 1594 set down new and precise regulations concerning dress, particularly for the standard-bearer, the priors, and the chancellor. The standard-bearer was exhorted to dress himself with

> a gown of coarse black wool with a collar cut in the civilian style that [came] below the knee, with purple lining or at least with the lining showing at the cuffs of the sleeves, a matching velvet hat . . . a wool

hood . . . to be worn thrown over the shoulder in sign of recognition of the community [of Poppi], cloth or leather slippers. And the clothes worn underneath to match these as much as possible, according to the possibility of each.[57]

The select priors also were required to wear a "gown" of black wool; the general priors had simply to wear a "long mantle with gathers held at the neck with a fastening, without the black collar."[58] All priors were to wear black hats "with three sides."[59]

The reform of 1594 reflected the awareness of the ruling families of constituting a new urban patriciate. Occupying the office of standard-bearer or prior conferred a degree of nobility on the holder and on his descendants. As in sixteenth-century Prato, after 1594 the position of standard-bearer carried the title of "Molto Magnifico Nobile et Honorando[,] . . . which nobility entitle[d] him and his descendants henceforward to be reputed and treated as nobles here and abroad."[60] Moreover, descendants of a former standard-bearer acquired the right to be admitted to that same office.[61] The priors received the title of "Magnifici et Honorati" as well as the right to be included among the candidates for standard-bearer; here, too, the privilege was extended to their descendants. Councilors were awarded the title of "Magnifici" and were made eligible for other minor offices.[62]

Now, for the first time, the notion that certain activities were unworthy of public officeholders also appeared. It was decreed, in fact, that it was "not lawful nor permitted for anyone while wearing the Worthy gown [occupying major office] to wear openly aprons, smocks or other distinguishing marks of the artisan or the shopkeeper."[63] This passage shows that under the luxury of the new gowns and velvet hats some of the officials were still "shopkeepers" and "artisans." As in Prato, but not Pistoia, Arezzo, and Borgo San Sepolcro, Poppi shopkeepers, especially druggists, remained eligible for public office at least throughout the sixteenth and part of the seventeenth centuries, testifying to a local tradition defining what constituted a patriciate.[64]

The council also passed other articles that focused on the issue of *danno dato*. These had clearly the purpose of shielding the interests of the ruling families in the community and defining and promoting the pursuits of a new local patriciate. In 1568 it was decided that wool dyers and leather workers could not use the water in the main cistern in town during the grape harvest season, between the months of September and October, a policy intended to benefit those among the ruling families who had recently begun to invest heavily in land.[65] Also in 1572, an article established the nomination of four outsiders to work as guards to protect the vineyards during the summer until harvest. Although this regulation benefited the propertied families of the ruling elite, the salary for the four guards was paid by the government.[66] Overall, throughout the second half of the sixteenth century, the local ruling families paid considerably more attention to keeping the town streets free from the activities of shopkeepers who had always washed leather or butchered animals just outside their shops.

These reforms also introduced direct financial benefits for local notables, such as suspension of payments of debt for standard-bearers and priors. These two offices also conferred the privilege of immunity from incarceration for public debt or from incarceration and confiscation of property for private debt.[67] In 1594 immunities were extended to include the "Fisco o Gran Camera di Sua Altezza Serenissima e Magistrati Cittadini."[68] The general priors, however, were immune only from incarceration, not from confiscation of their property.[69]

Through participation in office holding the Poppi ruling families were able to strengthen their symbolic status and privileged position in local society. By the end of the sixteenth century, participation in the Ordinary Council indicated both membership in the new local patriciate and a means of controlling the management and distribution of public income. Reforms were aimed at increasing the status and privileges of those officeholders controlling the local government.

The Poppi elite used public funds and the administration of charitable and religious institutes to benefit themselves and their own families. The central government, contrary to the situation in other towns, had granted Poppi the right of supervising "all income and donations belonging to the community and its people."[70] In 1560 a new article of the local statute made it possible for officeholders to manage the communal businesses while in office.[71] The Poppi ruling families extended favors to one another through control of public funds, and thus it became common for them to make donations to the municipal government. The Convent of the Santissima Annunziata, founded in 1563 to give hospitality to daughters of prominent families, was mainly subsidized by public and private donations. Between 1563 and 1567 the commune and the vicariate contributed respectively 1,482 and 350 lire for its construction. One of the principal donors was Dianora Pauolozzi, considered the "founder" of the convent, who contributed 2,536 lire.[72]

It also became common practice for the ruling families to make donations to the city rather than to religious organizations and for the city council to extend loans and gifts to members of the elite. In the 1560s Vincenzo Amerighi, burdened by debt, asked the local government for a loan to continue his studies in medicine at the University of Pisa. Considering him a man of "good will and promise," the municipal government awarded Vincenzo a grant of fifty scudi. Vincenzo never forgot his patrons; still a bachelor, upon his death in 1600 he bequeathed to Poppi a town house in Borgo degli Albizi in Florence and several farms in the Casentino, income from which was to underwrite the education of three young men, as well as to provide a salary for the town's schoolteacher.[73] During the seventeenth century, the donation from Dr. Vincenzo Amerighi was used exclusively for the purpose of educating the sons of Poppi elite at the University of Pisa. From 1613 to 1661, nineteen grants were distributed to eleven ruling families.[74] The leading families used public institutions to reinforce their social and political supremacy over local society, thus creating and strengthening mutual interests and promoting the well-being of relatives and friends.[75]

In the reform of 1594, offices were created with the specific intent of distributing charitable and private donations. For the ruling families these offices played a crucial role, since they provided new sources of control. The charitable activities of high-ranking public officials set them and their families apart from the rest of the population, furthered their legitimation as a ruling elite, expressed their superiority in local society, and helped them attain public support.[76]

The offices controlling religious and charitable institutions grew in number with the 1594 reform. For example, ten more positions were added to the two overseers of the Opera degli Ospedali: two for the Opera of Beato Torello and four each for the Convent della Santissima Annunziata and the Capuchin Convent. The growing number of operai (overseers), whose task was to provide good management and administration of the properties of these institutions, went hand in hand with an expansion in the possessions of the institutions in their charge. While the overseers of the Opera degli Ospedali and of Beato Torello were chosen by imborsazione and remained in office

for one year, the others were nominated for life by the General Council.[77] The operai administered the holdings of the institutions "as
would a real owner and proprietor" and appointed employees.[78] They
selected a rector, a doctor, a surgeon, and a druggist to operate the
hospital and a manager and a chancellor to administer the hospital's
possessions. Furthermore, together with the standard-bearer and the
priors, the operai could bestow a dowry on two underprivileged girls
of the community under the conditions of a donation made by Father
Sebastiano Salvini.[79]

The increase in the number of offices controlling religious and
charitable institutions went hand in hand with the increased wealth
of the institutions they managed. No less important, however, the
multiplication of operai mirrored the new presentation of the ruling
class as benefactors of the poor and the underprivileged and keepers
of public order.

In 1594 the local government established new offices whose holders, as in the case of the operai, received no salary. Each year two
"Visitatori delle Carceri" were selected by *imborsazione* and were
charged with looking after jailed prisoners, ensuring them medical
assistance and, in case of death, burial *"con decentia."* Furthermore,
they organized and administered donations made for the support of
prisoners.[80] Another new office was that of "Paciari e Conciliatori
d'Inimicitie Sedatori di Tumulti e Seditioni et Compositori di Liti e
Differenze" (Peacemakers and Conciliators of Enmity, Pacifiers of
Tumult and Sedition, and Mediators of Litigation and Differences).
Nominations for this office were made by the General Council; the
term of office was one year, with the possibility of renewal.[81] The two
paciari were charged with the responsibility of trying to resolve "all
civic, criminal and mixed litigation among kin" without recourse to
the interference of the vicar.[82] These and other positions were created
by the Poppi elite to bestow upon those who filled them and their
families an authority that not only set them apart from the rest of
the population but also brought them respect and honor.

Those eligible for office were to be "well-intentioned men, fearful
and zealous of the Love and honor of GOD, of public welfare and of
their neighbors; and of highest consideration, authority, reverence,
respect and reputation."[83] Those who took on these responsibilities
did so "for charity and for love of Our Lord and for interest in the
public and universal good and well-being, counting only upon Di-
vine Aid and favor which [would] not be lacking" and accepting in

exchange only "honor, respect and reverence" on the part of the people.[84] Once invested with one of these unsalaried positions, a man and his descendants had the right to be admitted to all other offices, including that of standard-bearer. In addition, he was given the title of "Religious Pious Noble Magnificent Honorable" of the community.[85]

The new positions also represented the symbolic reappropriation of the local system of justice, particularly after the 1580 reform of the judicial system by Florence. By overseeing the treatment of prisoners and the functioning of jails, and by arbitrating local disputes, the ruling families invested themselves with a new form of judicial authority. Through these new positions the ruling class created a source of authority alternative to that of the central government. Poppi families provided local means for the execution of justice, faced the mounting pressure of centralization, and kept control over local society.

The scholarship has emphasized how a lessening exercise of local power corresponded to an increase in economic advantages and status of officeholders. In particular, by monopolizing municipal offices, local ruling families benefited in the redistribution of income from local religious and charitable institutions.[86] In Poppi, during the sixteenth century, office holding as defined by the statutes and as practiced by the ruling families assured their appropriation of public income. Office holding, however, also helped them create an alternative and parallel power system to that of the central government. This system helped to establish, extend, and reinforce their social and political position and maintain control over the community. The elaboration of new ways of local politics gave prominent families legitimation as benefactors and protectors of the community and fostered the loyalty and respect of the population at large. The elite families used local institutions to create new symbolic sources of status and authority. Finally, by monopolizing the local government, Poppi ruling families redefined the nature of their authority against centralizing reforms.

In Poppi, the sixteenth century was a period of important social and political change. As the centralization of the Medicean state advanced, a group of families strengthened its control of local politics. The consolidation of these families bolstered the political and social stability of the community. Unquestionably, the presence of the central government became increasingly more pervasive throughout the state. However, even though Florence curtailed the legislative and executive power of local institutions and the economic privileges of the community, the local ruling families were able to manipulate to their advantage the power that was left to them. They also conceived new forms of control to create a substitute source of authority to face the mounting pressures of centralization. The Poppi ruling class created and maneuvered public institutions as a means to strengthen and expand its authority. By manipulating local institutions, the Poppi ruling families were able to exercise their power without violating the confines of central authority and to establish an oligarchic regime that provided social and political stability in the community. This system, however, by containing a patrimonial definition of political participation, viewed municipal offices as private property, thus reinforcing local patterns of abuse and privilege.[87]

II

✦

The Emergence of Local Elite Families

Most of the sixteenth century coincided with dynamic and formative years in the socioeconomic life of Poppi, when the same group
of families that monopolized office holding and redefined political
participation emerged as the local elite. During the later decades of
the century, however, a number of factors threatened the social position, economic situation, and political supremacy of the ruling
families. The economic depression between the 1590s and the early
decades of the seventeenth century, the demographic decline from
the 1550s to the 1630s, and the central government's restrictive measures on wool manufacture significantly altered the financial interests of local ruling families. From artisans and shopkeepers they
became landowners. No less important, in conformity with new notions about nobility, the title of notary lost the prestigious connotation it once enjoyed and ceased to provide the emerging local elite
with renewed prestige.[1] Consequently, the notarial title was superseded by that of lawyer, in particular for higher-ranking positions in
the state bureaucracy.[2]

For most of the sixteenth century, matrimonial strategies reflected
the growth of the Poppi families as they were becoming financially
stable, professionally qualified, and locally more powerful. During
most of the century, the elite families combined endogamy with
marriage alliances with provincial families from other parts of the
state. This changed during the 1580s as elite families emphasized
endogamy and limitation of marriages, seeking to preserve their social, political, and economic identity in the face of changing circumstances. By the end of the sixteenth century, it became apparent that
mutual support through family connections and friendship ties provided the basis upon which to define and strengthen a new political
administration intended to further the collective interests of the local ruling families.

The example of the Lapucci family points to these important developments in the life of the local ruling families. Ser Francesco
Lapucci was a member of one of the oldest families of Poppi. Between
the second half of the fifteenth century and the beginning of the sixteenth, Ser Francesco and his son, Ser Agnolo, divided their time between caring for family properties, a wool shop and some land, and
practicing the notarial profession as private local notaries and officers of the Florentine bureaucracy.[3] In the next generation, however,
Ser Agnolo's son, Jacopo, did not follow the traditional profession in
the law but instead concerned himself exclusively with the family

business. During the 1550s Jacopo combined a careful policy of land investment with the family's activity in the textile industry. His two sons, Pierantonio and Torello, expanded their father's land investments and further consolidated the family patrimony.[4]

While building a secure economic foundation for their family, Jacopo Lapucci and his two sons also consolidated the social and political position of the family in the community. The Lapucci became very active in local political life. Between 1448 and 1556 they held twenty-three of the highest offices in the municipal government (3.9 percent of the total).[5] Between 1574 and 1632 the next generation of the Lapucci occupied forty-two positions (5.2 percent of the total).[6] At the same time, the Lapucci demonstrated their newly established socioeconomic position in Poppi by buying and renovating a new home and building a family chapel in the Church of San Fedele.[7] In addition, Torello Lapucci bequeathed a substantial sum of money for the construction of a new Capuchin monastery in 1586. These initiatives bestowed on the family honor and the status of leading benefactor in town.[8]

During most of the Cinquecento the family's matrimonial strategies reinforced its socioeconomic position. Jacopo Lapucci and his wife, Cassandra, married off all of their children. The three daughters married into prominent local families, thus reinforcing class solidarity within the community. The two sons established close ties, one with a family of notaries from Florence and the other with one of small but prosperous landowners of a nearby community. In the later decades of the century, however, only two of the four daughters of Pierantonio Lapucci married; the other two entered a convent. The two sons contracted matrimony with local women.

The following chapters illustrate how thirty-one surname groups, among which were the Lapucci, gained control of local wealth, distinguished themselves by their ancient lineage and traditions and by their professional qualifications, and went through a process of self-definition. They emerged as the Poppi ruling elite.

✦

FOUR

The Wool Industry and Its Crisis

During the sixteenth century the financial position of the ruling families improved as they consolidated their interests in commercial and artisanal activities, in particular those connected with the wool industry. During the middle decades of the sixteenth century, when the social status and economic position of the ruling families strengthened, income from industrial enterprises was supplemented by that from land holdings. In the years straddling the sixteenth and seventeenth centuries, however, famine and plague, a general crisis of commerce and industry, and restrictive measures of the Florentine wool guild challenged the socioeconomic stability of the leading families.[1]

The example of Poppi provides new insights into the motivation that led lesser provincial elites to withdraw from industrial activities and invest in land. Traditionally historians have striven to understand how and to what extent the Italian urban economy fell from splendor to decline at the end of the Renaissance. During the sixteenth and seventeenth centuries, it has been claimed, the lessening in industrial investments corresponded to an increase in speculative investments in land. The modification in the economic interests of urban elites was caused by a crisis in the industrial sector of the economy, as reflected by a "refeudalization" of Italian society as well as its economy.[2] In more recent years, some scholars have not only questioned the magnitude of Italian economic difficulties in the commercial and industrial sectors but have also begun to doubt that a process of "refeudalization" was at the basis of such difficulties.[3]

In Poppi, withdrawal from industry was not the result of a parasitic attitude by the Poppi elite, nor was it, at least initially, the result of a decline in industrial activities. The Poppi leading families had other reasons to start investing in land. By almost completely abandoning industrial activity and, as shown in Chapter 7, by seeking economic well-being on landed property, at least some of the Poppi ruling families succeeded both in surmounting a phase of economic and demographic depression and in protecting their social position. Landownership represented a source of food as well as a way to spread financial risk. Particularly toward the last decades of the sixteenth century, prices of industrial products declined as a consequence of a shrinking market. Conversely, bad harvests and epidemics combined to increase the prices of foodstuffs and to facilitate the expropriation of small peasant-owners. Land became not only a good investment but also a less risky financial venture. Furthermore, landownership conferred prestige and status. Thus, withdrawal from industry was the result of external events such as the plague, government intervention, and the general economic conditions of the late sixteenth and early seventeenth centuries. It was also a calculated strategy elaborated by the elite families to defend their threatened social and political prominence in local society.

I

During the fifteenth century and most of the sixteenth, financial success was founded primarily on manufacturing and commerce and on keeping retail shops for the sale of local products and foodstuffs. Wool manufacturing was the most important industry in town, which accounted for most of the financial stability of the Poppi ruling families. Until the 1550s several families did not hesitate to invest their capital in the industry and to open new wool shops in town.[4] Its vitality bestowed a degree of financial success and social prestige on the leading families. Their financial investments reflected the development of a new social self-consciousness as they began to project an image of themselves as the Poppi ruling elite.

The Cascesi family was among the most ancient and honored in town.[5] The Cascesi had been wool merchants and manufacturers since the fifteenth century, and by the early 1500s the family became one of most active in this industry in Poppi. In 1590 Valerio Cascesi owned three wool workshops and his cousin, Leonardo, two.[6] Together these accounted for 31 percent of the shops dealing with wool processing. But the Cascesi branch of Valerio, son of Giovanni, enjoyed greater wealth and prestige than did Leonardo's father, Niccolò. In the early sixteenth century Giovanni was described by local chroniclers as "an excellent merchant, expert in negotiations," and as "an expert business manager, already merchant and financier."[7] He owned a storehouse for the wool, a workshop with looms and dye works at the foot of the hill near the Arno "with two cauldrons and their apparatus." In addition, he possessed a kiln that produced cement and roof tiles, was a major landowner, and had become a financier.[8] The chronicler, Lapini, recorded his thoughts about the profitable wool business of Giovanni Cascesi and, quoting "*le voci de' vecchi*," described the entrance of the wool-carrying mule trains into town, so numerous that "when the lead mule had arrived at their house, the last had not as yet entered the Badia Gate."[9]

The growing fortune of the Cascesi family was mirrored by a change in lifestyle. In the first half of the sixteenth century, Giovanni gave up his old family home, "comfortable but not suitable to the wealth and business position" he enjoyed, and bought the house of Ser Alfonso, last male descendant of the Turriani family. In no time, Giovanni had his new home remodeled, "turning it into a palace worthy of his station."[10] As Richard Goldthwaite noted, investing in domestic architecture was a common characteristic of Italian elites starting with the fifteenth century. Local ruling families in Venice, Florence, and other, smaller towns, having achieved political stability, became confident that investing large sums in building family palaces would further strengthen their position of power.[11]

With the next generation, the Cascesi further displayed the self-consciousness of the family as an urban elite when Valerio leased out the kiln that he had theretofore managed.[12] In 1572, probably on the occasion of his marriage to the Florentine Ginevra Guasconi, he further expanded the family's new residence by purchasing an adjacent house.[13] This new image of the Cascesi as local elite was also supported by investing in the education of their sons. According to the chronicler, Lapini, "they [Cascesi] could afford to spend money in educating their young and to support them away from home and [set them up] in important businesses."[14]

The financial strategies and investment in a family palace undertaken by Leonardo Cascesi typify even more the ascending social and political consolidation of the Poppi ruling elite during the period. Toward the 1560s Leonardo had been simply an *artiere di calzoleria*, a shoemaker, living at Borgo a Badia in one of a cluster of modest houses occupied by a group of five families. His social and economic rise in the following decades is symbolized by his purchase of all the houses surrounding his own and in his remodeling them to form a single dwelling.[15] The social ascent and financial success of Leonardo were based on a number of factors. His marriage and, later, those of his sons brought the family cash, land, and prestige, all indispensable for the series of investments which Leonardo was to undertake. The ability of Leonardo himself is not to be underestimated since he was, according to Lapucci, a man of "great soul and spirit, articulate and extraordinarily active in his business."[16] Finally, the ancient lineage of the Cascesi must be kept in mind as well as the social prestige derived from the name and, perhaps, the fortune of the wealthier branch of the family, that of his uncle Giovanni. By the early seventeenth century, Bernardo Lapini wrote of Leonardo and his wife, Eugenia Lapini, that although the family fortune of the former was inferior to that of his wife, the Cascesi enjoyed a higher ranking in the social hierarchy of the community and were "*messi secondi in ordine et i Lapini i quinti*" [second to the Lapini's fifth].[17] By the early seventeenth century, in short, Leonardo's family was considered among the most prominent in town.

A few years after his marriage, Leonardo invested the twelve hundred scudi his wife had inherited upon the death of her brother, a priest, in the purchase of two shops—one a leather shop and another, the larger, a wool shop.[18] Close ties with the other branch of the family were extremely useful to Leonardo in introducing him into Tuscan manufacturing and commercial circles. As witness to this, on the occasion of the marriage of his cousin, Valerio, to Ginevra Guasconi, Leonardo, although of much humbler circumstances, found himself seated at the main table together with all the Florentine "*gentilhomini*" invited to the wedding banquet. Thus it was that when embarking upon his new activity, Leonardo encountered no difficulty in becoming established among the merchants of Pisa and Florence.[19] Business must have been good for him in the years to follow, since he decided to use a *casetta* of his, a small house, as a storehouse.[20]

The fortunes of the Cascesi began to decline in the troubled last decade of the century. For Valerio, business took a turn for the worse, forcing him to enter the Florentine prison (Le Stinche).[21] After his release, Valerio continued to live very comfortably, although a few years later, when his daughter, Clarice, wed Ferrante Niccoletti in

1599, he closed down his wool storehouse and signed over the house in which it was located to Clarice as part of her dowry.[22] Then, in the first decades of the seventeenth century, the sons of Valerio, perhaps "more inclined to a contemplative than an active life," began to re-structure completely their industrial activity. Of the four brothers, only Ercole and Giovanni continued to look after the reduced family business.[23] Francesco, with a doctorate in theology from Pisa, lived for many years in Rome, eventually returning to Poppi to become director of the Convent of the Santissima Annunziata. Bernardo, doc-tor of law, did not take to the family's business and rested his finan-cial security on the laurels of its celebrated ancestors. He was the only survivor of the plague of 1632 and left no traces other than that he was a bachelor and at sixty became a cleric.[24] At his death, a few years later, he left the interest from his estate to his mother's cousin, Bernardo Guasconi, until the latter's death, after which the Cascesi patrimony was to go to the Opera degli Ospedali of Poppi.[25]

Also for Leonardo, the first signs of trouble were visible in the final years of the century. In the late 1590s, Leonardo, as in the case of his cousin, Valerio, submerged by debts, had to turn himself over to deb-tor's prison (Le Stinche) in Florence, but thanks to the intervention of relatives and friends, he was released and "with more caution car-ried on his business."[26] Early in the seventeenth century the fam-ily's brief crisis was reversed after its fortune was boosted by the marriages of Leonardo's sons, Giovanni and Niccolò, to heiresses—Giovanni to Dianora Buondi of Poppi and Niccolò to Dianora Ulivi from Borgo San Lorenzo—who brought into the families cash and land.[27] The latter marriage was particularly advantageous to the family in that Dianora Ulivi brought with her a dowry of almost one thousand scudi and, after the death of her brother, a group of farms in the Mugello Valley which provided "so much grain and fodder that his [Leonardo's] house was annually filled with goods and the wool business profited thereby."[28]

Despite the investments made by Leonardo and the providential marriages of Niccolò and Giovanni, in 1612 the wool storehouse was closed, and in 1627 both the wool shop and the leather shop were permanently shut down.[29] The lack of offspring from Niccolò and Dianora and the plague almost wiped out this branch of the family. By 1632 the only surviving member was Paolo, son of Giovanni and Dianora Buondi, and he, too, died childless shortly thereafter, but not before he had completely dissipated what was left of the family fortune.[30]

During most of the sixteenth century, crafts and trades boosted the financial position of many of the ruling families. Economic stability further supported their political ascent and, in line with other Italian elites, also encouraged the unfolding of new ways to strengthen their image as local ruling elites.[31] Investment into private architecture bolstered the external representation of their power. It reinforced the new public role that the Poppi elite was fashioning through the manipulation of charitable and religious institutions observed in Chapter 3. In a second instance they refrained from some of the minor industrial activities. But for all their social ascent, the Cascesi, together with the other families, did not give up the wool trade until important events threatened the industry and consequently their social and political stability.

II

The scarce and fragmentary information available relative to Poppi businesses and industries reflects the difficulties that first appeared in the 1590s and deepened in the first half of the seventeenth century. Examination of the surviving evidence, such as variations in the number of shops open for business and the impressions of contemporary observers, provides essential information on the downward trend in these sectors of the local economy. In 1590 the Nove Conservatori of Florence requested a list of all the shops in town, "both those run directly by their owners and those rented out."[32] The survey resulted in a list of sixty-three shops in Poppi, fifty-eight in operation and five closed. In the succeeding decades the number of shops decreased to such a point that in the 1630s only thirty-six were still functioning and twenty-seven were closed.[33] In little more than thirty years, 43 percent of the shops had ceased any kind of activity (table 4.1).

Not all the commercial and industrial activities followed a downward trend; although some were completely wiped out, others were reorganized on a smaller scale. Shops linked with everyday life, such as those of the barber and the druggists, continued to operate. Other enterprises connected with the rise of a more sophisticated lifestyle remained active during the period in question, such as the tailor shop and the kilns, which produced bricks, tiles, and vases, suggesting that a fair amount of construction and renovation supported this industry.

TABLE 4.1

Total Number of Shops (Percentage) and Shops Owned by the Ruling Families in 1590 and 1630

Shops	1590						1630					
	Open		Rented		Closed		Open		Rented		Closed	
	Total	Rul. Fam.	Total	Rul. Fam.	Total	Rul. Fam.	Total	Rul. Fam.	Total	Rul. Fam.	Total	Rul. Fam.
Wool	14 (22.2)	10 (15.9)	2 (3.2)	2 (3.2)			8 (12.7)	5 (7.9)			8 (12.7)	7 (11.1)
Kiln	1 (1.6)		1 (1.6)	1 (1.6)			1 (1.6)		1 (1.6)	1 (1.6)		
Leather	3 (4.8)	3 (4.8)	1 (1.6)	1 (1.6)					1 (1.6)	1 (1.6)	3 (4.8)	3 (4.8)
Druggist	2 (3.2)	2 (3.2)	1 (1.6)	1 (1.6)			2 (3.2)	2 (3.2)	1 (1.6)	1 (1.6)		
Grocery	9 (14.3)	4 (6.3)					7 (11.1)	3 (4.8)			2 (3.2)	1 (1.6)
Bakery			2 (3.2)	2 (3.2)					1 (1.6)	1 (1.6)	1 (1.6)	1 (1.6)
Butcher	2 (3.2)	1 (1.6)					1 (1.6)				1 (1.6)	1 (1.6)
Blacksmith	4 (6.3)	1 (1.6)					4 (6.3)			1 (1.6)		
Haberdasher	1 (1.6)										1 (1.6)	
Wood	1 (1.6)										1 (1.6)	
Barber	1 (1.6)						1 (1.6)					
Tailor			1 (1.6)	1 (1.6)					1 (1.6)	1 (1.6)		
Cobbler			1 (1.6)	1 (1.6)							1 (1.6)	1 (1.6)
"Shop"	1 (1.6)	1 (1.6)	10 (15.9)	8 (12.7)	5 (8)	5 (8)			7 (11.1)	3 (4.8)	9 (14.3)	11 (17.5)
Total	39 (62)	22 (35)	19 (30)	17 (27)	5 (8)	5 (8)	24 (38)	10 (16)	12 (19)	9 (14.4)	27 (43)	25 (39.8)

Hardest hit was the leather industry, once important to the Poppi economy.[34] Of the four shops active in 1590, only one remained open in the seventeenth century.[35] The decline in leather crafts was probably associated with the one in the wool industry. As Judith Brown noted in the case of Pescia, the success of the leather industry there was related to the proximity of cheap raw material, in particular sheep skins.[36] The decrease in wool production and thus in the supply of raw material had important repercussions on the leather crafts.

Wool manufacturing, the most important industry in the community, underwent a major reorganization. The sources rarely indicate the precise function of the shops, which are usually referred to as *botteghe della lana*. In this category were included all those shops involved with the various phases of wool production. Few of them, however, appear to have carried out a complete cycle of production, and most were involved with one specific operation, such as wool beating or retail. Assuming that a variation in the number of shops actively engaged in wool manufacturing is indicative of a general trend in the industry, in Poppi, in the decades after 1590 wool production declined. In fact, of the sixteen shops operating in this sector in 1590, only half were still functioning in the 1630s, and these had not grown in capacity after the loss of so many competitors.

A large part of the industrial activities was controlled by the ruling families. In 1590 eighteen of the leading families supervised approximately 70 percent of the urban economy, since they were owners of forty-four of the sixty-three shops (table 4.1). Of these, twenty-two were owner operated, seventeen rented out, and five closed. In contrast, in the 1630s, the ruling families held only ten shops, rented out nine shops, and owned twenty-five shops that had been closed (table 4.1). Thus the percentage of shops the ruling families operated directly went from 35 to 16 percent, and those rented out from 27 to 14 percent; the greatest change occurred in the percentage of closed shops—from 8 to 40 percent of the total. Furthermore, at the earlier date the ruling families controlled 75 percent of the wool industry, operating twelve and renting two of the sixteen shops in town. Later, only five were still operative, none had been rented out, and seven had been closed.[37]

These statistics confirm the keen awareness of contemporaries of the severe decline in the industrial sector. In 1613, with perhaps a certain amount of exaggeration, the monks of the Badia of San Fedele

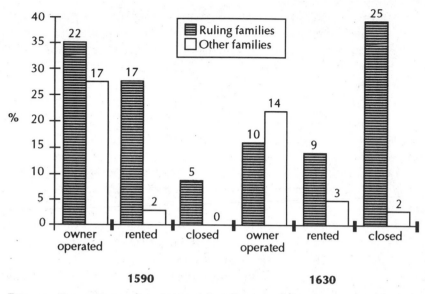

FIG. 4.1. Frequency and percentage distribution of shops in 1590 and 1630

affirmed in a letter to the grand duke that "in Poppi's territory more than 100 shops [were] closed."[38] In the years following the plague of 1631–32, Ser Bernardo Lapini, careful observer of local society, wrote, "[Suppliers of] lumber, leather, Spices, Cloth, wool products, livestock were numerous even within our memory. . . . Wool fillers and kilns were plentiful; [these shops are] today reduced to ground floor rooms as evidence that prosperity is at an end, souls are humiliated and minds grown idle."[39] The downward turn in the industrial sector reflected, in particular, the withdrawal from it by the ruling families. In 1590, of the total number of shops operative in town, nineteen were rented out and the remaining thirty-nine were managed directly by their owners (fig. 4.1). By the 1630s, of the thirty-six functioning shops, twenty-four were under owner management. The percentage of active, owner-operated shops had fallen from 62 percent to 38 percent of the total and those rented out from 30 percent to 19 percent. The shops that were closed had risen from 8 percent to 43 percent (fig. 4.1). The percentage of shops directly managed by the ruling families dropped from 35 to 16 percent, whereas the percentage of shops controlled by other families dropped only from 27 to 22 percent. In the 1630s the leading families also rented out almost twice the number of shops of the previous period, whereas other families in town rented only one more shop. Consequently, the downturn trend in town depended mostly on the gradual disengagement from artisan and commercial activities on the part of the ruling families.

III

In the preceding pages we have described the vitality of Poppi textile manufacturing. But in the last years of the sixteenth century, a number of factors determined the decline of the industry in the minor centers of the state. Doubtless, the disappearance of merchant families such as the Cascesi as a result of the plague contributed to the closing of wool shops in town. These, however, were not taken over by new families. By the first decades of the seventeenth century, the crisis in this sector common to Tuscany and all of Italy did not make the wool industry a profitable venture.[40] Moreover, restrictive measures emanating from the textile guilds of Florence significantly influenced the local economy. During the early 1500s, as proof of the vigor of the local wool industry, Florence felt the need to protect itself by imposing restrictive laws on the production and commerce of Casentino wool. In the long run, however, Florentine intervention in the local economy did not facilitate the growth of the industry in Poppi.[41]

Since the fifteenth century the Poppi manufacturers were exempted from paying registration fees to the Florentine guild. The local wool industry also enjoyed some privileges not accorded most other communities of the state. A law of 1536 limiting the commerce of local cloth decreed that "all types of textiles produced in the Dominion [could] not be transported from place to place within the territory, but [had to] be used in the same place wherein they [were] made."[42] This limitation was applied to the communities of the state in different manners. The merchants of the Casentino were allowed "to transport wool of their own manufacture . . . throughout the Florentine Dominion and abroad."[43] But if producers of the cloth of Casentino could sell freely throughout the territory and "abroad," they were restrained—as were others in the state—in the type of cloth they could produce, which was largely of low grade and made solely with local wool. A general law intended for provincial wool producers fixed the price of cloth at forty soldi *a braccio,* "to enable the poor to clothe themselves."[44] The best cloth produced in the Casentino, called *pannina fina*, was valued at three lire and ten soldi *a braccio* and was permitted to be sold at the markets of Prato and Impruneta.[45] The other restriction that applied to the Casentino producers, as well as to many others who came from the provinces, was the ban on the sale of any kind of cloth within a radius of six miles around Florence.[46]

The commerce of Casentino cloth at Prato dated from earlier times. In 1535 Prato producers stated that "this had been the custom for such a long time that there [was] no memory of its ever having been otherwise."[47] But in 1541 Prato wool producers enacted a series of protectionist measures to safeguard their industry and to control the production and commerce of Casentino wool. They decreed that no cloth could be introduced into the local markets with the exception of wool coming from Romagna at twenty soldi *a braccio*. As for the cloth from Casentino, the Arte della Lana of Prato, despite the requests made by local *"righattieri"* and *"fondachieri,"* forbade its entrance except during the time of fairs.[48] These regulations favoring Prato were not well received by Poppi manufacturers, who, together with producers from outlying areas, continually but unsuccessfully appealed to central authority.[49]

The limitations on the price and consequently on the quality of the cloth of the Casentino did nothing to facilitate the development of wool production. One of the main problems facing local producers, however, was the lack of outlets for their products. For this reason, there were instances of evasion of the restrictions imposed on the Casentino cloth. In 1551 Valerio Cascesi illegally sold cloth he produced at the market of Garbo. The cost of the cloth was within the legal limits of three lire and ten soldi *a braccio*, but its "leek green" color was not usually produced in the Casentino.[50] By manufacturing a different kind of cloth, Valerio was able to expand his market and thus broaden his participation in the commerce of wool. Local producers also expanded their outlets by protecting the best cloth they produced, the *pannina fine*. For this reason, on August 5, 1579, a committee of wool producers of the vicariate of the Casentino wrote the grand duke a letter in which they asked to use a stamp to differentiate their good cloth from others.[51]

Proclamations concerning the limitations forced upon the Casentino producers were repeated periodically in the following years, indicating that the orders continued to be eluded. In 1599 Florentine officials renewed the prohibition on bringing into the podesteria "items forbidden now or in the future and especially foreign cloth."[52] By the early seventeenth century, restrictions from the central government intensified as a result of a decline in the wool industry of Florence.[53] At this time more laws obstructed the sale of Casentino cloth within the state. Guild officials were mostly concerned about the competition of Casentino textiles, especially the *pannina fine* valued at more than forty soldi. Consequently they sought to control the frequent instances of illegal production and sale of contraband cloth. For this reason they intensified enforcement of old restrictions. In 1604 the law prohibiting merchants from the Casentino from transporting within the state cloth worth more than forty soldi was reinstated, and in 1608 local merchants were obliged to procure a special permit when traveling near Florence carrying cloth valued at more than the allowed amount (forty soldi *a braccio*) to "avoid scandals and to clear up as much as possible the doubts that [arose] daily concerning the transportation of Casentino cloth . . . to Prato or to Impruneta or from these back to the Casentino."[54]

In 1630 Florentine officials confirmed the crisis in the wool industry and at the same time provided an explanation for it. In a letter to the Pratica Segreta they stressed how in the rural communities of the dominion the production and sale of *panni bassi* (low-grade cloth) had declined and added, "Particularly in the Casentino, where at Poppi and Pratovecchio there formerly existed numerous workshops of this sort, today, [they] are reduced to a few and those have difficulty in placing their small production, and we believe the reason lies in their not having outlets for their cloth."[55] The central government, at the same time that it encouraged the development of local woolen industries, was careful that these did not in any way compete with the wool production in the capital and in so doing greatly controlled the development of the Poppi wool industry and certainly did nothing to promote its progress.

Obliged as it was to concentrate production on low-grade cloth for local sale, the Poppi industry was limited to a largely self-sufficient rural market, and consequently it was extremely sensitive to any variation in the agricultural sector.[56] If lower-class income decreased, so did industrial production on which local markets chiefly depended. Moreover, the demographic decline among the rural population of Tuscany during the late sixteenth century lessened the demand for lower-grade industrial products.[57] Any reduction in their buying power necessarily had repercussions on local industries.[58]

IV

Restrictive measures alone were not responsible for the industrial depression in Poppi and the Casentino. The generally unfavorable economic conditions of the late sixteenth and early seventeenth centuries also played a role. Famine, plagues, and the rise in the price of agricultural products caused a deterioration of lower-class economic conditions. The widespread malaise in both the industrial and agricultural sectors which characterized the Tuscan and European economies had repercussions also on the fortunes of the ruling families and led to a curtailing of industrial and commercial activities.

Hardship for lower classes had already begun during the first decades of the sixteenth century, and in 1521 problems arose concerning the provision of grain to the town's poor. The local government set up the Monte di Pietà, which was managed by the Opera degli Ospedali, with the intent of providing grain to the poor by raising money through loans from the local wealthy families.[59] The plague then raging throughout the Casentino struck Poppi only in 1530; thus in January 1528, upon the request of the Signori Otto of Florence, the local government was able to organize loans both to the poor of the town and to the community of Stia, already hit by the plague.[60] There was apparently no lack of grain in Poppi. The Niccoletti, Sociani, Cascesi, Rilli, and Soldani, to name but a few of the prominent families that contributed to the loan, were able to offer aid while at the same time sending grain to nearby markets.[61]

Between 1535 and 1560 Poppi, like the rest of Tuscany, found itself prey to an alternating cycle of famine and plague, further aggravated by the war against Siena.[62] Locally produced grain was no longer sufficient to fill the needs of the population, and therefore the local government began requesting subsidies in grain and fodder from the Magistrato dell'Abbondanza in Florence.[63] In 1535 Poppi paid the Abbondanza 376 lire for a loan of 94 *staiora* of grain.[64] In 1540 a request to the central government for 1,500 *staiora* from the whole podesteria forced Poppi to seek a loan of 100 scudi from the prominent families to repay the Florentine officials.[65] Requests for grain were renewed in 1541, 1542, 1543, 1549, and 1551. In the meantime, Poppi was stricken by plague at least twice—in 1550 and 1555.[66] For the Poppi ruling class, however, the economic crisis did not have overly onerous consequences, since, in 1542, the city council approved a proposition to create a livestock market at the nearby Ponte a Poppi and, in 1552, one to contribute to the poor with a loan of grain rather than cash.[67]

Then, at the end of the sixteenth century, throughout the Mediterranean area a series of conjunctural elements—unfavorable climatic conditions, resulting bad harvests, rising prices, and population growth—combined to destabilize the already precarious balance between resources and population and contributed to increased pauperization.[68] Poppi was not spared the consequences of this general trend. Near the end of the century signs of increasing hardship in the local agricultural economy appeared.

In Tuscany the years 1579–80, 1583, 1589–90, 1591–92, 1596–97, and 1600–1601 were characterized by crop failures and famine.[69] Prices of agricultural products and raw materials skyrocketed.[70] In 1581 and again in 1588, to assure a reserve of foodstuffs, Ferdinand I issued a series of proclamations forbidding the export of cereals.[71] Following the serious crisis of 1590 which paralyzed agricultural commerce in Tuscany as well as the rest of Italy, new orders against the exportation of *grascie* (foodstuffs) were issued.[72] To make these laws more effective in border areas, the Casentino among them, where the problem of contraband was most evident, the central government assigned special commissioners to carry out the restrictions.[73] Cases of contraband were frequent, particularly between periods of famine, and were directed toward the Papal States, Urbino, Piombino, and Lucca.[74] Grain and mostly chestnut flour from the Casentino were often smuggled into the Papal States, where they were subsequently sold at a much higher price than in Tuscany.[75]

To control the export of grain, the central government added limitations on internal sales. Producers could sell to local markets only with the authorization of the Ufficio della Grascia. In addition, grain dealers were obliged to register all their transactions and to provide the Ufficio della Grascia with a monthly summary. A law of 1591 issued by Ferdinand I, moreover, established fixed prices for commercial products.[76] Apart from making sure that the people of Tuscany had enough grain for their needs, these laws gave the grand duke larger control over any attempts at grain speculation.

The famine that stalked Tuscany at the end of the sixteenth century did not spare Poppi. Despite controls and protective measures, the grain supplies of the community were finally depleted, and its requests to the Ufficio dell'Abbondanza for loans in cash or in grain became more frequent. In 1594 municipal officials described the situation as "calamitous times" in which the poor were reduced to eating "grass and fodder destined for livestock and drop[ped] from hunger and exposure in the streets and villages."[77] The local government, in consideration of these circumstances, set up a permanent office of the Soprastanti e Grascieri to see that the territory was never without grain.

In the early 1600s, bad grain crops and a poor harvest of chestnuts—the mainstay of the diet of the rural population—forced the council to request again loans of grain from the Ufficio dell'Abbondanza.[78] In February 1607 a loan of 2,000 *staiora* of grain was followed by the order to punish anyone who exported from the podesteria "grain, fodder, chestnuts and livestock," indicating that those who still had products to sell were trying to gain the most from them. Everywhere in Italy food shortage pushed grain prices higher than usual, and local landowners tried to take advantage of the situation by selling their crop outside the community.[79]

Famine recurred in the 1620s.[80] Crop failures between 1621 and 1623 occasioned renewed requests to the Monte di Pietà of Florence for the purchase of 3,000 *staiora* of grain to meet the needs of the entire podesteria.[81] Difficulties persisted in the following years to such a point that in 1629 the "poverty of this town was abated by the pious and holy hand of [His] Highness [Ferdinand II] who sent alms to be distributed in large amounts."[82] In March 1630 Giorgio Scali, a commissar nominated by Grand Duke Ferdinand "to visit his happy domain" and to report on economic conditions, wrote that in the Casentino there remained "a part of uncultivated but very well tended land."[83] Despite every effort, the grain and fodder crops were "*scarsissime*" [meager], and with the first signs of plague appearing in Tuscany, livestock and textile markets virtually ceased to be held.[84]

In this unfavorable economic situation the plague of 1631 erupted with violence.[85] It devastated an economy already characterized by a precarious balance between resources and population. With the plague, the collapse came, and in Poppi the results were upheaval and radical change within the social structure.

V

The plague, raging in Europe since 1628, first appeared in Italy at the end of 1629, carried across the Alps from the west by French troops and from the north by Germans engaged in the war of succession of the duchy of Mantua.[86] Between 1629 and 1630 the epidemic spread with tragic consequences from northern to central Italy.

In July 1630 the plague reached the environs of Florence. By November, Arezzo, Prato, Empoli, Pistoia, and Lucca were infested. With the onset of winter the epidemic abated, only to break out with renewed violence in the spring.[87] Throughout 1630 there was no sign of plague in Poppi, although precautionary measures were being taken to protect the area from contagion. On January 12, 1631, when there was still reason to believe Poppi might be spared from the ravages of the disease, the first steps were officially taken to set up a sanitary barrier.[88] Sanitation officers were elected, initially only three, and successively three more were added: Filippo Grifoni, Giovanfrancesco Rilli, Lodovico Lapucci, Feliciano Sociani, Scipione Mannucci, and Alamanno Soldani, all from elite families.[89] Regulations were laid down for issuing "health certificates" authorizing freedom of movement to those unaffected by the plague, and guards were set up at the town's gates to control movement to and from outlying towns.[90]

The situation gave no cause for alarm until April 11, when the sanitation officials confined to quarters Matteo Riccianti, a druggist, and one Acciai, a tavern keeper, who had sold certain medicines and offered hospitality to a traveler from Figline Valdarno who subsequently died of plague. At this point the situation was still calm, and the two men, who showed no evidence of illness, were released from house detention on April 18. But by the end of the month, the plague had begun to cut down victims in small outlying communities.[91] Consequently, proclamations were made forbidding the commerce of "used wool or linen cloth" in Poppi and its territory without permission from the sanitation officials, requiring that all dogs be killed or kept chained, and ordering the streets to be kept clean and trash carried away at least twice a week.[92] Movement from one place to another was restricted; no one could enter the town or escape the surveillance of the guards at the gates without a *"bulletta"* or other official certification of good health. But these measures were to no avail, and from May 18 it was no longer possible to check the rising tide of the disease, whose victims were increasingly numerous, even if still limited to the countryside. By May 27 the situation had become sufficiently serious to forbid holding fairs and markets. Of course, these measures, aimed at totally isolating the sick and avoiding any possible contact, caused almost complete economic paralysis.[93]

On May 31 the plague appeared within the gates of the town; two people died in the parish of San Lorenzo, the poorest in town.[94] Immediately the school was closed, and all forms of communal life virtually ceased.[95] From the first to the twentieth of June more than eighteen cases of disease were registered, and from the twentieth to the end of the month eighteen houses listed one or more cases. Altogether, therefore, by the end of June the number of deaths must have exceeded 77, since by June 18 all the houses in the San Lorenzo neighborhood with the exception of two had been quarantined.[96] With the heat of summer the plague spread like wildfire, and in July 218 deaths were registered.[97]

In mid-July a proclamation ordered all infected persons, of whatever class or condition, into the *lazaretto*, although most of the prominent families ignored the order and remained in their homes.[98] A break in the weather brought the number of deaths in August down to fifty-seven.[99] By September conditions in general had improved to the extent that no deaths were registered.[100] "Today, October 13, with the help of God and the Glorious Virgin Mary and of Beato Torello, honored in our country," wrote the officer of the *sanità*, "the women's *lazaretto* at Ponte a Poppi at the place called 'La Tinta dei Cascesi' has been closed." On November 4 the officials closed the convalescent hospital for men.[101] In mid-November public life and commerce resumed in the podesteria, and fairs, markets, and the school were reopened. On January 2, 1632, a proclamation brought from Florence announced "business as usual" throughout the state, and at the end of the month all four of the town's gates were opened without restriction.[102]

In Poppi the disease was particularly severe. During the three months of intense contagion, the deaths had exceeded 352. According to a comparison of this figure with the census of 1562, approximately one-third of the town's population perished. Considering that the population was already declining by the end of the sixteenth century, we can suppose that the effect of the 1631 plague was around 32 percent. Poppi numbered among the Tuscan towns with the highest percentage of mortality in Tuscany, which varied between 33 percent in Pescia, 25 percent in Prato, and 10–17 percent in Florence.[103] The local officials reconfirmed the devastating result of the epidemic by requesting the central government to decrease the amount of salt usually provided the community from 250 to 100 *staiora*, offering as justification, "One half of our population is dead."[104]

In time of plague the wealthy and the public officials often abandoned cities and sought comfortable refuge in their country houses. The upper classes were therefore almost immune to the ravages of epidemic. In Prato, for example, the plague spared almost all local government functionaries and many well-to-do families.[105] Contrary to patterns in other cities, in Poppi the plague struck both the poor in the parish of San Lorenzo and the wealthy, whose comforts and privileges were not sufficient to immunize them. Quite the opposite was true, since they, as community leaders invested with the task of applying preventive measures, were perhaps in greater risk of contagion than others.

In May 1631 Filippo Grifoni in his role as sanitation official did not hesitate to travel throughout the countryside accompanied by a *cerusico*, a "surgeon," to ascertain the progress of the disease.[106] The same was true of the other officials, such as Lodovico Lapucci, Giovanfrancesco Rilli, and Jacopo Crudeli. Grifoni was the first to die, on June 21, followed in short order by several other town leaders. By the end of that month the homes of almost all the sanitation officials had been quarantined following the deaths of their wives and children. The home of Giovanfrancesco Rilli was closed off on June 1 after the death of his wife. The following day the homes of Jacopo Crudeli and Lodovico Lapucci were quarantined and, subsequently, those of Niccolò Soldani, Alessandro Martini, Luca Niccoletti, Alamanno Soldani, Vettorio Martini, Domenico Sociani, Annibale Rilli, and Egidio Rilli.[107]

The plague completely wiped out seven of the twenty-two families that had held the greater number of government offices between 1556 and 1633.[108] Another two families had become extinct prior to the appearance of the disease.[109] Furthermore, by midcentury, in other families—the Lapucci, Grifoni, and Lapini—only women were left.[110] At this time, of the ten remaining ruling families, only six were from the original group of Poppi ancient *casate* which had been at the summit of the municipal political and economic life since the end of the fifteenth century; the others were *uomini nuovi*.[111]

During the first decades of the Seicento, protectionist measures on agricultural and industrial products, famine, and plague aggravated the already precarious urban economy and threatened the economic situation of local shopkeepers and wool producers. But those of the ruling families who survived the plague shaped new financial strategies and reemerged from the crisis having all but abandoned any sort

of artisan and industrial activity. Conjunctural events not only influenced political developments by tightening control both from central power and from local rulers. They also significantly altered the
social structure of peripheral towns. As the economic gap between
local leading families and the remainder of the population widened,
peripheral societies further revealed hierarchical and elitist forms of
organizations.

   In the same period another important transformation threatened
the aspiration for social advancement of the lesser state functionaries
who lived in provincial towns. As the political role of notaries in provincial bureaucracy lessened, the social values attached to the notarial profession also declined.

FIVE

✦

Bureaucrats and Notaries

Current scholarship stresses the relevance of careers in the bureaucracy both as vehicles of social mobility and as means for the formation of a regional Tuscan elite. According to this interpretation, provincial elites found in the notarial profession and in bureaucratic positions a means to gain esteem and status both in the local arena and in the broader environment of the regional state. However, in most cases, only those families that, by the early sixteenth century, had already established themselves as local patricians were rewarded with high honor. The Medici rulers often granted Florentine citizenship to wealthy provincial merchants, businessmen, and large landowners, in recognition of their loyalty. For these elites a career in the bureaucracy meant further access to high-ranking positions in the grand-ducal administration and in courtly services. Thus, professional success in the state bureaucracy and close ties with the Medici grand dukes allowed the transformation of provincial notables from a local to a regional elite.[1]

Before and during most of the sixteenth century, confirming this general interpretation, the sons of the Poppi ruling families who pursued a professional career most often became notaries. Training in the law or the notarial arts provided admittance into the state bureaucracy and bestowed on provincial elites important social and public roles.[2] By the late sixteenth century, however, a number of factors significantly influenced the social and political status of provincial notaries. The title of notary faded in importance as a means of advancement into more influential bureaucratic positions. At the same time the Poppi youth were not offered many career options. Until the 1640s the notary and the church remained the only two career paths open for those who wanted to remain in town. Some chose not to. Others abandoned any form of professional activity.

During the late sixteenth and seventeenth centuries, the career strategies of lesser provincial elites reflected a split in their social composition, indicating diverse economic conditions and financial choices. The changes in career policies were both consequences of external circumstances and by-products of the ruling group's development of a sense of itself as a new local patriciate. These new strategies revealed a redefinition of the self-image of the Poppi elite, which broadened to include both the local and the regional context.

I

Beginning in the early sixteenth century, provincial elites became increasingly aware of professional qualifications as instruments for maintaining and consolidating their social and political supremacy and for creating a class base in local politics. In Poppi, as in Prato, this awareness was reflected in the importance that local ruling families bestowed on education.[3] The position of the town schoolteacher acquired further prestige. No less important, the municipal government and private benefactors created new incentives to boost the education of the local youth.[4]

In 1448 the schoolmaster was paid 60 lire per semester. In 1521 a government reform decreed that, "considering how important [were] the virtues which surpass all other riches," the teacher of grammar and rhetoric be given usufruct of a house for the period of his employment in addition to a salary of 105 lire per semester.[5] In the last years of the sixteenth century, teachers enjoyed increasing prominence, and thanks to a bequest by Doctor Vincenzo Amerighi, their salaries doubled to 30 scudi (210 lire) per semester. Moreover, in 1568 the council offered new incentives to increase the number of notaries, doctors, and teachers. It awarded a prize of 10 lire to anyone with a doctorate who had lived in the community for ten years.[6] In 1600 an additional bequest by Amerighi to fund doctoral studies at the University of Pisa for three youths from Poppi was a further encouragement to higher education.[7]

Education and professional expertise were also used as a means to define political rights and justify concentration of power. The popularity of the notarial profession depended on the prestige it enjoyed in local society. As reflected in the regulation concerning the rights and qualifications to occupy major public office, professional status was an important element in the eyes of the Poppi leaders. At the beginning of the century, the need for a more efficient administration performed by "*huomeni pratici e discreti*" promoted the administrative superiority of Poppi magistrature over the rural district.[8] By the 1590s the council consolidated this position by granting the professions of teacher, notary, and doctor the right of election to all major public offices and providing them and their descendants the title of "Religioso, pietoso, nobile Magnifico Honorando."[9]

Both in their public and private capacities notaries occupied important local administrative positions, such as that of riformatore or of chancellor of the municipal government.[10] In these positions they supervised the entire political-administrative process by overseeing electoral procedures, council meetings, and the elaboration of new statutes. They further legalized all personal and public transactions such as wills, dowry agreements, marriage contracts, and business deals. Their influence was also strengthened by their role as teachers of the Poppi youth. The notarial profession thus empowered those who practiced it to unravel the actions and goals and to guide the relationships of the inhabitants of the community.

Notaries were therefore instrumental in the elaboration of a new political language that prized education and professional skills above everything else as the necessary prerequisite for "good government." In their position as riformatori, notaries used the professional qualification of the Poppi ruling families to present an image of the town as the center of education and of political expertise in the podesteria and the vicariate. With this new rhetoric the Poppi ruling class rationalized and legitimized its practice of politics and reinforced its leadership and domination over local society.

II

Besides exercising their profession locally, Poppi notaries filled the positions in the lower ranks of the bureaucracy of the state as chancellors and judges at the service of the vicars and podestà in the peripheral towns of the Florentine state.[11] The development of bureaucratic structures of the Tuscan regional state provided many provincial families with new employment opportunities. During the fifteenth century, after the territorial reorganization of the Florentine state and the consequent expansion of peripheral structures, positions for notaries at the service of peripheral functionaries expanded. This trend continued in the following centuries. Litchfield indicated that between 1551 and 1723 the provincial bureaucracy increased from 81 positions of captains, podestà, and vicars, each accompanied by lesser notaries, regular justices, and chancellors, to about 450–500 officials.[12]

For Florentine patricians office holding in the state bureaucracy offered good forms of employment for younger sons who could not count on inheriting the family patrimony.[13] Also for provincial elites, a bureaucratic career was important both for maintaining social status within the community and for attaining such economic advantages as derived from it.[14] In Poppi a secure income represented an additional support for family resources. No less important, employment as staff members of provincial vicars and podestà promoted the exercise of the private profession of provincial notaries, who offered their legal services to a larger body of clients than the one they served in their hometowns. Families that numbered notaries among their members thus achieved a balance between professional and financial endeavors which strengthened their social and political position in local society.

In the early years of the sixteenth century, the Poppi ruling families linked a notarial career with administration of their families' business and created a beneficial combination of interests. Those who became notaries and were in the employment of the Florentine state were absent from the community for long periods of time. Their brothers and fathers, who stayed at home, not only looked after the financial interests of the family but actively pursued office holding in the local government. Finally, by pursuing a career in the peripheral bureaucracy the Poppi families broadened their municipal outlook as they began to shape a web of new social interactions with people of other provincial towns.

For the Lapucci family state employment provided additional revenues to supplement the income they drew from their professional activities with their textile investments. In the late fourteenth century, Ser Giovanni was in the service of Count Ruberto Guidi in Bologna. Subsequently, Ser Giovanni, "antico e bellissimo scrittore," became known to the officials of the Florentine republic and moved to Florence.[15] In the following generations both his grandson, Ser Francesco, and his great-grandsons, Ser Giovanni and Ser Agnolo, continued in the family tradition of public service.[16]

At the beginning of the sixteenth century, however, the two brothers pursued similar professions but different career paths. Ser Giovanni, after a brief experience in local administrative offices, moved to Florence and became very active in the lower levels of the state bureaucracy.[17] Ser Agnolo stayed on in Poppi to look after the family properties, consisting of a wool shop and some land. He combined his business with active participation in the higher offices of the local government and the exercise of the notarial profession in town.[18] In the next generation, the two sons of Ser Agnolo followed a traditional pattern among the Poppi families. Whereas Jacopo concerned himself with family affairs, Ser Francesco, who had become a notary, entered the regional bureaucracy, filled the position of chancellor and notary in several provincial towns, and, in 1552, was appointed chancellor to the Signori Otto of Florence.[19] Unlike his uncle, however, Ser Francesco never permanently left Poppi, where his wife and children resided and where he still owned properties and interests in the wool trade. In addition, he continued to participate, albeit at irregular intervals, in the municipal political life, alternating this with his bureaucratic career. Thus, although he appeared in 1527 as chancellor at Cortona, and again in 1545 and 1550 as chancellor or notary in other provincial towns, in 1544 and 1548 he was select prior at Poppi.[20]

Two generations later, Ser Francesco followed in his grandfather's footsteps. His bureaucratic and notarial careers, however, were short lived. In 1580, at the beginning of his career, he was chancellor of the podesteria at Pontassieve.[21] In the following year, the young man was involved in a brawl and was expelled from Pontassieve and consequently from his position.[22] Ser Francesco appealed directly to the grand duke "to do him the favor of substituting him for this period, so that [he might] continue to practice in the . . . League [of Bagno a Ripoli] in order to support his family and to continue to serve [His] Serene Highness."[23] We know little of the fate of this Lapucci after his appeal was rejected. His register of notarial acts, however, was interrupted after the first months of 1581, indicating that he died shortly thereafter, leaving behind a son, Giovanbattista, and a daughter, Margherita.[24]

Between the 1580s and the early decades of the seventeenth century, a deterioration of the financial position of this branch of the Lapucci led to a decline in their participation in local politics and to their withdrawal from the notarial profession. Giovanbattista, the father of the ill-fated chancellor of Pontassieve, did not get an education and instead managed the family interests in the wool trade, a task he later passed on to his other son, Vincenzo, who also did not follow the traditional profession of the family. Family records suggest that this branch of the family did not invest in land, as did many of the other ruling families, and continued in the wool industry. In the estimi of 1588–98, this branch of the Lapucci owned only 21 hectares of land, as opposed to the 117 hectares owned by their cousins, Pierantonio and Torello.[25] Thus it became particularly vulnerable to the economic downturn that hit the textile sector at the end of the century.

This branch of the Lapucci family was not as active in local politics. Its involvement in politics further declined beginning in the 1580s. The last in the family to sit on the town's council was Giovanbattista, son of Ser Francesco, who was elected general prior on August 1, 1630.[26] Toward the end of the sixteenth century, careers in the notarial profession allowed the Lapucci to retain the social prestige that the family had long since acquired within the community, without, however, in any way increasing it. They did not give the Lapucci long-term material advantage. The reputation of the family tradition, however, was undoubtedly one of the main considerations that led the local council members to grant the next generation of the Lapucci the Amerighi scholarship to study in Pisa.

Demoralized by the outcome of their family's professional careers, those Lapucci males able to pursue education, however, preferred ecclesiastical to notarial careers. Of the four sons of Vincenzo, only one, Lapuccio, received an education. In 1620, thanks to the Amerighi legacy, he obtained a theology degree at Pisa, where he became rector of the Church of Santa Margherita.[27] Not much is known about the other sons, who remained in town, married local women, and did not participate actively in the local political scene. In the next generation, the only one of the Lapucci to undertake an education was the nephew of Lapuccio, Giovanni, who also received a degree in theology and became prior of the parish of San Lorenzo at Poppi.[28] The lack of information concerning the Lapucci males after the plague of 1632 is an indication that the family was particularly hard hit by the deadly epidemic. After this calamity the only surviving Lapucci were Margherita, daughter of Ser Francesco, and Verginia and Alessandra, daughters of Giovanbattista.[29]

The crisis in the wool industry and the lack of a solid landed economic base led to the economic and political decline of this branch of the family.[30] By the end of the sixteenth century, to improve their conditions the sons of the Lapucci brothers would have needed both a stronger financial foundation based on landownership and a different profession. They met only half of these preconditions. Their departure from the notarial career typified a trend that was characteristic of most elite families.

III

During the fifteenth and sixteenth centuries, lesser provincial elites—small landowners, artisans, and shopkeepers—increasingly gained notarial qualifications and filled the lower ranks of the state bureaucracy. But toward the end of the sixteenth century, these elites followed a pattern that conformed to the choices of Florentine patricians, and a career in bureaucratic positions lost popularity. Following a Tuscany-wide trend, the number of Poppi ruling families that pursued the legal profession declined.[31] The lessening popularity of careers in the state bureaucracy was a common phenomenon in provincial Tuscan towns, as shown by changes in the requirements for holding a position as state functionary. A Florentine provision of 1469 established that only notaries over twenty-four years of age could hold office in the lower state bureaucracy.[32] At the beginning of the seventeenth century, however, a shortage of notaries made exceptions to the rule necessary; it was not unusual to find unfilled positions in the various towns of the state, where "no eligible candidates could be found to assume these posts."[33] Younger notaries therefore had to be selected to fill the positions.

A number of factors accounted for the declining trend in the participation of notaries in the state administration. The notarial profession and career opportunities associated with it lost the prestigious connotation they once enjoyed and ceased to provide the emerging local elite with necessary prominence to improve one's social status. No less important, however, internal developments in the local contexts significantly influenced the choices and actions of rising provincial elites.

In provincial Tuscany, a career in the bureaucratic apparatus was, for the most prominent citizens, limited to the lower-level positions of judge, chancellor, and notary, with only a small minority holding important posts.[34] For the high-ranking positions in both provincial and central administration, Florentine citizenship was an essential prerequisite. Florentine citizenship was granted by the Medici to provincial elites in recognition of their loyalty. However, only those families that, by the early sixteenth century, had already established themselves as local patricians were rewarded with such an honor.[35] Overall, the dukes offered Florentine citizenship in limited numbers to provincial elites of smaller towns.[36] In Poppi, no one was awarded Florentine citizenship by Cosimo or Francesco. The Soldani family alone enjoyed such a title because they originally lived in Florence.[37] In time, thus, as shown by the demise of the Lapucci family, social mobility through a bureaucratic career became increasingly difficult.

Participation in the minor positions of the bureaucracy also required long periods of absence from local affairs and local politics, which in time became essential preconditions for local prestige and privilege. By the end of the sixteenth century this disadvantage was combined with a lack of substantial monetary gain in return, since the stipends of state functionaries remained fixed despite the inflationary trends of the period. During the seventeenth century, according to Litchfield, salaries of state functionaries increased. The increase, however, was registered among higher-ranking rather than lower-ranking officials.[38]

Finally, the decline in participation in the state bureaucracy was paralleled by a lessening of the notarial training as a means to achieve important positions in the bureaucracy. Consequently the notarial profession retained little prestige and honor, and the number of provincial families who undertook this profession decreased. If, in the fifteenth century and part of the sixteenth, the title of notary had been essential for social mobility and for holding minor bureaucratic offices, in the following century it was replaced by that of lawyer.[39]

The notary had always had a lower social prestige than the lawyer.[40] During the sixteenth century, this gap further widened. In conformity with new notions about nobility, the title of notary was superseded by that of lawyer, particularly in relation to attaining higher-ranking positions in the state bureaucracy. Because the law profession required formal university training in legal studies for about five years, sixteenth-century writers numbered lawyers among the ennobling professions. The notary achieved his legal training by practicing the profession as the assistant of an older notary. After a number of years a successful examination in front of a commission of notaries and a lawyer permitted matriculation to the art of notaries. At times, as in the case of the Poppi elite during the seventeenth century, an aspiring notary enrolled in the university for a couple of years of training.[41] The notarial profession thus retained characteristics of the medieval craft and consequently fell into the group of "ignoble" activities scorned by elites aspiring to nobility.

In 1612 the formation of the Collegio degli Avvocati further enhanced the new social status enjoyed by lawyers. During the preceding centuries the legal and notarial professions were represented by the same guild, the Arte dei Giudici and Notai. The new Collegio, however, admitted only lawyers from Florentine noble families, thus setting them apart from the notarial profession and identifying them as an exclusive group. In the long run the establishment of the Collegio deepened the gap between lawyers and notaries and conferred on lawyers a much more prestigious position.[42]

The elevated status and career possibilities offered to lawyers in the Medicean state led to a trend of migration to Florence by provincial elites. Here, non-Florentine lawyers could hope for positions in the city's permanent offices, which were filled for the most part by lawyers from the dominion.[43] They also had to contend with higher competition. Often, as in the case of the Rilli of Poppi, a career as a lawyer in Florence meant having to leave one's hometown with no guarantee of improved prestige. Thus, Costantino and Federigo Rilli, both lawyers, vanished into the more competitive Florentine environment. After they moved to Florence during the 1630s, they never held important positions in the permanent offices of the capital, nor did they advance in courtly services, and they did not gain membership into the Order of Santo Stefano. They thus joined the number of those non-Florentine lawyers who migrated to the capital in large numbers hoping for career advancement and social acceptance.[44] Instead, they encountered anonymity and the same itinerant notarial career of their predecessors.[45] Costantino's bureaucratic career was rather irregular. From 1651 to 1654 he held the post of judge at Colle Valdelsa, San Gimignano, and in Val di Chiana. He practiced as a lawyer, probably in Florence, at least from 1650 on.[46] From that point until 1664, when he was nominated to the same post at Borgo San Sepolcro, I have been unable to find traces of him among the state civil servants.[47]

IV

The changes in legal requirements led to a decline in the participation of many provincial elites in bureaucratic offices. Between the 1450s and the 1630s, Poppi produced at least sixty-nine notaries, forty-nine of whom came from the ruling families. From the 1630s until the end of the eighteenth century, only eighteen notaries came from Poppi. This tendency is exemplified by those who were awarded the Amerighi scholarships. Between 1613 and 1661, fifteen students received, in some cases over long periods, grants of 350 lire per semester to pursue their studies at the University of Pisa.[48] As Litchfield emphasized in the case of Florentine patricians, it is quite difficult to establish the exact number of students who went to Pisa to study law because many did not complete their degree.[49] Among thirty-two Poppi youth that received a degree from Pisa, eight graduated in theology and entered a career in the church, and seven who already had a theology degree undertook legal training (table 5.1). Five students became doctors, two pursued military careers, and the remaining twelve became notaries, even though, contrary to their predecessors, they had formal training at the university.[50]

During the second half of the sixteenth century, the transformations in the legal profession and in prerequisites for career advancement also influenced new patterns of participation which corresponded to significant local developments. As the Poppi families reached economic and political stability in the community and developed a self-consciousness of their social status, a position in the minor ranks of the bureaucracy and little prospect for career advancement ceased to fulfill aspirations of social mobility.[51] The conjunctural events of the 1590s threatened the economic conditions and influenced a reconfiguration of the financial strategies of the Poppi ruling families. In the same years, a parallel transformation occurred in the approach to career choices. Thus, in particular at the turn of the century, several local families, such as the Lapucci of Jacopo, abandoned any form of professional specialization and ceased to participate in the state bureaucracy. Instead, they concentrated their attention on preserving their threatened socioeconomic status. They expanded their land investments and rationalized their landholding. By the time the textile industry became less profitable, they had already reorganized their investments and were able to rent the woolbeater shop without major consequences for the family's financial

TABLE 5.1
Degrees Granted to Poppi Residents at the University of Pisa
between 1613 and 1674

Year	Name	Degree
1613–17	Francesco di Egidio Rilli	Law
1614–20	Bartolomeo di Alexandro Martini	Law
1620–26	Domenico di Francesco Lapini	Philosophy and Medicine
1620	Lapuccio di Vincenzo Lapucci	Theology
1620	Filippo di Lorenzo Grifoni	Law
1621	Giovanbiagio di Ottavio Martini	Law
1623	Soldano Soldani	Law
1625	Domenico Lapini	Philosophy and Medicine
1627–30	Jacopo di Bernardo Lapini	Theology
1629	Carlo Niccoletti	Law
1632–33	Agnolo di Bernardo Lapini	Theology
1633	Bernardo Lapini	Law
1635–40	Pierfrancesco di Niccolò Lapucci	Theology
1640	Rev. Costantino di Annibale Rilli	Law
1640–42	Marcantonio di Feliciano Sociani	Theology
1641–45	Giovanni di Giovanbatista Lapucci	Theology
1641	Rev. Pierfrancesco Lapucci	Law
1641	Rev. Marcantonio Sociani	Law
1645–48	Francesco di Domenico Folli	Philosophy and Medicine
1648	Rev. Girolamo di Domenico Folli	Law
1649–51	Assuero di Giovanfrancesco Baldacci	Theology
1650–57	Giuliano di Giovanfrancesco Rilli	Law
1651–61	Carlo di Giovanbatista Nardi	Theology
1651–60	Piero Soldani	Philosophy and Medicine
1657	Giuliano di Domenico Folli	Law
1657–60	Antonio di Jacopo Crudeli	Law
1670	Tommaso di Raffaello Tommasini	Philosophy and Medicine
1671	Antonio di Raffaello Rilli	Law
1672	Rev. Giovanfrancesco Sociani	Law
1673	Annibale di Raffaello Rilli	Law
1673	Rev. Domenico di Soldano Soldani	Law
1674	Rev. Torello di Jacopo Crudeli	Law

Source: AVP, *Ragioni e saldi dell'eredità di Vincenzo Amerighi, Medico Fisico,* 1500; ASP, *Università,* Seconda Serie D.II.4, 1610–35; Serie D.II.5, 1636–82; Serie D.II.6, 1682–1707.

status.[52] In the short run, withdrawal from the notarial profession allowed the Lapucci to devote all their energy to strengthening their socioeconomic position in town. In the long run, the combination of the professional and financial redirection of their interests and their consolidated local status supported the reconfiguring of new professional interests as the young Lapucci entered the army.

Throughout the seventeenth century, despite the declining prestige of the notarial profession, the title of notary retained a certain professional honor within local society. It also continued to be a crucial means for gaining entry and acceptance into the Poppi elite. Reflecting a broader regional trend, in Poppi, newcomers who were still seeking to define their social status locally and were in the process of consolidating their financial condition replaced the older elite families in their position as lesser officials in the peripheral bureaucracy.[53] For those families, like the Baldacci, for whom the profession of notary and the local municipal scene represented the basis of their social prestige and economic well-being, a career in the peripheral bureaucracy still retained important advantages. At the end of the seventeenth century, a bureaucratic career in the regional state apparatus provided the Baldacci with the means to consolidate their social and political dominance at home.

During the second part of the sixteenth century, Ser Mariotto Baldacci, a notary from Anghiari, without much wealth but thanks to his profession and an astute marriage to a prominent local woman, entered the ranks of the Poppi ruling families. At the beginning of the seventeenth century, however, affected perhaps by the general economic decline of the 1590s, family members set aside their notarial profession and concentrated on the more profitable activity of spice trading, which they had inherited from their Poppi great-grandmother's family, the Manfidi. The aim of the Baldacci was not only to affirm themselves within the political leadership of the community. They also hoped to retain and possibly strengthen a strong position in local society, both economically and socially. In the second half of the seventeenth century, once the family became financially secure with the accumulation of some land properties, four sons of Giovanfrancesco Baldacci undertook ecclesiastical careers, and the fifth, Federigo, became a notary and a state bureaucrat.[54]

The career of Federigo Baldacci was not dissimilar to that of other provincial notables who had chosen the same occupation. Periods of regional office holding followed years dedicated to the private practice of the notarial profession and to participation in local political life.[55] From 1664 until 1700 Federigo Baldacci went from one provincial center to another, from podesteria to podesteria, from vicariate to vicariate, sometimes as notary, sometimes as chancellor. In the ten years, spread over time, during which Federigo did not occupy positions in the state bureaucracy, we find him as prior and standard-bearer in the city council.[56] The occupational strategy of the Baldacci and other prominent families demonstrates that keeping a controlling position within Poppi itself was an objective of equal importance. As in the case of the Prato elite, the local scene remained both the base of their landed wealth and the source of their social prestige. Thus in 1695, toward the end of his career, Federigo refused the post of chancellor at Castelfiorentino in order to take the apparently less prestigious position of select prior in Poppi. In 1642 another Poppi notable, Soldano Soldani, did not hesitate to resign from the office of chancellor in the podesteria of Pratovecchio to assume that of standard-bearer in Poppi.[57]

The examples of the Lapucci and the Baldacci reveal the changing professional patterns of provincial elites between the sixteenth and seventeenth centuries. Many provincial families followed a notarial career to consolidate their socioeconomic and political position in their towns. Families such as the Lapucci of Ser Francesco, following a decline in their economic fortunes, opted for careers in the church as a way of retaining a hold on local society while at the same time not dispersing the small patrimony they possessed, even if such a decision ultimately entailed the extinction of the male line of the family. Other families, like the Baldacci, newcomers whose economic position was still emerging and uncertain, exploited a career in the lower positions of state bureaucracy first as a way to gain entry and acceptance into the local ruling group and later to improve their local privileges.

The life of state bureaucrats must not have been particularly serene and fulfilling. They, as Giorgio Chittolini demonstrated in the case of the Milanese state, often experienced the contradiction of the imperfect state system and of their position as both state functionaries and members of local ruling elites.[58] On the one hand, as state functionaries they experienced the frustration of their position and the animosity of local people for having to enforce the order of central power against local autonomy. On the other hand, however, the dual role they performed placed them in a position to develop a new sense of identity with other local elites who shared similar constraints, aspirations, and values. Overall, thus, for Lorenzo, Federigo, and Soldano, as for other provincial notables who undertook similar paths, a bureaucratic career in the regional state apparatus was important. As in the case of the Poppi ruling families a century earlier, it increased opportunities to broaden their legal service and assured stable salaries. Most of all it provided them with the means to enhance their social and economic dominance at home and thus take advantage of the privileges connected with it.

A career in the bureaucracy fulfilled the aspirations of social advancement of many of the elites of provincial Tuscany whose power was defined within the local community and who tried to improve their social status with unstable financial means and without the determination to abandon the local environment. Common professional qualifications as well as the private and public roles that notaries occupied in the community bound local families together and provided them with a strong sense of cohesion, creating a class base in local politics and society. No less important, the notarial profession enabled ruling families to integrate more easily into the social context of other provincial towns. Service to the state thus favored contacts with local ruling families from different provincial towns, conferred upon lesser elites a new legitimacy, and led to the emergence of a new collective social identity.

V

The withdrawal from the notarial profession and the departure from the hometown were strategies intended to retain and possibly improve social and economic status during difficult years in the life of the Poppi elite. Some families left their hometown and sought social and economic improvement elsewhere. But leaving the municipal world and moving to the capital did not necessarily imply successful entrance into the regional world.[59] Some, such as Costantino and Federigo Rilli, joined the numbers of the other provincial elites who, having abandoned their place of origin, made it to the capital but never to the top. Others, like Annibale Rilli, also left town but found in military service an effective way to combine the search for greater economic opportunities with an adventurous inclination.

In the mid-sixteenth century, one of the sons of Matteo Rilli followed a different career path, but unlike other local young men who still sought bureaucratic careers, he chose a career in the army. In 1547 Raffaello, the elder son of Matteo, abandoned the notarial tradition of the family and, while taking an active part in family and

political affairs, began to participate in the local militia as a lieutenant. His brother Costantino, on the other hand, became a notary.[60] In
the 1570s Annibale, son of Raffaello, followed in his father's footsteps and entered the army, but he decided to abandon Poppi and
sought his fortune elsewhere. Following a trend common among
other young men from provincial towns, he chose Rome, where he
served as a mercenary.[61] This dramatic choice was crowned with success, and in the course of the century, Annibale "became so rich, so
high in grandeur and respect that he was made a Roman noble."[62]

The branch of the Rilli family of Matteo had broken new ground
in choosing careers in the army. The reasons for doing so were multiple. Social and professional ambition and a desire for success outside the municipal world and in broader regional contexts lay behind
Annibale's decision to leave Poppi. The professional change and the
ensuing decision to leave town occurred at a time when the local
militia was still being consolidated and did not yet offer the possibility of high placement in town. No less important, the local scene
possibly did not satisfy Annibale's social and professional ambitions.

In the early 1600s Agnolo and Raffaello, sons of Annibale, extended the military involvement of the family while improving its
traditional standing in the legal profession. Both also renewed ties
with their father's hometown. Agnolo was for a time a lieutenant
in the grand-ducal militia before becoming an ensign of the galleys
of the pope. But he also participated in the political life of Poppi,
and between 1612 and 1624 he was standard-bearer twice and prior
seven times. Raffaello became a lawyer, and after his marriage with a
woman from Poppi, he alternated between Florence and Poppi, occupying major civic offices in the latter on several occasions.[63]

A strong incentive to keep close contact with Poppi was the large
holdings the Rilli had accumulated during their successful careers
and which at the beginning of the eighteenth century placed the
family as the largest landowner in town.[64] Moreover, Poppi housed
the family chapel and ancestral home. In successive generations, Raffaello and Lisabetta's children maintained some contact with their
place of origin, although by now they had definitively integrated into
the broader regional worlds of Florence and Rome, where they resided.[65] The subsequent story of this branch of the Rilli was marked
by notable achievements. Any account of it, however, would take us
away from the community.[66]

The decision of the Rilli to pursue a military career established a

pattern that would be followed by the majority of Poppi's young notables in the next decades. Those who emerged from the difficulties
of the 1590s–1630s, having consolidated their economic and social
status locally, now ceased to pursue a career in the state bureaucracy
and found in the army the means to enhance their social position
both in the local arena and in the broader regional environment.

The experience of the Poppi families shows that provincial elites
were not a homogeneous group. The consolidation of lesser provincial ruling families came from the diverse professional and financial
strategies devised within their local societies. It also came from participation in the administration of the state. Provincial elites followed different paths to achieve success as members of both their
communities and the regional state. These paths varied according to
changes that occurred in the social, cultural, and economic world of
provincial Tuscany. No less important in forging these strategies
aimed at increasing success were changes in the process of state consolidation in the periphery, in particular the development of the
grand-ducal militia. Although some sons of the Poppi elite became
doctors, clergymen, and lawyers, many more opted for a career in the
militia.

At the end of the sixteenth century, three important factors caused
profound transformations in Poppi society and threatened the social
position of the ruling families. In conformity with new notions about
nobility, attainment of the higher-ranking positions in the state bureaucracy necessitated the holding of the title of lawyer. At the same
time, the decline in prestige of the notarial profession as a vehicle of
social mobility coincided with difficult years in the life of the Poppi
elite, characterized by economic and demographic depressions. As a
way to overcome these crises, many among these families reexamined both their professional and financial strategies. In addition they
also modified their matrimonial policies according to both their own
socioeconomic values and traditions and the modified social, political, and economic circumstances.

SIX

✦

Strategies of Matrimony

During the late sixteenth century, provincial families, coping with difficult times, revised their financial and professional policies and elaborated new political strategies. First, they began to spread financial risk by cutting back their investments in industrial enterprises and increasing landownership. No less important, as a result of the decline in prestige of the notarial profession, some of the families abandoned it. They also configured new matrimonial patterns. The new policies were consequences of external circumstances and by-products of the ruling families' self-awareness as a new local patriciate. They were necessary for creating a new class solidarity and, at the same time, were the outcome of families' calculations of how best to strengthen their position of power.

Poppi families, seeking to preserve and consolidate their political, social, and economic identity in the face of changing circumstances, devised and adapted two distinct matrimonial policies. During most of the sixteenth century, matrimonial strategies reflected the growth of the Poppi families as they were becoming financially stable, professionally qualified, and locally more powerful. Initially, they combined endogamy with marriage alliances with provincial families from other parts of the state. This changed during the late 1580s, when elite families emphasized endogamy and limited the number of marriages, especially those of daughters, as a way to preserve their status and their wealth.[1]

I

The sixteenth century was the most dynamic and formative period in the social and political life of Poppi, when a new group of families gained control of local wealth and politics, began a process of self-definition, and emerged as the local ruling elite. A combination of endogamy and exogamy for both sons and daughters reflected this newfound dynamism of the Poppi families as they searched to expand their connections within a larger provincial setting while at the same time strengthening their hold over local society. By making useful and productive marriage alliances with other provincial families from similar socioeconomic backgrounds, Poppi notables established for themselves social recognition. Equally important, a tight network of local marriage alliances contributed to the formation of an exclusive social group. At the same time, endogamy provided the preservation of their newly consolidated wealth, since economic stability was an important means for maintaining a position of power and reinforcing the prerogatives associated with it (fig. 6.1). Finally, through these marriage strategies the Poppi ruling families were able to provide for the settlement of all their children.

The custom of marrying all the children, in particular daughters, departed from practices followed by other elites. During the sixteenth century, the self-consciousness of many Italian and other European elites of representing an exclusive rank influenced strategies aimed at reinforcing dynastic and patrimonial concepts by emphasiz-

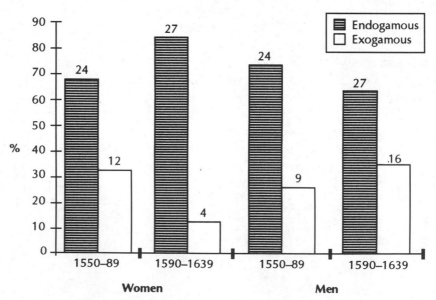

FIG. 6.1. Marriage patterns of the Poppi elite between 1550 and 1639

ing primogeniture, limiting the number of marriages, and preventing alienation of patrimony.[2] The desire to attend to the marriages of all the children was an indication that, although in the process of configuring a more exclusive image for themselves, Poppi ruling families emphasized a collective identity over the superiority of the lineage.

The concerns and desires of the Poppi ruling families were reflected in the marriage strategies of the Lapucci, Martini, and Cascesi families. Early in the sixteenth century Jacopo, son of Ser Agnolo Lapucci, married Cassandra (fig. 6.2). Jacopo and Cassandra raised four children, two boys and two girls, all of whom were married by the early 1560s. At the end of the 1540s, Torello, the older son, married Romana, daughter of Francesco Sociani from Poppi.[3] Within a few years, however, the premature death of Romana led Torello to remarry, this time to Caterina, daughter of Simione Gaetani of Florence, also from a family of notaries.[4] The exercise of their mutual profession as minor bureaucrats in the provincial towns was the basis for the relationship between the Lapucci and Gaetani, which was strengthened in the 1550s with the marriage of Torello to Caterina. As notaries, the Lapucci were active in the state bureaucracy. In 1552 Ser Francesco, Torello's paternal uncle, was nominated chancellor of the Signori Otto di Guardia of Florence.[5] The marriage, occurring as it did at the zenith of the Lapucci bureaucratic career, strengthened the social and professional ties of the family with lesser notables from Florence and thus corroborated the social status and sense of exclusiveness of the family in the community.

Although not much is known about the Gaetani, they probably came from the group of Florentine families employed in the lower ranks of the state bureaucracy. The notarial profession and service in the state gave them social recognition that was not, however, necessarily backed by a stable financial condition. In the 1560s the widowed mother of Caterina and her brother, Luigi, found themselves in economic straits. After the death of his father, Luigi was unable to raise the money necessary to cover certain expenses occasioned by his nomination as knight of the Order of Santo Stefano. His mother thus came to Luigi's aid and, putting up her own dowry as collateral, requested a loan from her son-in-law, Torello.[6] Despite the economic difficulties, Luigi Gaetani was later identified by the local chronicler as "a Florentine gentleman, worthy knight of the illustrious order of Santo Stefano."[7] Participation in the state bureaucracy, in particular during the first half of the sixteenth century, reinforced a network of

FIG. 6.2. Genealogy of the Lapucci, branch of Jacopo

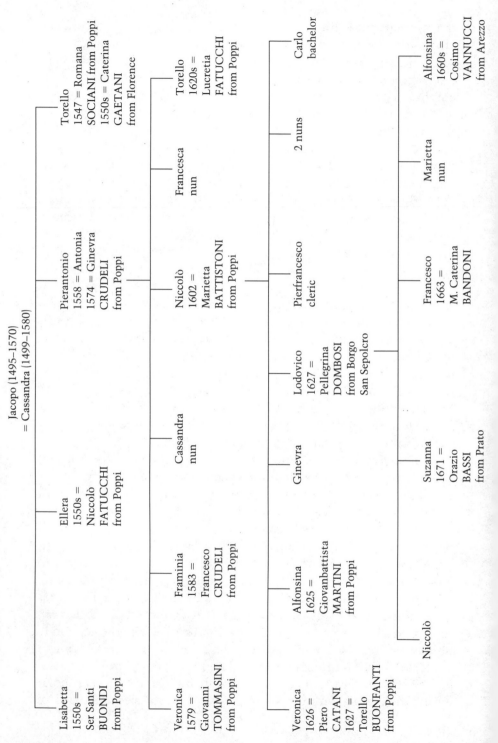

social solidarity among provincial notables who shared similar career choices.

The matrimonial strategy of the Lapucci was not unique. The Martini—notaries, landowners, and wool manufacturers—were among the most prominent families of Poppi. As notaries, members of the family were active not only in local government but also as minor officials in the Florentine state, particularly in the first half of the sixteenth century.[8] The basis for the friendship between the Martini and Riccomani, notaries from Arezzo, was, as in the case of the Lapucci, the exercise of their mutual profession as bureaucrats in the provincial towns of the dominion.[9] Connections between the two families were consolidated in the middle of the sixteenth century by the marriage of Ser Biagio Martini and Donna Bartolomea Riccomani (fig. 6.3).[10] Reciprocal obligations based on marriage and friendship bound the members of the elite together by creating a strong sense of cohesion and a collective identity both at the local and at the provincial level.

If similar professional careers served as the basis for initiating marriage connections, so did financial interests. These, rather than professional motivations, were behind the marriage of Pierantonio, second son of Jacopo and Cassandra Lapucci, to Antonia, the only daughter and heiress of Biagio and Manfreda, small but prosperous property owners from Corsignano on the outskirts of Poppi. In 1558 Antonia brought her husband a dowry of more than two hundred scudi as well as the family patrimony, consisting of a house and several acres of land inherited from her father.[11] It was not a coincidence that the marriage occurred at a time of extensive acquisition of land in Corsignano by Pierantonio's father.[12] In 1574 Antonia died, leaving Pierantonio with two small daughters, Framinia and Veronica.[13] A few months after his wife's death, Pierantonio signed a marriage contract with a local woman, Ginevra Crudeli. In this case as well, ties between the Lapucci and Crudeli families were longstanding. Pierantonio and Ginevra were fourth cousins on the maternal side, and the church prohibited such unions.[14] Reflecting a common phenomenon in other provincial towns, however, the necessary papal dispensation arrived within a few weeks.[15] Ginevra brought to Pierantonio a dowry of three hundred scudi, of which two hundred was paid immediately and one hundred was to be paid within a year from the marriage.[16] Ten years later the Crudeli were still in debt to Pierantonio for the remaining one hundred scudi. In 1584 the debt

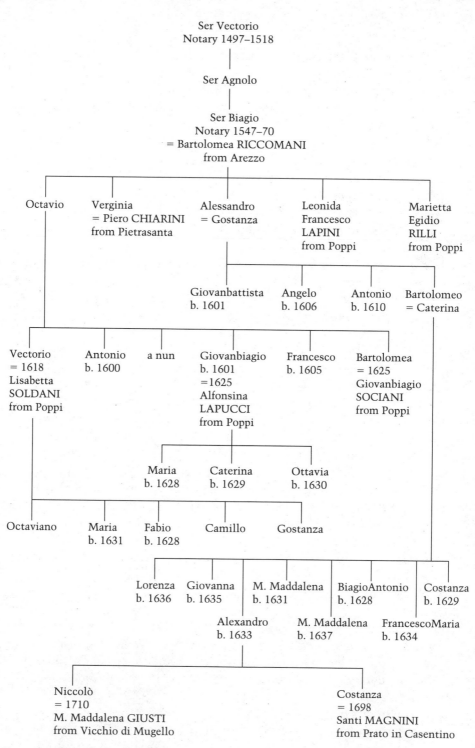

FIG. 6.3. Genealogy of the Martini

was finally settled, a year after the marriage of Pierantonio's daughter, Framinia, with Ginevra's younger brother, Francesco.[17] In the short run, the marriage of Ginevra and Pierantonio brought less immediate economic benefit than his previous marriage to Antonia. In the long run, however, this union strengthened the existing cooperation between the Lapucci and Crudeli families, consolidated their position as part of the town's elite, and permitted the marriage of younger generations.

Similar choices were also made by the Cascesi. In the first half of the century, Giovanni Cascesi had many interests that took him beyond the horizons of the community. As a wool merchant he traveled extensively, and with his partner Giovacchino Guasconi, a merchant from Florence, he also traveled to Germany on business ventures.[18] In the first half of the sixteenth century, Giovanni married first Alessandra Niccoletti from Poppi, with whom he had one son, and later Penelope Mazzoni of the lords of Urbecco, with whom he had six daughters.[19] Five of Giovanni's seven children married, and two daughters joined religious orders. Around the 1570s, when the possibility of consolidating their business partnership arose, Giovanni and Giovacchino strengthened their friendship by arranging the wedding of Giovanni's only son, Valerio, and Giovacchino's only grandchild and heiress, Ginevra, who brought her husband a substantial dowry of one thousand scudi.[20]

Little distinguished the marriages of the sons from those of the daughters of the Poppi elite, although daughters preferably, but not exclusively, married within the town's elite. This strategy was necessary to prevent the loss of dowries, which often took the form of real estate and could have thus led to a fragmentation of patrimonies. Ellera and Lisabetta, daughters of Jacopo and Cassandra Lapucci, married within prominent local families. In 1551 Ellera, with a dowry of about two hundred scudi, wed Niccolò Fatucchi.[21] Earlier Lisabetta had married Ser Santi, notary and sole survivor of the Verdiano Buondi line.[22] The mutual support that originated from marriage ties was crucial, for it strengthened the material conditions of the families while at the same time expanding their prestige. The influence gained by Poppi families was not based on individual power but on cooperation between families connected by ties of kinship and friendship.

The marriage pattern of the three Martini girls was different. The two youngest girls, Marietta and Leonida, followed a traditional practice and married respectively into the distinguished Poppi families of the Rilli and Lapini.[23] The eldest daughter of Biagio and Bartolomea, Verginia, unlike her sisters, married a militia captain from Pietrasanta who was temporarily stationed in Poppi.[24] Similarly, in the Cascesi family, two of the four daughters of Giovanni and Penelope were united with members of the Poppi elite: Ipolita with Captain Francesco Soldani, and another, whose name is unknown to us, with Francesco Pauolozzi. The other two, however, were married to men of important families from other areas of Tuscany: Argentina to Captain Carlo Pichi from Borgo San Sepolcro, and Smeralda to Conte Mutio della Massetta.[25]

During the Cinquecento, economic well-being as well as professional and commercial connections with the outside world widened the range of matrimonial exchanges among provincial elites. Torello Lapucci, Verginia Martini, and Valerio, Argentina, and Smeralda Cascesi did not hesitate to marry outside the community. As with sons, instances when daughters married outside the community occurred in particular when the union brought prestige to the family. The professional standing and social status of husbands and wives from other towns conferred local distinction and offered the possibility of reaffirming the social superiority of the Lapucci, Martini, and Cascesi families.

These marriage patterns thus reinforced the image that provincial elites were constructing for themselves in this period. Together with the building of new domestic residences and the withdrawal from the notarial profession, exogamous marriages were part of the same scheme of self-assertion. The Poppi ruling families used these strategies to attain public recognition and approval both within and outside municipal boundaries. The marriage of daughters with "foreign" men in particular revealed the socioeconomic consolidation achieved by the Poppi families as well as by other provincial elites. Fathers did not hesitate to provide substantial dowries for their daughters, even if they left town. Indeed, the presence of women from Poppi in other towns and of "foreign" women in Poppi guaranteed the participation of their families in a collective experience.

A combination of endogamy and exogamy allowed the elite families to expand their alliances within a larger provincial setting, while at the same time permitting them to achieve considerable hold over local society. A preference for endogamy among the elite daughters made this group highly cohesive, ensuring political monopoly and consolidation of wealth and guaranteeing social supremacy. By the 1560s all the Lapucci children had married. Within a few years Biagio and Bartolomea Martini had also succeeded in settling all of their sons and daughters, as did the Cascesi. Successful intermarriage made it possible for these and other Poppi families to succeed in providing for their offspring, to establish themselves as the town's elite, and at the same time to reinforce group solidarity. The intricate network of marriage exchanges thus contributed to a maturing awareness of common political, economic, and family interests and, consequently, to the shaping of a new collective identity.

II

By the late 1580s the marriage strategies of the Poppi elite began to change. Both internal and external factors threatened the economic, social, and political balance achieved by the elite families. The demographic decline between 1550 and the 1630s, the new restrictive measures of the central government, and the general economic depression shared by all Italian states caused profound transformations in Poppi society. Financial difficulties exacerbated fears of economic and social decline and deepened the desire for preserving the family line. As in the case of other urban elites both in Tuscany and in Italy, these concerns manifested themselves primarily in a decline in the number of marriages of daughters, especially with men from outside the community, and in a shift toward endogamy as the cornerstone of marriage policy.[26] Before the 1580s, a certain number of women from families with professional and financial ties with the outside world married outsiders; in the final decades of the century, those few who married outsiders tended to be men. The matrimonial directions of the Poppi elite conformed to earlier trends of other provincial elites. In Pescia, for example, similar patterns had distinguished the marriage alliances of women and men of the elite at the beginning of the sixteenth century.[27]

Between the 1580s and the 1640s endogamy preserved the social and political supremacy of the Poppi elite. Endogamy guaranteed cohesion and ensured and protected the political monopoly of provincial families. It allowed them to face the mounting pressure of centralization by keeping control of the community and elaborating new political strategies that relied on the cohesiveness of the group. No less important, local marriage alliances helped provincial families consolidate wealth, in particular landownership, by transferring the patrimonies of families that were dying out to other family groups with whom the former were connected by matrimonial ties. At the same time, however, the marriages of sons with women from other towns brought the Poppi families important economic advantages.

The matrimonial policy pursued by the Lapucci family reflected all of these advantages. In the early 1600s the Lapucci's marriages were aimed, as before, at creating and reinforcing connections with preferential families, in particular the Crudeli, Tommasini, and Fatucchi, and thus at consolidating the family patrimony. However, contrary to their earlier family strategies in which they sought to marry all their children, the Lapucci began to limit marriages of daughters, whose survival rate, in accordance with wider European trends, had exceeded that of sons.[28] Family men, lastly, contracted matrimony either with surviving female heiresses or with women who came from other towns (fig. 6.1).

Framinia and Veronica Lapucci, daughters of Pierantonio from his first marriage, were the only two of his four daughters to marry. The premature death of their mother had provided the young women with small inheritances, making them desirable matches and placing them in a position to strengthen family connections. In 1579 a marriage contract between Veronica and Giovanni Tommasini—a fourth cousin—specified a dowry of 380 scudi. In addition, on her father's death, Veronica was to inherit one-half of the possessions at Corsignano which had constituted her mother's dowry.[29] Four years later, on March 13, 1583, Veronica's younger sister, Framinia, married Francesco Crudeli, brother of her father's second wife, with a dowry similar to her sister's.[30] However, whereas the first dowry had been paid in cash, albeit in three installments over a period of two years following the wedding, for the second dowry Pierantonio and Francesco Crudeli arrived at a special agreement.[31] Francesco would receive 150 scudi for Framinia's trousseau and a field at Corsignano valued at 100 scudi. The remaining 100 scudi would be paid by the cancellation of the outstanding Crudeli debt arising from the unpaid portion of Ginevra's dowry from almost a decade earlier.[32]

At the time of Framinia's marriage, the widespread malaise in the industrial and agricultural sectors which characterized the Tuscan and European economies was having major repercussions on the fortunes of Poppi's leaders, including Pierantonio. This crisis first manifested itself in a lack of cash. The revival of endogamy and marital exchanges among a preferred group of families set in motion a circular movement of dowries which eventually returned patrimonies to the possession of original owners, and in particular to the male lineage. In the short run this strategy enabled the daughters of the Poppi families to marry even if their fathers had a shortage of cash. The long-term result, as was the case in other Italian regions, was that patrimonies of those families that were dying out were concentrated in the hands of other family groups with whom the former were connected by matrimonial ties, thus consolidating land wealth.[33]

New matrimonial alliances were devised to protect the local interests of elite families. The decision of the Poppi families to limit the exogamous marriages of daughters was paralleled by an increase in the number of unions of local men with women coming from other provincial towns. Whereas exogamous marriages of local women would have drawn wealth away from their families, those of men brought needed cash to their hurting businesses in the form of the dowries of their foreign brides.

In the latter part of the sixteenth century the dowries of women from other towns who married into the Poppi elite were larger than those of local women. Thus, while elite daughters who married within Poppi received a dowry varying from 350 to 700 scudi, women who married into the town brought dowries of 800 to 1,500 scudi. Only toward the middle of the seventeenth century, confirming a general trend of dowries seen elsewhere, did this gap narrow, with women from within and from outside Poppi equally bringing into their marriage between 1,000 and 2,000 scudi.[34]

The two sons of Pierantonio and Ginevra further strengthened the connections of the Lapucci with other prominent local families through marriage and simultaneously consolidated their holdings through the incorporation of new patrimonies. In 1602 Niccolò, the older son, married Marietta, last descendant and heiress of Lodovico Battistoni.[35] In addition to her dowry of 850 scudi, Marietta inherited on the death of her parents her father's entire patrimony and one-half of her mother's.[36] Torello, the younger brother of Niccolò, died of plague along with his wife Lucrezia Fatucchi and their five-year-old daughter in 1632.[37] With his brother's premature death and his unmarried sisters in a convent, Niccolò became heir to all of his father's estate, plus that of his uncle, Torello, who had died without issue. With his marriage, furthermore, Niccolò acquired the Battistoni patrimony.[38] By the 1630s the entire Lapucci patrimony was concentrated in the hands of Lodovico, son of Niccolò.[39]

Niccolò Lapucci and Marietta Battistoni had at least eight children. Of their four surviving daughters, two married and two took the veil. In 1625 Alfonsina married Giovanbattista, son of Ottavio Martini, with a dowry of 730 scudi.[40] The following year, on September 10, Veronica married Maestro Piero, son of Maestro Giovanbattista Catani, with a dowry of 600 scudi. After her husband's death five months later, Veronica married Torello Buonfanti.[41] Of the surviving sons, Pierfrancesco was a "cleric" and rector of the parish of Fronzola, and Carlo, a bachelor, died of plague. Lodovico was the only son to marry. In 1627, following in his father's footsteps, he wed Pellegrina, last descendant and heiress, together with her sister, of Maestro Francesco Dombosi of Borgo San Sepolcro.[42] From this marriage Lodovico received the substantial dowry of 1,100 scudi and one-half of the Dombosi family's estate upon the death of his father-in-law, therefore easing the family's chronic lack of cash.[43] Thanks to their matrimonial policy, the Lapucci, like other elite families, succeeded in overcoming the financial difficulties that beset them at the end of the sixteenth century. No less important, they established interfamily connections that provided all families involved with a group solidarity destined to last through the next century, guaranteeing the continuity and stability of the Poppi elite.

The Martini, who in the earlier part of the century engaged in matrimonial exchanges with prominent outsiders, now followed the same tactics as the Lapucci, in the hope of reinforcing family ties with members of the Poppi ruling elite. By the 1620s the marriages of the children of Octavio Martini reinforced the connections of the family with the Sociani, Soldani, and Lapucci families. Furthermore, in line with the tendency to limit the number of marriages, at least three of his other offspring, two daughters and one son, did not marry.[44] In 1625 Bartolomea, sole among Octavio's daughters to wed, married Giovanbiagio Sociani, of a prominent local family. By marrying only one daughter, Octavio was able to contribute a substantial dowry of 1,000 scudi.[45] Of the two sons who wed, in 1618 Vectorio married Lisabetta, only child and heiress of Fabio Soldani and of Margherita, daughter of Ser Francesco Lapucci.[46] In 1625 his brother Maestro Giovanbiagio married Alfonsina, daughter of Niccolò Lapucci and Margherita's second cousin.[47]

The limitation in the number of marriages and the shift toward endogamy were, in part, the result of broader socioeconomic and demographic difficulties. They also reflected family strategies aimed at defending political and economic prerogatives, maintaining local hegemony, and preserving class solidarity.

III

The tendency to keep marriages of daughters within the municipal boundaries and to marry sons with either local heiresses or women from nearby towns was accompanied by a decrease in the number of marriages of both daughters and sons. This phenomenon was reflected in an increase in the number of women who entered convents and men who undertook ecclesiastical careers or remained bachelors. The increased number of nuns was a common phenomenon in Tuscany and elsewhere in the sixteenth century, accounted for by a smaller number of men interested in and available for marriage and by an increase in the cost of dowries. These two factors obliged many women to either enter religious orders or marry below their social scale.[48]

Pierantonio Lapucci had four daughters, two of whom married. The other two, Cassandra and Francesca, took religious vows at the Convent of the Santissima Annunziata at Poppi.[49] Pierantonio apparently never pressured his daughters to take such a step. Cassandra was initially sent to the convent "to learn." The custom of sending their young daughters to study in the convent was common among the Poppi elite. This was also the practice among upper-class Florentine girls, who entered the convent for a limited period of time to receive an education.[50] Only later did Cassandra decide to take vows. Pierantonio promised Francesca a dowry of seven hundred scudi and the freedom of making her own choice as to her future.[51] Unfortunately, her father's open and egalitarian attitude clashed with reality. Francesca's choice—either to marry or to enter the convent—was ultimately restricted because there was not enough money for a marriage dowry.

Without doubt the years between the Cinquecento and Seicento were especially troublesome for the Lapucci family as they experienced financial difficulties. Pierantonio's activity in the wool industry had almost ceased, and his profit in land investment and money lending slowed down considerably. When Cassandra took vows in

1601, Pierantonio tried in vain to give the convent a field in lieu of the requested dowry of four hundred scudi. The bishop of Arezzo refused to accept the exchange, and Pierantonio was forced to pay Cassandra's dowry in cash. In 1612, when Francesca entered the convent, her brother Niccolò had to take out a loan with the Monte di Pietà of Florence in order to pay the convent his half of his sister's dowry.[52]

In 1565, as a consequence of this widespread difficulty in settling marriageable daughters, the new Convent of the Santissima Annunziata of the Order of San Agostino was built at the bidding of the town's elite. Spaces filled quickly, and by the early seventeenth century applicants far exceeded vacancies. Thus, Cassandra's father had to double her dowry to four hundred scudi as the cost of admission to the convent.[53] In Pescia the dowry requested by convents was smaller than that required in marriages.[54] In the latter half of the sixteenth century, however, Poppi elite families settled upon their marriageable daughters dowries varying from 350 to 700 scudi. The 400 scudi ultimately provided for Cassandra, even if on the lower end of the range of dowries established for local women, would have been sufficient to permit her to marry. Both financial considerations and the inability to find a suitable husband within the family's rank, then, must have accounted for the Lapucci's decision to enter Cassandra in the religious order.

In early-seventeenth-century Poppi, the number of women entering religious orders was related, in part, to both the diminished number of marriageable males and the attending difficulty associated with the absorption of women in the matrimonial exchanges among the Poppi elite, since men married a higher number of foreign women. Equally important, the strong collective identity shaped by the ruling families and fear of social decline restricted the choice of husbands. Since marriage served to protect social status, it was unthinkable that women of this class could marry beneath their social rank.[55] Placing daughters in religious orders was an economic burden, but one with the advantage of keeping the status of the family intact.

The matrimonial strategy of Poppi's ruling families as revealed in the reduced number of marriages together with an increase in premature mortality among the men of the group led to the extinction of a great number of the town's leading families. The plague of 1631 further accentuated the high mortality rate among Poppi notables. Between 1552 and 1562 the population of Poppi declined from 323 households and 1,450 people to 270 households and 1,107 people. During the following century, unlike the situation in other parts of Tuscany, the local population continued to fall, and in the entire Casentino it declined from 21,880 to 18,247 mouths. These broader trends paralleled more specific demographic characteristics that the Poppi elite shared with elites elsewhere. From 1560 to 1750 a demographic crisis also struck the Sienese nobility, particularly the lesser nobility, which diminished by 70 percent. In the same period only 48 percent of the Venetian nobility survived. In Poppi, after 1640, 61 percent of the elite disappeared as a consequence of demographic conjunctures and matrimonial policies.[56]

Several prominent families of Poppi were wiped out, among them the Cascesi. Despite the fact that eighteen children had been born to Valerio Cascesi and Ginevra Guasconi, only one son and one daughter married—Ercole with Bianca, daughter of a knight of the Order of Santo Stefano from Borgo San Sepolcro, and Clarice with Ferrante Niccoletti, a local man. The other three surviving sons of Valerio Cascesi and Ginevra Guasconi remained bachelors. Francesco became a priest, Bernardo a lawyer, and Giovanni looked after the family business.[57] If on the one hand limitation of marriages preserved wealth and status, it also had serious consequences for the family. In 1607 Ercole died prematurely, leaving three children— Camilla, Maria, and Valerio—all of whom perished before or during the plague of 1631. After the plague only Bernardo survived as the sole descendant of this branch of the Cascesi family.[58] But Bernardo had not married, and after his death the family disappeared.

By the mid-sixteenth century the branch of Maestro Leonardo Cascesi, cousin of Giovanni, was also nearing extinction. Leonardo and his wife, Eugenia Lapini, had six children, five sons and one daughter, Caterina, who entered a convent. Of the sons, Paolo died in a brawl, Francesco was sent to study at Pisa and later took religious orders, and only two—Niccolò and Giovanni—married. Niccolò's wife Dianora, daughter of Francesco Ulivi from Borgo San Lorenzo, died childless during the plague along with her husband.[59] Giovanni married a local woman, Dianora, who, with her sister, was the last descendant of Ser Santi Buondi.[60] From his union with Dianora, Giovanni inherited one-half of the remainder of the Buondi estate.[61] Of the ten offspring born to Giovanni Cascesi and Dianora Buondi, only one, Paolo, survived the plague during the 1630s, only to die shortly thereafter without children.[62] Elite family strategies were necessary for maintaining class solidarity and were the product of families' calculations of how best to strengthen their position of power. But the reduced number of marriages, particularly in regard to sons, together with the frequency of the latter's premature demise, further aggravated by the plague of 1631, led to the biological extinction of several lineages.

When Niccolò Fatucchi drew up a will in 1642, the surviving members of the family were his wife, Piera Cavaccini from Borgo alla Collina, two daughters—Maddalena, who was unmarried, and Alessandra, wife of Bartolomeo Sociani—and a granddaughter, Lisabetta, daughter of his only married son, Antonfrancesco, who had died of plague.[63] The Catani experienced a similar fate. Agnoletta, granddaughter of Ser Mariano Catani, was the only one in the family to survive the plague. In 1633 she married Pietro Scorsoni from Montalcino; after his death, in the 1640s, she married Francesco Riccardi from San Piero a Lecore.[64] The familial policies of the Poppi elite promoted strong group cohesion and guaranteed the defense of social prerogatives, but the defense of power was achieved at the expense of the destruction of the male line. These strategies, rather than sustaining the patrilineage, reinforced a collective identity of the family, which included both the maternal and paternal line.

IV

Between 1580 and 1640 the Poppi elite devised matrimonial policies that were fundamental to its consolidation. These policies were strengthened by the method of transmission of the family patrimony. Thanks to their inheritance practices, ruling families were able to concentrate and consolidate the patrimony of the family in the surviving female lines. In the process, the concept of lineage was reconfigured.

Inheritance was stipulated by *fideicommissum*. This provision regulated the practice by which the patrimony was passed down with the intent to restrict the alienation of property outside the family. The inalienability of the patrimony, however, did not prevent its partition during the lifetime of the heirs, and thus the practice of primogeniture was not imposed on the legacy. During the sixteenth century the emergence of a heightened sense of lineage among patrician families was manifested in a new interpretation of *fideicommis-*

sum which entailed both inalienability of patrimony and a hierarchical definition of lineage by favoring primogeniture.[65] In Poppi the elite families continued to divide their property. The family patrimony went from sons to grandsons and subsequently, in case none of them survived, to daughters and their sons and finally to granddaughters. In the absence of direct male heirs, then, family wealth passed on to daughters and subsequently to their male heirs in preference over nephews and male cousins. In more than one instance, in particular during moments of high mortality such as the years around the 1630s, sisters-in-law were often included in the hierarchy together with their sons.

As in the case of fifteenth-century Florence, the inheritance policy of the Poppi elite traditionally divided the family patrimony equally among all the sons. In October 1570, shortly after the death of their father, Jacopo, Pierantonio and Torello Lapucci met with their mother, Cassandra, to carry out the division of the family property according to the deceased's last will and testament. As was the custom among the Poppi families with adult offspring, Cassandra was provided with an annual income in cash, grain, hay, and wine. It was further stipulated that she would stay with Pierantonio but would live separately in the "rooms below with a small outbuilding and garden."[66] Further, the two brothers divided up with their mother the *masseritie*, "furnishings," of the house, consisting of "wool and linen cloth, beds, trunks, strong boxes, copper brass and tin utensils, plates, glasses, wine containers and tools."[67]

Once having carried out their father's wishes by assuring Cassandra the necessities for a serene and comfortable life, Pierantonio and Torello proceeded to divide the family's estate. To Torello went the Lapucci's new house in the Borgo di Badia, the farm at Ponticelli, the lands at Casalino, and one-half of two vineyards on the town's slopes. To Pierantonio went the family's old house over the wool beater's shop, the two "small farms" at San Marco, the lands at Corsignano, several scattered fields, and the other half of the two vineyards. In addition, the brothers divided the shop's furnishings.[68]

In the early 1600s Pierantonio also divided his patrimony between his two surviving sons, Niccolò and Torello, who were given the obligation of supporting their younger sister, Francesca, and providing her with a dowry on the occasion of her marriage.[69] Pierantonio's brother, Torello, departed from the traditional inheritance pattern and left all his property to his brother's older son, Niccolò. In sixteenth-century Tuscany the practice of primogeniture had already begun, but an equal distribution of the estate among male heirs was a common procedure during the fifteenth century.[70] In Poppi, thus, in contrast to larger urban centers in sixteenth- and seventeenth-century Tuscany, the case of Torello Lapucci was one of only two instances in which primogeniture was favored. Torello was childless, and consequently, as was common in this case or when minor children were involved, his wife, Caterina Gaetani, was named usufructuary and administrator of all her husband's holdings, "leading an honest life befitting a widow."[71] Nevertheless, and this is unique among all other wills encountered, Torello had adopted the principle of primogeniture, *maggiorasco*.

Upon the death of Caterina, Torello's estate would go to his oldest nephew, Niccolò, and should Niccolò not survive, to the younger nephew, Torello. In the event that the male line of his brother, Pierantonio, became extinct, the whole patrimony would have gone to the firstborn cousin.[72] This procedure differed markedly from that usually followed in Poppi, and the anomaly was bitterly remarked upon by Pierantonio in his *Libro di Ricordi*: "And after her [Caterina's] death he left Niccolò, my son, all his estate together with many obligations and legacies, while to me and my other children he left nothing with no reason whatsoever, which was in the wrong and may God forgive him."[73] It is not to be overlooked that connections with the Florentine family of Caterina influenced Torello's decision in favor of primogeniture.

Despite the difference in the transmission of the patrimony, during the following decades the family's wealth was not only totally concentrated in the hands of a single branch of the family, that of Pierantonio, but also, with the death of Torello the younger in 1632, in the hands of Niccolò and then in those of his only surviving son, Lodovico.[74]

Tuscan society of the fifteenth and sixteenth centuries was founded on a strong patrilinear basis wherein the agnatic relationships of the group prevailed. According to Klapisch-Zuber, women were confined to a role of dependence first on the paternal family and then on that of the husband. The possibility of a fifteenth-century Florentine woman inheriting real estate was practically nonexistent. At most, upon the death of her brothers and nephews, she could inherit one-fourth of the estate, with the remainder going to the agnatic group. As a consequence, an heiress was a rare figure in Florentine Renaissance society.[75] The inheritance strategies of the Poppi elite differed from those of other sixteenth-century provincial elites, for whom genealogies as well as inheritance patterns were strictly patrilinear. In Pescia, rather than see the family name die out, the sole survivor of a prominent family adopted an illegitimate son. In other instances, a woman could inherit her father's patrimony on the condition that she leave it all to her sons and that these adopt their mother's surname.[76]

In Poppi the female line was not excluded from inheriting land. The plagues that raged throughout the sixteenth and part of the seventeenth centuries, the early death of many of the elite's sons, and the general economic malaise of the 1590s contributed to the growing sense of precariousness among the leading families. These circumstances intensified the awareness of the Poppi families of belonging to broader family groups and of extending their lineage to include the families of married daughters. Thus, in 1594 a regulation that prohibited relatives from holding the same public office reflected an understanding of lineage which departed from the practice of other urban elites. Unlike the situation in Florence, the local statutes considered father-in-law and son-in-law as relatives to whom it was denied contemporary holding of public office.[77]

During the sixteenth century, an inheritance practice that ignored primogeniture, patrilinear descent, and the superiority of the agnatic group could have resulted in a fragmentation of wealth and the disruption of the family unity.[78] It did not, however. In Poppi this inheritance strategy, combined as it was with the practice of limiting the number of children who could marry and an increase in premature mortality among the men of the group, had the result of concentrating and consolidating the family patrimony in the surviving female lines.

Unable to rely exclusively on sons to transmit the family name and patrimony, fathers conferred upon daughters the privilege of preserving both the family patrimony and the ancestral line. The experiences of the Niccoletti, the Grifoni, and the other families with whom they intermarried exemplify the inheritance pattern of the Poppi elite with particular clarity.

In the mid-sixteenth century the two Teri sisters, Camilla and Caterina, entered Poppi society first by joining the newly established Convent of the Santissima Annunziata for the purpose of receiving an education and then by virtue of marriage into the Niccoletti and

Soldani families. Camilla wed the ensign Jacopo, son of Carlo Niccoletti.[79] The Niccoletti were already nearing extinction in the early
decades of the seventeenth century. Of Carlo's six surviving children,
two had taken religious vows; Ferrante had married Clarice, daughter of Valerio Cascesi; Antonio had married Giulia Gatteschi from
Strada; Jacopo, Camilla Teri; and Malaspina, Captain Giovanbattista,
son of Francesco Soldani.[80] In a will of 1619, Antonio Niccoletti had
named as heirs by *fideicommissum* first his sons, then his daughters, and, should his direct line die out, his nephew Carlo, son of
his brother Ferrante.[81] Luca, Antonio and Giulia's only son, died of
plague without heirs. On June 28, 1631, Luca had made out a first
will naming as heirs his little sisters, Jacopa and Camilla, both of
whom died of plague. Following their death, Luca had made a second
will whereby he left his estate to his cousins Margherita and Jacopa,
daughters of Jacopo Niccoletti and Camilla Teri. After the plague,
the sole surviving members of the Niccoletti family were Margherita
and Jacopa, daughters of Jacopo and Camilla, and Maria Maddelena,
daughter of Ferrante, a nun.[82]

Thanks to the inheritance policy that left the patrimony first to
sons and daughters and then to nephews and nieces, the two sisters,
Jacopa and Margherita, inherited the whole of the Niccoletti's estate.
Within a few years, in the 1640s, on the death of their uncle, Francesco Teri, they also inherited one-half of their mother's estate. The
other half of Francesco's estate went to the children of their aunt,
Caterina Soldani. Between them, the survivors were to divide at least
eight farms with houses and livestock in addition to three houses at
Bibbiena, of which two were old family residences.[83]

Endogamy and a network of preferential families as a source of
marriage partners enabled the Poppi ruling families to consolidate
their properties and strengthened their economic status. By the end
of the sixteenth century it became apparent that mutual support
through family connections provided the basis upon which to build
a family and a class base in local politics and define a new political
administration intended to further the private interests and the authority of the local elite. In the long run, the inheritance practices of
the Poppi elite permitted women who were the last of their lines and
heiresses on both the maternal and paternal sides to sustain the socioeconomic status of their families, otherwise threatened by premature death, plague, and financial difficulties. They also served to
expand matrimonial patterns from municipal endogamy to a broader

provincial exogamy. Finally, family wealth consolidated through these strategies permitted elite men to take up new careers in the grand-ducal militia.

Changing strategies reflected the need to reinterpret family traditions in light of new socioeconomic and demographic circumstances as well as central government intervention in local society. The new matrimonial policies were shaped by the elite's desire to preserve its social identity, maintain its political rights, and protect its newly accumulated land properties. During the last decades of the sixteenth century, Florence had curtailed local legislative and executive power and the economic privileges of the community. But the Poppi ruling families shaped new political practices to face the challenges of the Medici grand dukes and guarantee the perpetuation of their power. These practices were based on a heightened sense of collective interests and aspirations which, in turn, was sustained by their astute marriage alliances. A strengthened network of family relationships and loyalties and reciprocal obligations based on friendship bound the members of the elite together by creating a strong group cohesion and a collective identity. These ties allowed the elite families to preserve their threatened social status, reinforce their financial policy, and consolidate their political monopoly.

III

✦

The Consolidation of
a Regional Elite

During the sixteenth century the tactics shaped by the Poppi families in regard to their financial, professional, and matrimonial practices were intended to overcome short-term conjunctures and specific circumstances. In time these tactics became long-term strategies to maintain and reinforce a privileged social and political position in town. Commercial and professional ties with the outside world and relations with those few families that had migrated to Florence and Rome introduced the Poppi elite to new people and ideas that, over time, both influenced their own values and lifestyles and were adapted to the reality of daily life. During the seventeenth century, therefore, the Poppi families went through a redefinition of their financial and professional interests. These changes were sustained by new matrimonial and patrimonial strategies. The majority of the elite families abandoned their traditional artisan activities and the notarial career to form a provincial landowning military elite. The new choices of the Poppi elite became instrumental in the creation of a stronger political, social, and economic position in the regional state.

At the end of the Cinquecento the majority of the leading families abandoned artisan and industrial activities and concentrated their efforts on accumulating land. Prices of industrial products declined as a consequence of a shrinking market. Conversely, bad harvests and epidemics combined to increase the prices of foodstuffs and to facilitate the expropriation of small peasant owners. Concentration of landed wealth in the hands of a few families brought them economic stability. Landownership was a good investment and a way to spread out financial risks. The financial hazards of land investment were not as high when compared with those of commerce. Landownership also represented a source of food. No less important, it conferred prestige and status. The land passed down from generation to generation and thus became a tangible sign of family continuity and status. Finally, landed wealth further strengthened the hierarchical sociopolitical system erected by the Poppi elite in the course of the sixteenth century.

The transformation into a landed elite strengthened the economic and social position of the ruling families and led to a change in their professional pursuits. Many among them ceased to pursue careers in the state bureaucracy and found in the army the means to enhance their social position. During the seventeenth century, the consolidation of the grand-ducal militia in the Casentino contributed to the social advancement of many of the local families. A career in the army provided them a position of prominence both in the local arena and in the larger regional sphere. It also conferred on lesser elites a new sense of social exclusivity and helped create in Tuscany a wide social group bound by a common identity.

After the troubled decades of the seventeenth century, those families who survived the plague succeeded in maintaining their status and in consolidating their social, economic, and political position within the town. The basis of this success lay in the elaboration of new family policies.

To date, very little research on the early modern Italian family has been done. In conformity with other interpretative trends, the scholarship on the family tends to focus on either an earlier or later period.[1] Studies on the early modern Italian family are thus often limited to just a few general remarks. In Poppi the seventeenth century marked the beginning of a new trend as the consolidated social and economic position of the leading families was further strengthened by a change in strategies of matrimony and patrimony. Municipal endogamy was expanded to a broader provincial exogamy, in particular between the daughters of the Poppi elite and the sons of ruling families from other provincial Tuscan towns. Contrary to inheritance practices in the preceding centuries, women were excluded from the hierarchy in favor of a more rigid patrilineal pattern of succession.

By the end of the seventeenth century, strengthened state institutions, broad conjunctural factors, and reinforced ties of sociopolitical solidarity between provincial elites and central rulers led to the formation of new forms of control which promoted the exploitation of small rural landowners. The new patterns of domination also entailed the exclusion of women from participating in the success of their fathers, brothers, and husbands.

SEVEN

✦

Patterns of Landownership

In 1477 both Chimenti di Pauolozzo Pauolozzi, druggist, and Francesco di Piero Catani, tailor, declined the task of revising the estimo. They justified their refusal to the officers of the council because walking "over all properties surveyed in the register" was a full-time job that they could not perform, since it required them to "abandon their business and shops."[1] As time went on, the ruling families showed increased interest in controlling the management of the land survey, reflecting a change in their financial interests. The reform of 1501 established that every ten years the General Council would elect four officials "with authority to renew said tax register and to estimate, reevaluate and measure all said possessions and lands in said commune and jurisdiction of Poppi and calculate, draw up and complete at that time said tax register in such a way as they [found] acceptable."[2] In the following years the officials elected to revise the estimi were always chosen from among those families that would emerge as the local oligarchy. By 1507 the ruling families were so involved in protecting their enlarged land holdings that the municipal council required that two men from Poppi participate in calculating the estimo of the commune of Fronzola, since the amount of land possessed by Poppi families in that commune had increased considerably.[3]

The Poppi ruling families began to show interest in consolidating land properties in the early decades of the sixteenth century. At this time, the same families that began dominating the political life also stood out as the principal property owners. In the course of the century this trend became even more pronounced. Between 1517 and 1701, landed property was progressively concentrated in the hands of the ruling families and of civic and religious institutions.

The increase in landed wealth possessed by Poppi's leading families coincided with a decline in the amount of land owned by small proprietors. The recurrent series of plagues and famines in the 1520s and 1530s and again in the early seventeenth century caused considerable hardship in the Tuscan countryside. Hardest hit were small and medium-small landowners, those whose holdings did not exceed 3 and 10 hectares respectively. During the seventeenth century, incorporation of properties of related families who had been wiped out by the 1631 plague further consolidated the landed wealth of the survivors.

In the period between 1448 and 1556, the elite families who held most of the top government positions owned 82 percent of the total land surveyed in the estimi. In the period between 1556 and 1632, testifying to their astuteness in interpreting changing circumstances, the patrimonies of Poppi's ruling families increased to 90 percent of the total. Thus the same group of families which in the sixteenth century monopolized the wool industry in town had become by the seventeenth century the largest landowners.

I

In order to present a picture of the distribution of landed property in Poppi, I examined the local estimi of 1517, 1535, 1566, 1588, 1612, and 1701.[4] All local expenses both ordinary and extraordinary were based on the estimi, which were surveys of landed properties and represented the municipality's major source for calculating taxes. Every person who owned land was required to pay the *imposta*. The municipal council established that all the people

> who formerly were from the territory and commune of Poppi and its immediate vicinity and who were and lived in said place and equally each and every other person of whatever state, degree or condition who [did] not reside in said place and its jurisdiction but therein own[ed] and possesse[d] in any manner land and property which ha[d] been registered and described in the latest tax roll drawn up by the four officials elected, hired and delegated by the entire council of this commune according to the regulations contained in said old reform [were] held and obliged to pay in full without recourse to said commune or its Camerlingo every six months for the duration of the present reform . . . a tax

called imposta and every other tax that [would] be levied whenever necessary according to said regulations in lire and soldi in the usual manner on taxable income.[5]

The sum arrived at by applying the *imposta* to the actual value of the land represented the *massa d'estimo*. From this amount, which remained unchanged until a new estimo was drawn up, the *dazio*, or tax, was calculated. The tax was revised by the council every six months and increased or decreased in amount according to the needs of the community.

Throughout the period in question no property belonged to Florentine residents. Generally, Florentines preferred land closer to their city. In Prato, for example, where the percentage of Florentine ownership was lower than elsewhere in the contado, in 1512 Florentines owned 44.1 percent of the land.[6] In Pescia, Florentine proprietors were absent throughout the sixteenth century.[7] In Poppi a certain percentage of registered land was in the hands of residents of other communes of the podesteria or vicariate (table 7.1). Beginning with the estimo of 1566, ecclesiastical properties were also listed, both those acquired after 1517, to which taxes were applied, and the non-taxable properties acquired prior to that date.[8]

Only those citizens owning land appeared in the estimi. By comparing the estimi of 1566, 1612, and 1701 with the censuses of 1562, 1632, and 1745, respectively, it is possible to calculate the rough percentage of the households listed in the estimi and thus outline the parameters of landownership. Even though the lapse between the estimo of 1701 and the census of 1745 requires that we use caution in interpreting the results, this procedure does reveal general demographic trends and patterns in landownership.

In 1566, 138 families, or slightly more than half of the 270 households (1,107 people) listed in the 1562 census, appeared as landowners (fig. 7.1).[9] By 1632, following the plague, Poppi's population had fallen to 178 households (704 people), and according to the 1612 estimo 116 households owned properties.[10] At this time 65 percent of the surviving families emerged as landowners.[11] By the middle of the seventeenth century, a considerable increase in population was evident, and in the census of 1642, 214 households were listed.[12] In 1745 the population had returned to the level of the mid-sixteenth century, with 254 households and 1,329 people.[13] However, this demographic increase was paralleled by a decline in the number

TABLE 7.1
Land Distribution among Poppi Households, Lay and Ecclesiastical Institutions, and Outsiders, 1517–1701

| Year | Landowning Households | | | | Institutions[a] | | | | Outsiders | | | | Total | |
	Number of Owners	%	Hectares	%	Number of Owners	%	Hectares	%	Number of Owners	%	Hectares	%	Number of Owners	Hectares
1517	168	69	738	82	1	0	10	1	73	30	156	17	242	904
1535	164	67	724	80	1	0	10	1	79	32	171	19	244	905
1566	138	55	724	63	14	6	227	20	98	39	189	17	250	1,140
1588	140	56	702	60	18	7	257	22	94	37	218	18	252	1,177
1612	116	61	756	63	18	9	270	22	57	30	178	15	191	1,204
1701	79	74	627	49	21	20	522	40	7	6	143	11	107	1,292

[a]Ecclesiastical properties were included beginning with the estimo of 1566.

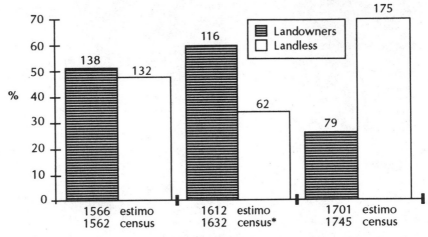

FIG. 7.1. Estimi and censuses of households for selected years. Because the plague of 1631 left the population of Poppi in 1632 smaller than it would have been in 1612, the reader should assume a 30 percent population decline.

of landowning households, which in the estimo of 1701 fell to 79 (31 percent).[14] At the beginning of the eighteenth century, then, in Poppi fewer than one-third of the families were landowners.[15] Between 1650 and 1750, despite the demographic expansion, the economic position of a large portion of the population had declined.

II

An analysis of the patterns of landholding confirms the trend toward the concentration of landed property into fewer hands. But while the number of households and the amount of land they held declined, the landed property of religious and lay institutions grew significantly. By 1701 religious and civic institutions had become major landowners (table 7.1). We have no information concerning ecclesiastical property in Poppi prior to 1566. In the Mugello area, between 1427 and 1498 ecclesiastical property increased at the same rate as that of the Florentines at the expense of the local small landowners. In the zone of Prato, by 1512 ecclesiastical holdings had already reached 36.9 percent of the whole, the highest proportion in all the Florentine dominion.[16] In Poppi, in the estimo of 1566 the 14 institutions constituted 6 percent of the landowners and held 20 percent of the landed property. By 1588, following these general trends, their share of land had reached 22 percent of the total, and by 1701 the 21 institutions registered (20 percent of the owners) possessed 40 percent of the surveyed lands.

In 1566 and again in 1588, the Benedictine monastery of San Fedele was one of the largest landowners in Poppi, with possessions totaling respectively 111 and 123 hectares. By 1701, the properties of the monastery had further increased to 142 hectares. Land accumulation was particularly noticeable in the holdings of the Convent of the Santissima Annunziata, which increased from less than 1 hectare in 1566 to 43 hectares in 1701. In the same period the Opera degli Ospedali offered the most spectacular pattern of land concentration. Between 1517 and 1588 its possessions increased from 10 hectares, equal to 1 percent of the total, to 38 hectares, or 3 percent. But the period of largest expansion of the property of the Opera was the seventeenth century. By 1701 the Opera owned 186 hectares, corresponding to 14 percent of the surveyed land.

This increase, however, partly reflected the change in the practice of taxation. In 1566 ecclesiastical holdings were subjected to evaluation for tax purposes for the first time. An important factor in the accumulation of land, particularly as regards the Opera and the Convent of the Santissima Annunziata, was the private legacies by the Poppi families (table 7.1). At the end of the sixteenth century, for example, Torello Lapucci instructed his heirs that should the Lapucci's male line die out, the estate would go to the Opera degli Ospedali.[17] A few years later, in 1632, in his last will Bernardo Cascesi, the last and only survivor of his family, also left the interest from his estate to his mother's cousin, Bernardo Guasconi from Florence, until he died. Afterward the Cascesi patrimony was to go to the Opera degli Ospedali.[18] The increase in pious gifts, in particular during tragic times, has often been underscored. There were other reasons that led the Poppi families to prefer the convent and the Opera over the monastery. Both institutions held a very important position in the life of the ruling families, who had also played a leading role in their foundation.[19]

The accumulation of land by lay and religious institutions was accomplished not only through pious bequests. The impoverishment and the extinction of many small landowners, residents in Poppi and nonresidents, further affected land redistribution. Between 1588 and 1701, for example, both the number and the extent of holdings of

forestieri—that is, residents of towns in other podesterie and those
of the rural communes in the podesteria of Poppi—declined respectively from 39 and 17 percent to 6 and 11 percent (table 7.1). The
amount of the property held by families living in the larger towns of
the valley did not change much—going from 12 to 11 percent of the
total. The sharp downturn registered in land distribution of nonresidents thus corresponded to the total disappearance of the small landowners living in the rural district of the podesteria from the estimo
of 1701.

Lay and ecclesiastical institutions not only gained land through
pious legacies and at the expense of small rural nonresidents. They
also gradually absorbed large portions of the land that belonged to
small and medium-small owners resident in Poppi.

Between 1517 and 1701 the number of landowning households in
Poppi fell from 168 to 79. The amount of land they owned dropped
from 738 to 627 hectares (table 7.1).[20] The estimi of 1566, 1612, and
1701 reflected preceding periods of major economic and demographic
depression: the plagues and famines of the 1520s and early 1530s,
which recurred in the early 1600s, 1620s, and 1630s, as well as the
general economic slump at the turn of the sixteenth century. These
estimi, testifying to the demographic downturn, showed a decline in
the number of landowning households while the pattern of land distribution remained consistent with the preceding years (table 7.1).
But by 1701, both the number of landowning households and the portion of landed wealth they possessed decreased further while the extent of land under cultivation increased. Judith Brown indicated that
in Pescia an increase in the land under cultivation coincided with a
population increase between 1427 and 1535. A similar phenomenon
occurred throughout Europe in the sixteenth century and has been
attributed to a combination of demographic increase and land improvements.[21] In the commune of Poppi, thus, since the overall
amount of land under cultivation increased between 1517 and 1701
from 904 to 1,292 hectares respectively, the decline in the number of
landowning households was particularly striking.

III

The decrease in the absolute value of the total amount of land held
by landowning households affected, above all, the smaller owners,

those with holdings amounting to less than 10 hectares. During the 1560s, more than half of the population were registered as land-owners in the local estimi (fig. 7.1). During the sixteenth century, thus, small ownership was a prevailing phenomenon in Poppi, as it had been in other Tuscan towns in the previous century. In 1427, in Piuvaca, near Pistoia, for example, more than 60 percent of the population was listed as owning property.[22] A comparison between Poppi and other towns in Tuscany must be made with caution, owing both to the century that separates the data I used from those of other historians and to the diverse nature of the fiscal records on which these data have been based. In fact, in Poppi the propertyless were defined as those owning no land, whereas in other cities the term was used for those with no taxable income. Herlihy and Klapisch-Zuber recently ascertained that in 1427 the number of families with no taxable income varied between 5.9 percent and 9.1 percent in Cortona, Arezzo, Volterra, and Pistoia, whereas in Pisa it reached 15.4 percent and in Prato the figure actually increased to 25.8 percent.

During the 1560s, in Poppi, the data reveal that of the 138 land-owning families, 119, or 86 percent, owned less than 11 hectares (table 7.2). Overall, whereas the number of landowning households declined between 1517 and 1588 from 168 to 140, the percentage of small and medium-small landowners declined slightly, from 88 to 86 percent. Their mean holding, however, declined from 2.1 to 1.7 hectares, revealing a wider imbalance in land distribution (table 7.2). In Poppi, small owners, those with properties amounting to less than 3 hectares, lost out during the seventeenth century. The amount held by medium-small proprietors (owning between 4 and 10 hectares) declined mostly during the sixteenth century.

Between 1517 and 1588, the number of households owning between 4 and 10 hectares had fallen from 35 to 20. The amount of land held by this group declined from 200 to 115 hectares (table 7.2). The decline in this category contrasted with the increase in the mean value of their properties. This not only remained steady throughout the sixteenth century, varying between 5.7 and 5.8 hectares, but it actually increased to 6.4 hectares in 1701. Their loss thus reflected a demographic decline that characterized the troubled years from the 1520s to the 1550s, affected not only by plagues but also by the Italian wars and the war of the Medici against Siena in 1554–55.

During the seventeenth century, the medium-small owners were able to retain their possessions, whereas those owning less than

TABLE 7.2
Land Distribution among Poppi Households Classified by Amount of Land Owned, 1517–1701

Year	Small <3 Hectares					Medium-Small 4–10 Hectares					Medium 11–30 Hectares					Large >30 Hectares				
	No.	%	Ha	%	Mean Hold.	No.	%	Ha	%	Mean Hold.	No.	%	Ha	%	Mean Hold.	No.	%	Ha	%	Mean Hold.
1517	113	67	109	15	1	35	21	200	27	5.7	16	10	249	34	15.6	4	2	180	24	45
1566	96	70	94	13	1	23	17	133	18	5.8	13	9	238	33	18.3	6	4	259	36	43.2
1588	101	72	91	13	0.9	20	14	115	16	5.7	13	9	231	33	17.8	6	4	265	38	44.2
1612	68	59	59	8	0.9	22	19	118	15	5.4	20	17	339	45	16.9	6	5	240	32	40
1701	42	53	43	7	1	19	24	122	19	6.4	13	17	241	39	18.5	5	6	221	35	44.2

3 hectares lost their land.[23] In 1517, small owners represented two-thirds of the total number of landowners and held 15 percent of the total land (table 7.2). Within this group, approximately one-half (49.4 percent of all owners) owned parcels measuring less than the median value of 1.35 hectares. In the same period, in Torano, in the contado of Imola, one-third of the landowners held parcels of less than 2 hectares. In the district of Ferrara, in the same period more than one-half of the proprietors had less than 3 hectares.[24]

During most of the sixteenth century the number of small proprietors with plots of less than 3 hectares remained stable, as did their share of the available land (table 7.2). But between 1588 and 1701, their number and the amount of land they owned fell sharply, their number declining from 101 to 42 (from 72 to 53 percent) and their portion dropping from 91 hectares (13 percent) to 43 hectares (7 percent). During the late sixteenth and early seventeenth centuries, the plagues and famines, combined with bad harvests, rising grain prices, and the decline in the textile sector, forced small landholders into debt and led to a loss of land and overall to the gradual decline of their socioeconomic position. Any variations in the agricultural and industrial sector as well as the demographic decline thus had major repercussions on the well-being of the small owners.

Especially at the end of the sixteenth century, small property owners of most of northern and central Italy not only lost their lands to urban investors, but within a few years their source of supplementary income afforded by *lavoro a domicilio*, "taking in cloth to work at home," withered away with the contraction in the wool industry. The living conditions among the rural lower classes declined dramatically, and the problem of survival became even more acute. First their land was expropriated by wealthy landowners. Then, once landless, they were exploited as cheap labor. The combination of these factors made many peasant proprietors destitute.[25]

The pattern in the distribution of landed wealth reflected the overall trend not only of land concentration but also of land consolidation at the expense of families who were becoming extinct as a result of the high mortality of the period and the general economic slump. Those owning in excess of 10 hectares were the least affected by the general decline of private landholding in Poppi.[26] As figure 7.2 displays graphically, the concentration of land increased drastically between 1517 and 1701.

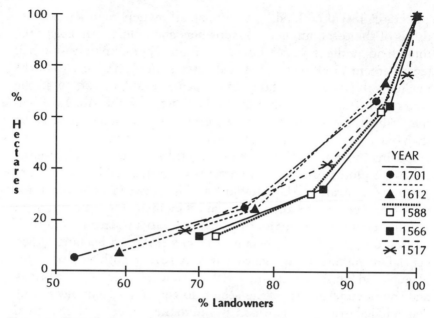

FIG. 7.2. Cumulative percentage of landowners among Poppi households classified by cumulative percentage of hectares. *Source:* From data in table 7.2.

IV

The beneficiaries of the situation outlined above were not only lay and religious institutions but also the large landowners of Poppi—those who owned more than 10 hectares. The same trend toward land concentration observed for lay and religious institutions was also evident in the pattern of property distribution among the wealthy landowning households from Poppi. Following a common trend among urban elites of other major Italian cities, the Poppi ruling families shifted their investments from the industrial to the agricultural sector.[27] In a period when wool production did not provide financial security and was threatened by protectionist measures from Florence, the rising prices of foodstuffs attracted investment in land.

Between 1517 and 1701 the number of the medium and large proprietors remained relatively stable, with variations ranging from 26 to 18 listed owners. The amount of property they possessed increased from 429 in the estimo of 1517 to 462 hectares in that of 1701 (table 7.2).[28] However, the concentration of property by the large landowners was not as much directed toward the territory covered by the estimi of the commune of Poppi as toward the countryside of the rural communes of the podesteria.

The years between 1560 and 1580 were relatively tranquil and co-incided with the period when prominent local families began investing an increasingly large portion of their capital in land, a strategy that was common among elites of the rest of Tuscany and, indeed, Europe in general. This initial period of acquisition and consolidation of landholding in turn coincided with a diminished participation in retail shopkeeping, although Poppi families kept their ties to wool manufacturing. Investments in real estate were part of a new search for profits with the intent of spreading out financial risks and taking advantage of an unfavorable situation among small rural owners. This policy of expansion and consolidation of agricultural holdings is exemplified in the new financial strategies of the Lapucci family.

Jacopo, born in Poppi in 1495, the son of Ser Agnolo Lapucci, had been active in the textile industry inherited from his father and grandfather. Around the 1550s, however, Jacopo began a careful policy of land investments which he combined with the management of the wool beater's shop.[29] Before that date, Jacopo had owned approximately 7 hectares in the commune of Poppi and 73.75 in that of Poppi Fuora.[30] By the time of the estimo of 1566, Jacopo had increased his possessions to more than 40 hectares.[31] By the end of the century, Jacopo's two sons, Pierantonio and Torello, owned between them more than 42 hectares of land in the commune of Poppi and more than 74 hectares in the outlying rural areas of the podesteria.[32] When in the 1580s the Lapucci rented out the wool beater's shop, the economic strategy of the family was clearly directed toward the consolidation of its land holdings and away from manufacturing.

In the 1535 tax roll, Jacopo owned 5 hectares of cultivated land—partly ruined by the Arno River—in the parish of San Marco, commune of Poppi.[33] In the following decades he increased these possessions to 14 hectares, as recorded in the 1566 estimo.[34] In 1570 Pierantonio inherited from his father *"due poderetti a San Marco"* consisting of 19 hectares, in addition to land at Corsignano.[35] Torello, Jacopo's other son, was left the farm at Ponticello, which Jacopo had slowly consolidated by buying small parcels of land from a certain Berto del Grosso between 1535 and 1566.[36]

The acquisition of property begun by Jacopo was carried on by

Torello and Pierantonio, who consolidated and rationalized the family holdings between 1560 and the 1570s.[37] Torello concentrated his holdings in the commune of Fronzola, where Jacopo had never owned property and where, by the end of the century, Torello had acquired more than 55 hectares.[38] In the early 1560s, Pierantonio married Antonia, an only child who, upon the death of her father, inherited a house and farm.[39] Pierantonio, as soon as he took control of this property, set about reconstructing the fragmented patrimony by selling or exchanging parcels of land included in Antonia's dowry to acquire plots bordering on his possessions. In 1561, for example, with one Santi d'Agnolo from Corsignano he exchanged two cultivated fields of 2 hectares at Corsignano for four parcels of land of equal size and type bordering on property he already held in the commune of Poppi Fuora.[40] In the years to follow, Pierantonio not only continued to swap the lands of the dowry of his wife but also began to invest in new lands in the commune of Corsignano. All the pieces of land accrued by exchange or acquisition bordered on lands already in his possession.[41]

Part of those lands that had served to consolidate the holdings of Pierantonio were acquired by means of *retrovendite*—that is, agreements that sanctioned the loan of money or grain in exchange for use of the land.[42] Evidence indicates that not only the Lapucci but many of Poppi's large landowners made frequent recourse to this practice. Often the debtor could not repurchase his land, in which case the original lender sold the land and the agreement to another party, thus extending the loan terms for the benefit of the owner in difficulty. On February 22, 1571, Pierantonio bought a vineyard of three *opere* for one hundred lire and a pact of *retrovendita* from Francesco di Giovanbattista Soldani.[43] The vineyard belonged to Lorenzo di Lazzero Beccai, who, finding himself in financial difficulty, had turned to Soldani for a loan. However, three years later, the agreement of *retrovendita* was about to expire but the Beccai had not yet been able to raise the cash necessary to repurchase the property. At this point, Pierantonio assumed the debt of Lorenzo from Soldani, the vineyard being contiguous to another of his properties, and undoubtedly useful to him, but also because Lorenzo belonged to an old Poppi family, part of the ruling class. In 1579, after Lorenzo failed in his attempts to repurchase the land, Pierantonio sold the vineyard to a certain Lorenzo from Partina.[44]

Families, like the Lapucci, whose members most often filled the major civic offices were also those whose economic condition was most solid. Nonetheless, as we have seen in Chapter 2, wealth was not a prerequisite for office holding, nor did it automatically provide admission into the Poppi ruling elite. Undoubtedly, landownership was of primary importance to the ruling class, as the pursuit of land accumulation and rationalization demonstrated.

V

To estimate the true extent to which the Poppi leading families were accumulating property, it is necessary not only to examine the Poppi estimi by households but also to add the properties that many of these families owned in the surrounding rural communes in the podesteria and to group individual households by surnames.

Conforming to a trend common among other urban elites in Tuscany and Italy, the largest urban landowning families expanded their holdings toward the countryside. As wealthy Florentines did a century before, the Poppi families invested in the rural districts of the podesteria.[45] They preferred the flat and fertile fields in the Arno Valley toward Arezzo to the south and Florence to the north, in the communes of Poppi Fuora, Fronzola, and Ragginopoli, which were well suited to agriculture.[46] The significance of the concentration of rural wealth into the hands of the Poppi elite lies not only in an enhancement in its economic position. It also reinforced forms of domination over the rural communes and their people, further strengthening the hierarchical structure of local society and politics.[47]

Economic well-being, though not by itself sufficient for inclusion in the ruling group, was an important condition, not as much for the individual as for the extended kin. Analysis of land distribution thus cannot be limited to individual households as single entities but must be broadened to consider the latter as part of a larger kinship group sharing a common surname (*casata*).

Once single households are grouped together, the long-term trends do not differ substantially from those observed in the case of individual households. The share of landed wealth of those families owning 11 hectares or less diminished. In contrast, those families with considerable holdings (with properties over 11 hectares) increased the percentage of land they owned from 78 percent to 84 percent of the total amount (table 7.3).

TABLE 7.3
Land Distribution among Poppi *Casate,* 1535–1701

| | 1–11 Hectares | | | | | >11 Hectares | | | | | Totals | |
Year	Number of *Casate*	%	Hectares	Mean Hold.		Number of *Casate*	%	Hectares	%	Mean Hold.	Number of *Casate*	Hectares
1535	94	82	158	1.7		21	18	566	78	27	115	724
1588	76	80	165	2.2		19	20	537	76	28.3	95	702
1701	41	72	98	2.4		16	28	529	84	33	57	627

Once the holdings from the rural communes are added, the general downward trend is reconfirmed for those owners with properties of less than 11 hectares. Conversely, the upward trend in the holdings of large owners is striking.

Complete estimi from the communes of Poppi Fuora, Fronzola, and Ragginopoli exist for the years 1535–40, 1588–96, and 1701–15. For table 7.4, I combined data from these estimi with those from Poppi in 1535, 1588, and 1701.[48] If the land that Poppi families owned outside Poppi in the 1530s is added to their holdings near the town, one sees their properties expand from 724 hectares to 1,227 hectares, which is the fuller measure of their ownership. If one includes such properties in the 1590s and the early 1700s, a similar expansion occurred, respectively from 702 to 1,221 hectares and from 627 to 1,579 hectares.

The fall of the small and medium-small owners was particularly dramatic. Between 1535 and 1701 the share of wealth of those proprietors with parcels up to 3 hectares declined from 5 to 2 percent and from 7 to 3 percent for the owners of parcels between 4 and 10 hectares (table 7.4). The beneficiaries of the wealth of the rural communes of the podesteria were the wealthiest families of Poppi. The increase in the amount of land held in the podesteria was all to the advantage of the very large property owners, in particular those with holdings over 100 hectares. In the years between 1535–40 and 1701–15 their share increased from 11 percent of the total (134 hectares) to 58 percent (911 hectares).

In 1534 the Niccoletti, the family with the largest land properties, had only 14 hectares in the commune of Poppi Dentro, but they held 120 hectares in the contado. In the same period, the Sociani owned only 2 hectares in the commune of Poppi but almost 18 in the countryside. The period of largest expansion, however, occurred between the second half of the sixteenth century and the early seventeenth. This was the time when the Grifoni began investing heavily in land, taking advantage of those of the ruling families who were nearing extinction. In 1559 Ser Raffaello bought from Antonio di Domenico Fontanini, member of an old family, 1 hectare of cultivated land in the parish of Largnano.[49] The following year, Antonio sold Ser Raffaello one-half of his farm at La Fonte in the same locality, consisting of an owner's residence, at least 7 hectares of land, "*lavorativa, castagnata e querciata*," six *treggie* of hay and eight of straw, and one-half of the interest in a cow, for a total value of 1,428 lire.[50] In the

TABLE 7.4
Land Distribution among Poppi *Casate* Including
Properties in Rural Communes, 1535–1715

Year	3 Hectares			4–10 Hectares			11–30 Hectares		
	Casate	Surface	Mean Hold.	*Casate*	Surface	Mean Hold.	*Casate*	Surface	Mean Hold.
1535–40	78 (68%)	66 (5%)	0.8	14 (12%)	82 (7%)	5.9	8 (7%)	190 (15%)	23.7
1588–96	65 (68%)	54 (4%)	0.8	6 (6%)	32 (3%)	5.3	12 (13%)	228 (19%)	19
1701–15	28 (49%)	31 (2%)	1.1	7 (12%)	48 (3%)	6.9	8 (14%)	162 (10%)	20.2

years to follow, Ser Raffaello bought from Antonio, the brother of Piero Fontanini, other property at Largnano, and in September 1574 he completed his acquisition of the farm at La Fonte with the purchase of the farmhouse, stable, pigeon loft, and kitchen garden together with 1 hectare of cultivated land and seven *opere* of vineyard—the whole totaling 1,718 lire.[51]

The landed patrimony of the Grifoni increased not only by incorporating properties of other ruling families but also at the expense of small landowners. In particular they took advantage of the consequences of the famines at the turn of the century and of the downturn in the textile industry, which had further worsened the living conditions of the lower classes.

Between 1553 and the early years of the following century, Ser Raffaello di Ser Lorenzo, notary, and his son Lorenzo built up a large estate, for the most part in the rural communities of the podesteria. The Grifoni, like the Lapucci, followed a policy aimed at consolidating and expanding their land possessions. Between 1552 and 1593, Ser Raffaello acquired more than 40 hectares in the commune of Fronzola, the greater part from small farmers who, with pacts of *retrovendita*, ended up so far in debt as to lose all or most of their land.[52]

In 1561, for example, the family of Renzo di Vangelista from La Fonte in the parish of Largnano, commune of Fronzola, was forced by financial difficulties to sell the greater part of its possessions to its wealthy neighbor, the aforementioned Ser Raffaello Grifoni. At first Renzo mortgaged small parcels of land in return for loans of twenty lire.[53] In time, however, Renzo's family could not escape the fate common to small farmers throughout Italy in this period: debt, loss of land, and proletarianization. Successively, both Donna Thea,

Table 7.4

(*continued*)

31–100 Hectares			>100 Hectares			Totals	
Casate	Surface	Mean Hold.	*Casate*	Surface	Mean Hold.	*Casate*	Surface
14 (12%)	755 (62%)	53.9	1 (2%)	134 (11%)	134	115	1,227
9 (10%)	540 (45%)	60	3 (3%)	367 (30%)	122.3	95	1,221
8 (14%)	427 (27%)	53.4	6 (11%)	911 (58%)	151.8	57	1,579

Renzo's widow, and her sons, Renzo and Giovanni, became indebted to the Grifoni to such an extent that on November 1, 1571, they sold them one-half of their house at La Fonte, "with what little kitchen garden they had," for two hundred lire.[54]

On May 17, 1586, Agnolo di Niccolò del Brisciaio, also from La Fonte, ceded to Ser Raffaello with a one-year agreement of *retrovendita* one-half of a hectare of land, "*lavorativa, querciata e sodo*," bordering on property already held by the Grifoni family, for 150 lire. A few months later, Agnolo succeeded in regaining possession of his land.[55] Shortly thereafter, however, on January 5, 1587, Agnolo and his son, Francesco, once again indebted themselves to Grifoni, this time for 500 lire exchanged for a hectare of cultivated land and a hectare of woods, all bordering on Grifoni property.[56] Two and a half years later, Agnolo del Brisciaio once again turned to Grifoni, this time putting up one-fourth of a hectare of land, "*lavorativa, vignata e fruttata*," for 350 lire.[57] The process continued implacably with yet another hectare ceded. Then, in November 1594, the Brisciaio family was overcome by debts and famine. Agnolo and his sons, Pasquino and Santi, sold for 100 lire of "a piece of land with farmyard and shed located at the fountain at the place called the Torcitoio comprising all that [remained to Agnolo] in said place."[58]

In the latter half of the sixteenth century, Agnolo di Mina, Giovanni di Baldo, Santi and Polito di Giovannotto, the widow Tognina, and others, all residents in the parish of Largnano, lost both their homes and their land holdings to Ser Raffaello. In 1593 the Grifoni owned some 23 hectares in the parish.[59] Within a few years the small owners of Largnano would also provide cheap labor to improve the Grifoni holdings.

Lorenzo, son of Ser Raffaello, carried on the work of consolidation begun by his father with the purchase of numerous pieces of land and at least two farms. In 1607 he bought the estate of La Selva at Ragginopoli for a thousand scudi and in 1614 that of Le Vignacce in the commune of Ortignano, podesteria of Castel San Niccolò, for three thousand scudi. The latter estate consisted of two houses—one for the owner, one for the farmer—and numerous head of livestock, including two oxen, two cows, two donkeys, one colt, forty sheep, five goats, and twenty-seven pigs.[60] Lorenzo did not limit himself to buying land but also undertook to improve it. In 1602, for example, taking advantage of low labor costs caused by the expropriation of land of small owners and further aggravated by the famine that devastated Poppi and Tuscany in general, he improved the terracing of an old vineyard. This property, which had long belonged to the family, had been recently augmented by the acquisition of adjoining land. In his account book, Lorenzo recorded the amelioration in fine detail.

> I remember how on February 11, 1602 and for all of March of that year I added to the vineyard of Le Mura three small vineyards and it took 2,000 maglioli and I made three walls together with that I had made under the vineyard that I bought from messer Jacopo Pucci and the work required 350 opere and also 42 opere of masons to build the walls and I gave the laborers a daily wage of one lira plus one half glass of dried chestnuts cooked each morning and to each mason one lira and five soldi plus expenses. In all I spent 60 scudi and the work was useful to the poor workers who helped me because in that year there had been famine.[61]

In May 1608, shortly after having purchased the farm La Selva, Lorenzo began to remodel the house, "that is, to reinforce the main room," and to improve some fields along the Sova River by building "drainage and irrigation ditches," improvements that required one hundred scudi and a year for completion.[62]

In the early decades of the seventeenth century, Lorenzo's branch of the Grifoni family owned a total of 171 hectares distributed in the communes of Poppi Dentro (11), Fronzola (68), Soci (11), Ortignano (22), and Ragginopoli (59). In this last commune, in the estimo of 1598, Lorenzo had been listed as possessing less than 1 hectare.[63] The investment choices of the Grifoni family reflected the economic principles adopted by the majority of the Poppi leading families, who abandoned commercial interests in favor of increasing and rationalizing their landholding. In the course of the Cinquecento a group of families who were among the largest landowners had consolidated their dominance by establishing economic control over the rural communes in the podesteria and economic supremacy in town.

VI

Toward the end of the sixteenth century, among a group of twenty-four *casate*, property distribution ceased to be as homogeneous, and the gap between the wealthiest and the less wealthy widened (table 7.5). The distribution of property within the ranks of landholders owning more than 10 hectares changed. Land distribution was more homogeneous and the group more compact in the period between 1535 and 1540. Only one family, the Niccoletti, owned more than 100 hectares, more than half of the families held property between 31 and 100 hectares, and the remaining eight families had single properties amounting to between 11 and 30 hectares.

By the end of the sixteenth century, a certain equality was lost in the group of the ruling families as the gap widened between the first and last family. The number of *casate* with more than 100 hectares grew remarkably, as did the share of the land they held. The Lapucci and the Rilli families doubled their property, from almost 68 to 138 hectares for the former and from 62 to 103 hectares for the latter, thus joining the Niccoletti in the group of major landowners (table 7.6). As few new patrimonies were accumulated, many others were dissolved and absorbed. The recurring plagues and famines in the Tuscan countryside not only undermined the economic position of the lower classes but also wiped out a number of Poppi's ruling families. Those who survived controlled an even greater portion of the land, having bought up the property of both peasant holders forced to sell out by hardship and families who were dying out and in financial difficulties. The estates of the Fatucchi, Lapini, Buondi, Fontanini, Beccai, and Ferruzzi families, which in the previous estimi were in the larger category, were now considerably reduced, since these families had become almost extinct. A few families, such as the Martini and Sociani, increased their holdings and moved from the lowest rank to the medium one; the Cascesi, Soldani, Pauolozzi, Grifoni, and Crudeli maintained their properties from the beginning of the century.

TABLE 7.5

Land Distribution among the Wealthiest *Casate*, 1535–1715

Year	11–30 Hectares				31–100 Hectares				>100 Hectares			
	Number of *Casate*	%	Hectares	%	Number of *Casate*	%	Hectares	%	Number of *Casate*	%	Hectares	%
1535–40	8	35	190	18	14	61	755	70	1	4	134	12
1588–96	12	50	228	20	9	38	540	48	3	12	367	32
1701–15	8	36	162	11	8	36	427	28	6	27	911	60

TABLE 7.6

Poppi Families Classified by Office Holdings and Patrimony between 1448 and 1715

Name	Hectares 1535–40	Offices 1448–1556	Hectares 1588–89	Offices 1557–1633	Hectares 1701–15	Offices 1634–1715
Baldacci			0	29	21.8	27
Barboni					32	58
Battistoni	20.4	20	25	16		
Beccai	51.6	26	12	17		
Bonilli-Nardi	20.6	27	63		29	2
Buondi	34.2	25	18	4		
Buonfanti			20	18		
Cascesi	77.2	35	81.6	61		
Catani	20		12.4	40		
Cavalieri				**21.4**		
Corsignani				**48**		
Cresciuti	29	13				
Crudeli	53.8	31	39.2	19	179.4	71
Durazzi					8	18
Falchi					**23.2**	
Fabbri					**88.8**	
Fatucchi	47.2	28	30	30		
Folli			18.2	14	42.4	34
Fontanini	69.4	30	17.8	14		
Ferruzzi	**38**		**13.8**			
Gatteschi					**58**	
Giorgi					133	20
Grifoni-Ducci	57.4	42	45.2	43	177.5	27
Lapini	31.2	13	23.2	35	15.7	
Lapuci-Bassi	67.8	23	138.4	60	76.8	14
Leoni					**23.4**	
Manfidi	7.6	11				
Mannucci			0.8	15		
Martini	37.4	21	96.6	43	44.8	36
Niccoletti	133.6	33	125.6	49		
Pauolozzi	44.4	36	52.5	34		
Poltri					**13.8**	
Rampini	23.5					
Rossi					**36.3**	
Rastrellini	27.2	15	14.4	30		
Rilli	62	41	103.4	56	187	63
Sociani	19.6	15	37.2	42	127	65
Soldani	83.2	11	73.7	52	107.4	54
Teri			**22.7**			
Tommasini			50.5	33	13.4	18
Turriani	29.6	5				

Note: The highlighted surnames belong to families who owned considerable property but did not participate in office holding.

The sole newcomers into the category of owners with properties of more than 30 hectares were the Tommasini, natives of Poppi, who were known in town as woodcutters. Sometime around the middle of the Cinquecento this family increased its property holdings from 5 to 50 hectares. The improvement in the family's financial status corresponded to an improvement in its sociopolitical status. During the 1550s the elderly brothers Domenico and Francesco, sons of Thomasino, entered the political scene by filling positions as general prior.[64] By the end of the sixteenth century, the family assumed the surname of Tommasini as it clearly became a member of the ruling group.

The pattern that emerged was one in which the same-surname families retained the highest positions in landownership. Most of these families maintained or increased their properties. This group figured prominently among the Poppi ruling class (fig. 7.3). In the 1535 estimo for Poppi, those twenty-one families that between 1448 and 1556 had provided the majority of public officials owned 513 hectares of the surveyed land of the commune of Poppi, or 71 percent of the total, and 491 hectares of the land from the rural communes, or 98 percent of the total.[65] In short, of the 1,227 hectares that Poppi citizens held, 82 percent (1,004 hectares) was in the hands of Poppi's ruling families.[66] In 1588 the twenty-four families that sat in the major offices of the local government held 581 hectares, or 83 percent of the surveyed land in the Poppi estimo, and the 519 hectares in the rural communes registered under Poppi citizens were in the possession of these same families. The leading families thus owned 1,098 of the total 1,221 hectares, or 90 percent of the total land wealth.

At the end of the seventeenth century, of the twenty-two major landowning families, only fourteen were part of the ruling elite. They represented 25 percent of listed owners and owned 75 percent of the total land wealth. Four of these families were part of the old ruling group. By now they had increased their property holdings, inheriting a large portion of the lands left by families now extinct.[67] Six new families moved into the ruling circle through their direct ties with Poppi's original families and with prestigious professions. A good part of the lands formerly belonging to the Lapucci and Grifoni families, for example, were assimilated by newcomers—the Bassi and Ducci—whose members married the last descendants of these ancient families and who inherited not only property but also social and political privilege. The agricultural patrimony thus remained

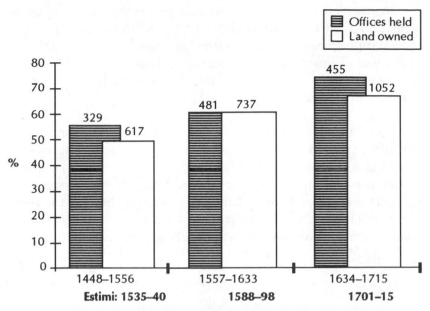

FIG. 7.3. Offices held and land owned (percentage and number) by the top ten families between 1448 and 1715

within the same group of families. Other new families also appeared among the largest landowners, but now economic and political predominance split. These newcomers had to wait until the 1730s before attaining political acceptance. Following a trend common among other Tuscan provincial elites, wealth alone was not enough to ensure entry into the ranks of the elite, and the correspondence between political predominance and economic supremacy withered away. By the early eighteenth century, political leadership was mostly dependent on tradition, marriage connections, and professional standing.[68]

The data presented above indicate the stability of the Poppi ruling elite throughout the two centuries under inquiry. The same group of eighteen surname groups maintained economic and political supremacy. The stability and homogeneity of the leading families derived from their monopoly of landed wealth not only within the confines of Poppi but also throughout the surrounding countryside. The economic preeminence of the leading families over Poppi's lower classes and over the rural communes of the podesteria contributed to the emergence of a hierarchical and elitist provincial society that mirrored the Florentine court society of the Medici grand dukes. The

developments in local society also underscored the successful transformation of the Poppi ruling class into a provincial elite. This polar-
ization influenced social and political relationships, favoring the development of a more authoritarian and paternalistic attitude toward
the community at large and fostering a new mentality as the Poppi
elite became increasingly aware of belonging to a new ruling urban
patriciate.

Acquisition and consolidation of real estate by Poppi's prominent
families, which intensified at midcentury, preceded the crisis in wool
manufacturing and the retreat from industry. Nevertheless, the redirection of capital from commerce into real estate was linked to transformations in the professional and matrimonial policies of the Poppi
elites which led them to reinterpret their concept of self-image and
redefine what it meant to be part of the ruling families.

EIGHT

✦

The Army

A Career for Success

The importance of the attraction of provincial elites to military careers and the social significance of the establishment of permanent military structures have been widely neglected by the scholarship of the Tuscan state. In part this is because the study of military organizations has been traditionally limited to monarchic states in which officers came from the aristocracy. During the sixteenth and seventeenth centuries in Europe, according to John Hale, a military profession did not represent a constructive career move because the highest ranks were limited to the nobility. Evidence from both Piedmont and France shows that only during the eighteenth century did a career in the army become an important vehicle for social mobility.[1] Military organizations thus have been studied to show the effect they had on the political development of states, in particular in fostering absolutism and centralization of power.[2]

During the seventeenth century, military careers, however, became important vehicles of social mobility for lesser provincial elites.[3] Particularly after the reorganization of the grand-ducal militia, an army career gave provincial elites the opportunity for locally based upward mobility and for new positions of leadership within the community.

I

At the turn of the sixteenth century, economic conjunctures, natural disasters, and administrative centralization threatened the socioeconomic and political position of the Poppi elite. But the leading families devised new political, economic, and matrimonial policies to protect their dominance over local society. After the 1630s in particular, it became apparent that the Poppi elite that survived the plague not only maintained its social and economic position but also retained its authority over local society without challenging that of the central rulers.

The same conjunctural forces also challenged the authority of the Medici grand dukes. Between the 1590s and 1640, economic instability and frequent outbreak of disease increased the possibility of social disorder, of urban and rural violence, and, particularly in the more peripheral mountainous areas such as the Casentino, of brigandage.[4] During these decades, in Italy and the rest of Europe, the gap between landless rural laborers and large landowners broadened. Everywhere, rulers strove to maintain order and stability and to contain the widening social imbalance between the poor and the rich. The scholarship has traditionally underscored the importance of this period for providing a significant input to centralization of power by European rulers.[5] In this unstable society, the Medicean government sought to control and contain possibilities for social unrest and thus maintain public order and peace throughout the dominion.[6] It reinforced a relief system for the poor and public provisioning policies to maintain a hungry population. It passed regulations to protect exports and the commerce of foodstuffs. But, as mentioned in Chapter 3, the peripheral administration met significant obstacles in enforcing the rules of law and order. Indeed, Fasano Guarini suggested that Cosimo's intentions in strengthening the militia were dictated by the need to face the inefficiency of the judicial system in the periphery.[7]

At the same time that central rulers created new ways to protect their authority in the face of economic conjunctures, local rulers were also shaping new forms of organizing their power. The same developments that promoted the intervention of central authority also influenced the actions of municipal governments. In the 1590s Poppi's ruling families established new offices to distribute charitable and private donations and thus maintain control of local society. They also established positions to provide for prisoners and to intervene in cases of local family disputes. The political strategies of the ruling families were intended to meet the constraints imposed on local elites by centralization of power. They were also forged to gain legitimation from the local population, strengthen their authority, and provide social and political stability in the community. Through these strategies the local elite projected an image of itself as benefactor of the poor and the needy and protector of peace and order.

The decades from the late sixteenth to the early seventeenth century framed a period of significant economic and social change for the Poppi elite. In this period, the majority of them abandoned commercial activities, withdrew from the notarial profession, and concentrated on expanding their landholding. To further consolidate their position in local society they also favored endogamy over exogamy, in particular in regard to daughters.

The means by which local leading families consolidated their socioeconomic and political positions combined, but did not conflict, with the central rulers' efforts to reinforce their hold over the state. The political and familial strategies of the Poppi elites were particularly advantageous to Florence. They contributed to the effectiveness of centralizing policies and secured the preservation of peace and order during difficult times. For its part, the central government remodeled its relationship with the local ruling families. The grand dukes and the local rulers grew together. Together they strove to maintain social and political stability in the community and in the state. As they elaborated new forms of authority, they also developed mutual goals and consolidated both state and local institutions. During the seventeenth century the shaping of new relations between central rulers and local elites was reflected in the consolidation of new permanent militias in the provinces.

II

Around the middle of the sixteenth century, central authority strengthened its hold over the state through the consolidation of new permanent militias in the periphery.[8] In 1534 Alessandro de Medici, in order to defend the Florentine state and the Medici regime from foreign troops and from exiles, created a more permanent military structure.[9] The militia was organized into districts (*bande*) corresponding to different recruiting areas and headed by captains who resided in the principal provincial towns. At the beginning of Cosimo's rule the militia consisted of nine *bande*, or military districts. In 1547 their number doubled, and they comprised about

15,000 enlisted men. By 1571 there were thirty-six districts, and the number of soldiers had risen to 25,519. Thirty years later, the number of enlisted men had increased to 44,189.[10]

The Casentino district was initially headquartered in Poppi and commanded by the captain of Arezzo, who also supervised the troops of Civitella and of the vicariate of San Giovanni in Valdarno. In 1547 the Banda del Casentino numbered 1,343 soldiers; by 1572 it had increased to 1,759 and was divided into two units, one stationed in Poppi and the other in Bibbiena.[11] By the early seventeenth century the Banda del Casentino increased to 2,879 soldiers, and new units were established in Stia, podesteria of Pratovecchio.[12] By the mid-seventeenth century, the increase in the number of soldiers corresponded to the creation of four military units—Poppi, Bibbiena, Stia, and Strada—each headed by a captain, a lieutenant, and six sergeants in the first two sections, four in the last two.[13]

The developments in the military structures paralleled changes in the dynamics of power between the central government and local rulers. During the early decades of the sixteenth century, Florence's military policy was guided by preoccupations similar to those concerning its relationship to provincial towns and their governing classes. The Florentine government feared that the militia might be used by local governments to challenge central authority. Local militias were thus composed of recruits from the surrounding countryside and districts. The officers were not selected from among the local notables but, for the most part, were people from Florence and provincial towns who held office for only six months. These measures were intended to avoid any possibility of insurrections. In the process, they also led to a weak military structure. The inefficiency of the system was based on the inability of the officers to control a very large district and thus to develop any kind of relationship with the local people. Captains often found it difficult to review the small troops in their district more than once. Consequently, a lack of discipline and competency among soldiers contributed to a weak military organization.[14]

A lack of cooperation from local people also contributed to a fundamental inefficiency of the system. The numerous wars of the late fifteenth and early sixteenth centuries, the commercial interests of many families, and the impossibility of holding positions higher than that of foot soldier discouraged participation in the militia. Consequently local citizens demonstrated aversion to military service, avoiding it whenever possible. In 1448, for instance, considering the continuous requests for foot soldiers made by Florence among the local people and the unpopularity of these demands, the Poppi government passed a new decree. The names of all men between the ages of eighteen and sixty were placed in special pouches, and as the need arose, their names were drawn. As in the case of Piedmont, however, exoneration was possible upon payment of forty soldi, a solution that was regularly used by local notables, shopkeepers, wool producers, and notaries.[15]

The growth of a more developed military structure paralleled the consolidation of Medicean authority over the dominion observed in Chapter 3. The reorganization of the grand-ducal militia was accompanied by reforms concerning the privileges of the armed forces. Unlike those of the preceding period, these reforms reinforced the interests of ruling families, and thus a military career became one of the most attractive to provincial elites.

During the rule of the first Medici dukes the militia assumed a role of increasing importance in the general strategy of strengthening central power. Since 1534, soldiers had been guaranteed special privileges, such as exemption from taxation, immunity from the confiscation of goods for private debts, and the right to trial for military matters, by the *commissario generale*. In the 1540s Cosimo authorized the creation of a special military tribunal within the Magistrato delle Bande headed by an *auditore* to ensure uniformity in the administration of justice for all soldiers and remove them from the reach of local jurisdiction.[16] Tax exemptions for soldiers were confirmed and extended. Officers and their fathers paid no taxes, and lower ranks paid only one-third of regular taxes owed. Civilians, on the other hand, were responsible for payment of the soldiers' unpaid tax quotas. Immunity from incarceration on troop review days and the privilege of paying only one-half the legal expenses in civil trials were added to immunity from private debt. Finally, officers could carry arms throughout the state, a right that made them at once distinct from and superior to the rest of the population.[17]

The intentions of the Medici in reforming the militia were clearly directed at assimilating provincial elites into the army. In 1548 Cosimo stated his aspiration of having in his army "dedicated and faithful soldiers . . . and not such as join[ed] the army to escape taxes and to enjoy privileges and profit and then to stay home when there [was] war."[18] Over the next century the Medici aimed at creating a military organization for the defense of the dominion and their regime. Their strategy also entailed the shaping of a structure that served to form a new body of personnel made up of volunteer officers selected from the ranks of provincial elites.

The need to transform local militias was reflected in the words of Commissario Generale Guicciardini, who in 1572 wrote about several provincial troops, among them those of Poppi: "This is not a good formation because there are too many peasants . . . and many controversies with Captain Pandolfo [Ricasoli]; these are people who often leave to do seasonal work in the Maremma."[19] The situation did not improve in the following years, although in 1577 an observer noted that, notwithstanding the soldiers' poverty, thanks to "reasonable officers" the *banda* was "well drilled and maintained."[20] Finally, in 1588 the captain of Poppi, Piero Chiari, in a letter to the *commissario generale*, suggested a strategy to improve the local troops: eliminate "diggers and farmers little inclined to discipline and to do service," the poor, the aged, and all those who left to do seasonal labor and encourage the enlistment only of *"persone facultose."*[21]

In the years following the suggestion of Captain Chiari, eight of Poppi's leading families, formerly notaries, chose the military as their main profession. These were the Grifoni, Rilli, Niccoletti, Fontanini, Lapucci, Martini, Soldani, and Sociani. But the heyday of military careers for the Poppi elite came later, in the years following the seventeenth-century plague. Between the 1630s and the first decades of the eighteenth century, members of thirteen of the town's eighteen ruling families held positions of command in the militia; the remaining five families—Tommasini, Crudeli, Folli, Barboni, and Durazzi—continued to pursue careers in the state bureaucracy.

III

The new choices of the leading families first manifested themselves in the 1590s with the beginning of economic hardship. Over the next fifty years, however, a career in the army became significantly more attractive for larger numbers of the Poppi elite because it also offered prestige and privilege without the need to leave town.

Among the first to take advantage of the opportunities for social advancement offered by a military career was the Rilli family. We have already traced the life story of the branch of Raffaello, who, given the lack of military positions in the local militia, departed for Rome in search of success. A military profession in the 1610s, however, allowed the branch of Ser Niccolò, cousin of Raffaello, to remain in the local scene and thus maintain and enhance the family's local power. In 1615 one of Ser Niccolò's two grandsons, Giuliano, became an ensign in the Casentino grand-ducal militia, headquartered in Poppi, where the other, Niccolò, was a sergeant.[22] In the following generation the Rilli youth followed two career alternatives: they entered either the church or the army. Jacopo and Niccolò, sons of Giuliano, were an infantry captain and a Vallombrosan monk, respectively.[23] The pattern was repeated with Jacopo's own sons: Giuliano became a cavalry officer, Antonio and Niccolò churchmen.[24]

Ser Niccolò's branch of the Rilli family was the only one to remain permanently in Poppi. The accumulation of large landholdings by the end of the sixteenth century provided a greater incentive to remain in town. The professional choices of the young Rilli of this line bear out this dynamic. On the one hand, an ecclesiastical career for one or more offspring promised to keep a family's patrimony intact.[25] On the other hand, a locally based military career for those sons destined to marry allowed them to stay close to their financial interests and to occupy a prestigious position within the community. In addition, entrance into the army gave them a series of privileges, including exemption from ordinary taxes on their agricultural holdings.

Similarly, when the Lapucci, following the troublesome decades at the turn of the century, decided to undertake a new career path, they did not enter the notarial profession but rather decided to enroll in the ranks of the grand-ducal militia in the periphery. By the 1580s Pierantonio and Torello Lapucci had chosen not to pursue a profession as notary, ceased any textile activity, and concentrated all their energies on managing their estate. In the following generations, the two surviving Lapucci men strengthened the socioeconomic position of the family by marrying wealthy heiresses. At the same time Lodovico, son of Pierantonio, undertook a new professional career and entered the military. In 1639 he was elected sergeant in the Casentino militia and was later field marshal in Prato, Pistoia, and Perugia. In 1643 he died of an illness while in service at Cortona.[26] Like his father Lodovico, Francesco, the last of the Lapucci males, undertook a military career, never left Poppi, and was for many years an ensign in the military unit of Poppi.[27]

A military career provided economic advantages that were particularly attractive to a rising landowning patriciate and was largely preferred over a bureaucratic one. The new career choices reinforced the possibility not only of reaffirming one's superiority—especially important at a time when traditional economic and professional interests were being redefined—but also of creating new areas of power within the local community. Through the reorganization of a permanent army the central government provided provincial elites with an alternative profession to the old notarial one by opening up career advancement through the higher positions of captain, lieutenant, and ensign in the local *bande*. By filling the cadre of the grand-ducal army, the Poppi elite gained new sources of prestige which strengthened its self-consciousness of representing an exclusive social group.

The career choices of the Poppi ruling families reveal an awareness of the prestige and worthiness attached to certain professional callings in Italian and other European societies of the period. Sixteenth-century tract writers who defended the interests of the nobility formulated theories in which possession of a doctorate and the exercise of "arms" were considered titles and professions that conferred nobility and were, therefore, the desirable professional paths of a nobleman.[28] Within the legal and medical professions, lawyers, judges, and physicians were highly respected. Other professions, such as notaries, procurators, surgeons, merchants, bankers, shopkeepers, and druggists, continued to be characterized as "lowly and repetitive trades" and consequently unsuitable for noblemen.

The Poppi elite, like others in Tuscany, creatively adapted generally shared notions to local contingent situations.[29] Throughout the sixteenth century, for many of the elites of provincial Tuscany, the sources of their power were defined within the local community, since the municipal scene represented the basis of economic well-being, social prestige, and political supremacy. Consequently, in Poppi, the professions of notary and schoolteacher were popular career choices, just as many druggists and merchants were part of the ruling families. It was only later, in the seventeenth century, that certain activities began to be considered unworthy of public officeholders. At the same time, another idea emerged—the notion that military honors conferred a superiority connected with a noble status—but even so, exception was made for "the category of druggists."[30]

In the seventeenth century, the decision to pursue a military career reflected the changing economic and social conditions of this group of families. The Poppi elite acquired a new patrician image and sought social mobility through distinct strategies like the ones employed by the Niccoletti family. Writing about the period following the plague of 1632, the chronicler Lapini described the Niccoletti family as having been at that time "highly reputed throughout the Casentino for their great wealth and family connections and for having had successively three ensigns among their members, even though since the beginning they had been merchants and druggists and, for the most part, notaries."[31]

Always active in public affairs in Poppi, the Niccoletti made their official entrance into the ruling families when Carlo, son of Bartolomeo, druggist, was elected riformatore in 1449.[32] In the six years that followed, Carlo was often chosen ambassador to Florence and also served as standard-bearer and riformatore in the local government.[33] In the years between 1535 and 1540 the Niccoletti had become the largest property owners in town, but in the ensuing years the social position of the family improved when Carlo's grandson and namesake began his career as a notary in Poppi.[34] In 1542, income from land, from a druggist's shop, and from the notarial profession permitted his son, Bartolomeo, to purchase a wool shop.[35]

The diversification that characterized the early economic successes and professional choices of the Niccoletti—druggists and property owners, notaries and wool merchants—was abandoned in the second half of the sixteenth century. A few years after enlarging his wool business, Carlo di Bartolomeo rented out the pharmacy that had been under family management since the mid-fifteenth century.[36] Simultaneously the male members of the family entered military careers, and the family began to assume more patrician attitudes. In the 1650s the chronicler Lapini, attentive observer of the local reality, described the social evolution of the Niccoletti, commenting on how the last generation, after having given up their shop "and having obtained military honors with Carlo di Bartolomeo and his son, Jacopo, considered themselves so noble as to be odious to the people."[37]

At the beginning of the seventeenth century, both Carlo and his sons, Jacopo and Antonio, were officers in the Casentino unit. Another son, Luca, took religious orders, and the fourth, Ferrante, was left to look after family affairs.[38] The professional choices of the three Niccoletti brothers were reflected in their matrimonial choices. Ferrante married Clarice, daughter of Valerio Cascesi, from Poppi; both Antonio and Jacopo married women from other towns in the vicariate.[39] The network of marriage exchanges exemplified by the Niccoletti family is indicative of the formation of new ties among provincial elites. These ties, which are further discussed in the following chapter, reflected the growing awareness of common political, economic, and professional interests among lesser provincial elites who shared similar experiences. As large numbers of rising local elites entered the army and became the pillars of provincial militias, they merged into one social group whose legitimacy was guaranteed by participating in the process of state consolidation. By sharing in a common experience they derived a collective identity as new regional elites.

IV

Doubtless the search for economic alternatives in the crisis years was an important factor in explaining the large numbers of Poppi youths who entered military careers. Not by chance did Ser Bernardo Lapini in his "Istoria" of the town, compiled after the plague, underline the need to "restore among the few youths who remain[ed] the discipline of undertaking an education, so necessary . . . since many arts, skills and trades had ceased to exist in [Poppi] which formerly used to keep it very comfortable."[40] An army career also answered the need and aspiration for social mobility into the regional world. No less important, changes in the strategies of the central government toward provincial elites influenced the new professional directions of the Poppi families. By the 1640s, after the regional state offered a growing number of higher positions in the new military organization, many among the lesser provincial elites chose a career in the army over one in the civic bureaucracy not only as the best vehicle for social mobility at the regional level but also as a means to maintain and extend their political supremacy within the community. A military career offered the possibility of creating new areas of power within the local reality by strengthening a new system of privilege.

Prior to 1640 only the lower-ranking officers were local men; the captain was an outsider stationed in Poppi.[41] Over the following years the provincial military units were filled with officers appointed from among local elites. Following the reforms of that period, the captains of each unit were selected from among the sons of the most prominent local families.[42] Furthermore, whereas initially the positions of captain, lieutenant, and ensign were designated only for one year, in time these ranks were made lifetime appointments and even became hereditary.[43]

We can see this in the experience of the Ducci, descendants of the Grifoni family. At the end of the seventeenth century, Lorenzo Ducci became captain of the Poppi *quarto* of the grand-ducal militia.[44] Lorenzo's son, Dario, followed in his father's footsteps and, having served in Bibbiena first as lieutenant and then as captain, succeeded upon Lorenzo's death in 1718 to the office of captain of the Poppi command.[45] In both cases, a military career permitted these men to remain close to home, supervise the family's holdings, and participate actively in the community's political and administrative life. Between 1678 and 1712, Lorenzo was standard-bearer three times and prior eleven times. Dario, too, was active in local government. He was prior twice, in 1709 and 1713, and between 1734 and 1747 was standard-bearer four times and prior five times.[46]

During the sixteenth century, the monopoly of local government allowed prominent Poppi families to establish, extend, and maintain their social and political superiority within the community. By creating a tight network of alliances based on friendship and marriage, the Poppi elite sustained the shaping of a local structure that perpetuated patterns of privilege and abuse. At the same time, though, this system provided political stability and social continuity. In the next century the Poppi elite established a similar monopoly of the commanding offices in the militia of the Casentino. Through participation in the offices of the local military structure the leading families extended and adapted the same system of privilege and abuse from a local to a regional dimension. They thus carved out a new area of power wherein they successfully combined the need for retaining economic and social control within the community with their desire to be part of the new regional reality.

By the 1640s the majority of Poppi's elite families abandoned their traditional artisan activities and the notarial profession to form a local landowning military patriciate. Their transformation into a landed elite further strengthened the economic and social position of these families and led to their entrance into military careers. The new professional choices were part of a new sense of social solidarity and exclusiveness among the Poppi elite families through which they sought simultaneously to enhance their professional success, preserve their socioeconomic predominance within the town, and reinforce new images of themselves as regional elites.[47] Through a career in the army the Poppi ruling families identified new areas of power aimed at consolidating relations of authority in local society. The experience of the Poppi families suggests that the backbone of the new state was not only the judges, notaries, and chancellors but also the captains and the lieutenants who filled the cadre of the local militia. The new officers of the state originated from local elites. Their members were drawn to the service of the state because it provided financial security during difficult times and allowed them to preserve local dominance. By broadening the social basis of support for the central authority, they played a crucial role in the consolidation of the Tuscan regional state.

Through the militia local and central powers jointly pursued their mutual interests and forged parallel strategies aimed at consolidating their authority and their control over society. For the Poppi elite the locally based military profession became a source of prestige and privilege and thus bestowed upon the men of the leading families a renewed sense of authority, which the process of centralization as well as the economic and demographic circumstances had partially undermined in the preceding period.

In the municipal context, a career in the army served to mask the increasing loss of traditional power and contributed to the symbolic legitimation of the authority of local elites. A military career served to reinforce a system of privilege through which local ruling families could exercise their power without infringing upon the authority of the central government. If the Poppi elite benefited from the creation of the grand-ducal militia, so did the central government. Through the militia the Medici rulers were able to offer the Poppi elite special advantages while still keeping their central authority intact. At the same time, by successfully strengthening central institutions in the periphery, the Medici and provincial rulers consolidated the state.

The case of Poppi shows that the political dynamics of state consolidation were not one sided. Unquestionably, in the local communities traditional political power connected with office holding diminished during the sixteenth century as central rulers extended their reach. The political dynamics of state consolidation involved a constant renegotiation of power between local elites and central rulers. Together they strengthened homogeneous and centralized structures that consolidated a decentralized system of power. Altogether, participation in the locally based regional militia provided the Poppi elite with strength, status, and legitimacy. Furthermore, it contributed to the formation of a new preferential relationship between the Florentine rulers and provincial elites. This relation was defined by dynamics of power and authority between Poppi and Florence which reinforced forms of social and political hierarchies in the local context and in the regional society, in the private sphere and in the public space of the Tuscan state.

NINE

◆

Strategies of Patrimony

In 1684 Giuseppe Mannucci, one of the local chroniclers, wrote of the requirements for office holding:

> To such a prestigious body [the community government] none but those similarly qualified are eligible since only the most civilized people can be promoted to the offices of Standard-bearer and Priors as heretofore has been the custom; and in conformity to ancient and honorable usage to these is given a noble title . . . to increase further their honor and to gain it by belonging to a civilized family . . . to enable yet another family to attain to such dignity, given that they have lived civilly and formed connections with the area's leading families.[1]

During the Cinquecento the defense of the patrimony and the solidarity of the family were fundamental features in the strategy of the Poppi elite to maintain its social and political predominance. In the following century this predominance was reinforced and extended to the regional level at the same time that the Poppi ruling families were elaborating new ways to define themselves through participation in the army.

In the course of the sixteenth century, the Poppi elite had been formed and strengthened within the boundaries of the municipal environment. Now new professions and extended matrimonial exchanges helped to create a new Tuscany-wide social group, bound by common economic and professional interests and strengthened by family connections. The entrance of elite families into provincial militias paralleled a change in the matrimonial and inheritance policies of elite families. Changes in these policies indicate the degree of socioeconomic and political strength achieved by provincial elites after the troubled decades of the seventeenth century. They also reveal their heightened sense of forming a new exclusive social group. Provincial families abandoned an outlook limited to the municipal context and instead developed a broader consciousness as members not only of a local ruling class but also of a regional elite.

The emergence of a new regional elite was exemplified by the new matrimonial connections attending the consolidation of the regional state. It was also displayed in modifications of inheritance patterns. The endogamy of the late sixteenth century was replaced by the broadening of matrimonial exchanges of local women with ruling families of other provincial towns. During the early years of the eighteenth century, the customary inheritance practices were also modified in favor of a more rigid patrilineal succession.

I

During the sixteenth and seventeenth centuries, an inheritance policy whereby property in the absence of direct male descendants could be transmitted to daughters in preference to nephews and male cousins guaranteed the continuity and transmission of elite wealth. The inheritance strategies employed by the Niccoletti, Grifoni, and Sociani families, for example, enabled the consolidation of the family patrimony in the hands of their daughters, last descendants and wealthy heiresses on both the maternal and paternal side.

In the first half of the seventeenth century, the two Niccoletti sisters were married—Jacopa to Giuliano, son of Giovanfrancesco Rilli, and Margherita to Antonio, son of Lorenzo Grifoni (fig. 9.1).[2] Antonio was the only child in the Grifoni family to marry and the one to inherit the large patrimony that his father, Lorenzo, and grandfather, Ser Raffaello, had accumulated.[3] Margherita, the last of her family's survivors together with her sister, brought to the marriage a dowry of 2,350 scudi, one-half of the Niccoletti patrimony and one-fourth of that of the Teri.[4] Between 1623 and 1647, Antonio and Margherita had fourteen children, twelve daughters and two sons. Their son Lorenzo died at eighteen in 1648, and Pierfrancesco died in infancy.[5] Most of the girls also died in infancy, with the exception of Lessandra and Maria Anna, who became nuns, and Camilla, Lisabetta, and Giulia, who in the middle years of the seventeenth century married into prominent provincial Tuscan families.[6]

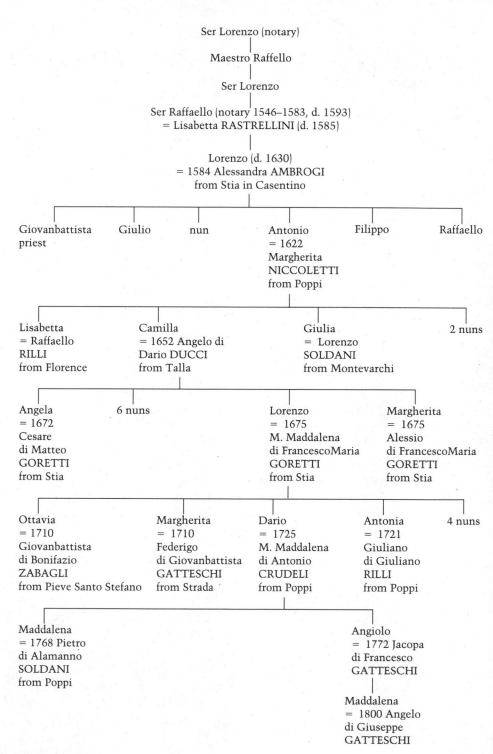

Ser Lorenzo (notary)
|
Maestro Raffello
|
Ser Lorenzo
|
Ser Raffaello (notary 1546–1583, d. 1593)
= Lisabetta RASTRELLINI (d. 1585)
|
Lorenzo (d. 1630)
= 1584 Alessandra AMBROGI
from Stia in Casentino
|
Giovanbattista   Giulio   nun   Antonio   Filippo   Raffaello
priest   = 1622
                                      Margherita
                                      NICCOLETTI
                                      from Poppi
|
Lisabetta   Camilla   Giulia   2 nuns
= Raffaello   = 1652 Angelo di   = Lorenzo
RILLI   Dario DUCCI   SOLDANI
from Florence   from Talla   from Montevarchi
|
Angela   6 nuns   Lorenzo   Margherita
= 1672   = 1675   = 1675
Cesare   M. Maddalena   Alessio
di Matteo   di FrancescoMaria   di FrancescoMaria
GORETTI   GORETTI   GORETTI
from Stia   from Stia   from Stia
|
Ottavia   Margherita   Dario   Antonia   4 nuns
= 1710   = 1710   = 1725   = 1721
Giovanbattista   Federigo   M. Maddalena   Giuliano
di Bonifazio   di Giovanbattista   di Antonio   di Giuliano
ZABAGLI   GATTESCHI   CRUDELI   RILLI
from Pieve Santo   from Strada   from Poppi   from Poppi
Stefano
|
Maddalena   Angiolo
= 1768 Pietro   = 1772 Jacopa
di Alamanno   di Francesco
SOLDANI   GATTESCHI
from Poppi |
                                          Maddalena
                                          = 1800 Angelo
                                          di Giuseppe
                                          GATTESCHI

FIG. 9.1. Genealogy of the Grifoni-Ducci

In the second half of the century, the Grifoni sisters became wealthy heiresses, having received the entirety of the Grifoni patrimony, one-half of the Niccoletti's, and one-quarter of the Teri's. Giulia married Lorenzo Soldani of Montevarchi; she later separated from him and, having no children, returned to Poppi.[7] Her sister Lisabetta first married Sergeant Niccolò Rilli, the younger brother of her aunt, Jacopa Niccoletti. Widowed at eighteen, Lisabetta married Raffaello, son of Annibale Rilli; Raffaello was a Roman aristocrat and lawyer residing in Florence but originally from that branch of the family which had left Poppi for Rome in the sixteenth century."[8] The only sister to remain in Poppi was Camilla, who on April 12, 1652, married the town doctor, Angelo, son of Ser Dario Ducci, of a prominent family from Talla, podesteria of Castelfocognano.[9]

Another interesting case is that of the Sociani. Toward the middle of the seventeenth century, Lieutenant Cristofano di Feliciano Sociani married Laura di Giovanbattista Gatteschi. At the end of the century, Cristofano's granddaughter, Laura Caterina, was designated heiress of her father, Giovanbattista. In 1716, following the death of two uncles, one a priest and the other a bachelor, Laura inherited the whole of the family's patrimony. Successively, the Sociani wealth went to Laura's sons, Ventura and Giovanbattista, by Ottaviano Ranucci, who was originally from Città di Castello but had moved to Poppi following his marriage. During the eighteenth century the Ranucci became one of the most prominent families in town.[10]

During the seventeenth century elite women, as heiresses of their families' patrimonies, held a significant position in the consolidation and transmission of elite wealth. They were also instrumental in the emergence of a new socioeconomic and familial solidarity among an extended network of provincial families. In smaller towns such as Poppi and Prato, endogamous marriages continued throughout the sixteenth and most of the seventeenth centuries.[11] But beginning in the 1650s, new families entered the ranks of the Poppi elite through intermarriage with women who were the last of their families' descendants. Returning to an earlier trend, and following the practices of other provincial elites such as the one in Pescia, matrimony between women from Poppi and men from other towns now became frequent (fig. 9.2).[12]

Several Poppi women married outsiders and left town, at least temporarily, but many brought their new families to Poppi. The experience of the Lapucci family again illustrates the new trend. The

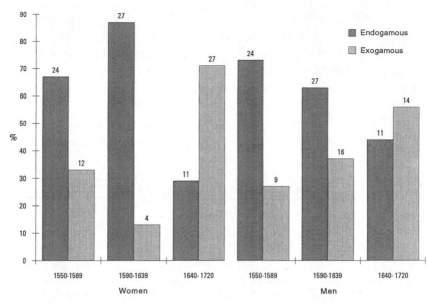

FIG. 9.2. Marriage patterns of Poppi elite between 1550 and 1720

decline of marriages and the demise of sons led to the extinction of the male line of the Lapucci family. In 1645 Lodovico Lapucci was outlived by his wife, Pellegrina, two sons, and three daughters (see fig. 6.2). Only one of the boys, the ensign Francesco, married, but he, too, died a "sudden death" in 1670 without issue.[13] With his death the male line of the family became extinct. By the second half of the seventeenth century, the family survivors were the three Lapucci sisters—Alfonsina and Suzanna, who wed officers of the regional elite, and Marietta, a nun.[14] After her wedding to Cosimo Vannucci, Alfonsina Lapucci moved to Arezzo but continued to maintain contact with Poppi. In the 1690s, for example, one of her daughters married into the Rilli family of Poppi.[15]

The case of Suzanna Lapucci was different. Together with her sister Alfonsina, Suzanna had inherited a large land patrimony in addition to the family ancestral home and chapel. Rarely in Florentine society was the paternal home left to a daughter. William Kent presents as an exceptional case that of Francesco Capponi, who left his house to his daughters only in the event that they were widows and "with the understanding [that] they [could not] take there any children, whether boys or girls."[16] In 1671 Suzanna, however, lived in her father's house with her new husband, Orazio Bassi from Prato in

Casentino. After the marriage Orazio sold his new house at Prato in Casentino and moved to the Lapucci's home in Poppi.

The motives behind Orazio's actions were multiple. Most important was that Suzanna had inherited a substantial patrimony. Although Orazio owned lands of his own in the podesteria of Castel San Niccolò, he also became the administrator of Suzanna's inheritance. For example, shortly after his marriage, Orazio contested Torello Lapucci's will of 1591, which stipulated that in case of extinction of the male line, all of Torello's estate would go to the Opera degli Ospedali of Poppi.[17] After considerable effort, Orazio succeeded in having himself considered *"la terza linea masculina"* and in obtaining for his offspring the use of the estate at Ponticelli and the house in town in exchange for an annual payment to the hospital of 135 scudi and three pairs of capons to the operai.[18]

Orazio had other reasons for settling in Poppi. He was an only child whose parents had died soon after his birth. After their death he lived with his grandfather, who left him a house in Prato and a small inheritance. Orazio carefully looked after his land, became a notary, and entered a career in the provincial bureaucracy of the Medicean government, acquiring sufficient means to build a house in Strada valued at seven hundred scudi.[19] But financial stability was only one of Orazio's aims. An ancient lineage and a continuous tradition complete with an old family home and chapel were all desirable to him as symbols of social status. As Suzanna's husband and thus heir of a prominent family, Orazio immediately was invested with all the honors and privileges accorded to members of the Poppi elite. In 1677 Orazio began to fill important civic offices as prior and standard-bearer. In later years both his son, Domenico, and his grandson, Francesco, held high local administrative offices and were active as lieutenants in Casentino's grand-ducal militia.[20] The new familial strategies exemplified by the Lapucci sisters guaranteed the continuity of the Poppi elite. In particular the inheritance strategies of the leading families enabled their daughters, last descendants and wealthy heiresses on both the maternal and paternal side, to establish new ties with families belonging to the elite of other provincial towns, bringing some of them into Poppi.[21]

In many cases, however, what made the expansion of matrimonial exchanges to the regional level possible was not only the accumulation of wealth and its concentration in the hands of those few remaining families but also new career options. During the latter part of the seventeenth century, matrimonial alliances and new professional choices reflected the growing awareness among provincial elites of a class solidarity that went beyond the confines of the community. Together they enabled the ruling families of the towns of Tuscany to shape a new public image of themselves.

The network of marriage exchanges of the Ducci family reflects the development of common professional, economic, and social interests that furthered the formation of new ties with the region's other provincial elites, many of whom were experiencing similar conditions. At the end of the seventeenth century, Lorenzo, Angelo and Camilla's only son, unlike his father but like his maternal grandfather, became captain of the Poppi *quarto* of the grand-ducal militia (fig. 9.1).[22] The offspring of Angelo Ducci and Camilla Grifoni were among the first to establish ties with an important family from Stia, the Goretti. Both Lorenzo and two of his sisters, Margherita and Angela, married members of the Goretti family from Stia, who, like the Grifoni, made the military their main profession.[23] In 1672 Angela Ducci married Cesare, son of Captain Matteo Goretti.[24] Three years later her sister, Margherita, and her brother, Lieutenant Lorenzo, married respectively the son and daughter of Ensign Francesco Maria Goretti.[25] Early in the eighteenth century, Antonia, daughter of Lorenzo and Maria Maddalena, married Giuliano, son of Giuliano Rilli and Pellegrina Vannucci.[26] At the same time, the Ducci's son, Dario, married Maria Maddalena, daughter of Antonio Crudeli.[27] Caterina and Assuero, Antonio's other children, married in this same period Domenico di Francesco Maria Goretti and Antonia di Domenico di Dario Ducci from Talla, Lorenzo Ducci's cousin. In 1710 the remaining two daughters of Lorenzo Ducci and Maria Maddalena Goretti, Ottavia and Margherita, married respectively Lieutenant Giovanbattista Zabagli from Pieve Santo Stefano and Poppi's district doctor, Federigo Gatteschi from Strada.[28]

In particular, as provincial elites entered the army, they became bound by a common commitment to the consolidation of the state. This alliance at the same time defined and sustained the matrimonial exchanges of Poppi women with men from outside the town. Building on this alliance, the Poppi elite, as in the case of the Ducci family, revived the sixteenth-century pattern of preferred matrimonial exchanges and expanded the pattern of local endogamy to the regional level.

II

The women of early modern Italy were not always as powerless as the historiography has traditionally emphasized. In her numerous articles on women and the family, Christiane Klapisch-Zuber has consistently underscored the patrilineal character of fifteenth-century Florentine genealogies and an inheritance system that relegated women to a marginal position within the household.[29] More recently, however, the scholarship has revised this representation of women as obedient wives, childbearers, and passive recipients of male domination.[30] For seventeenth-century Tuscany, Giulia Calvi suggested the hypothesis that the legal exclusion of women from the inheritance hierarchy enabled widows to assure their children a love that was free from pecuniary concerns. In this position, mothers were empowered with a new role as legal supervisors of their children's material well-being and carriers of the family's tradition.[31]

For the same period, Tommaso Astarita has also shown how Neapolitan aristocratic women enjoyed considerable rights over their dowries. This situation placed women in a privileged position, providing them with considerable influence over their families' pursuits.[32] According to Astarita, Neapolitan aristocratic women had as much "responsibility for their families' survival and success" as did their husbands and sons. Astarita's argument that despite this equal responsibility the "rules were set by men," however, obstructs any possibility that women may have translated their newfound influence into a more assertive involvement in decision making.

During the seventeenth century in Poppi, elite women gained influence over local society. Familial strategies placed women in a critical position within the family. First, having preserved elite wealth, they enabled the daughters of the Poppi elite to establish new ties with other provincial elite families. Women brought into town a new group of families, thus sustaining the continuity and stability of their families. Women also facilitated the emergence of a new socio-economic and familial solidarity among an extended network of provincial families. Finally, inheritance strategies, by providing women with control over their inheritance, entrusted them with the transmission and continuity of the lineage. The same patrilineal system that traditionally undermined women's position thus also provided them with new forms of control which sustained the shaping of new familial traditions.

During the second half of the seventeenth century, it was not un-usual for the ancestral line to be carried on by women. Virginia, daughter of Ser Alphonso Turriani, for example, together with her sister, Caterina, was the last descendant and heiress of the family. In 1579 Virginia married Lodovico, son of Ser Batista Battistoni. Of all their children, only two daughters survived and only one, Mari-etta, married.[33] During the 1650s, in his "Istoria" Lapini wrote how "the Turriani blood, after the loss of the family's men, was transmit-ted by Madonna Virginia to the Battistoni [her husband's surname] and thence to Madonna Marietta, the last daughter [of Lodovico Battistoni]."[34]

Following the interpretation of the lineage and kin elaborated by the canon legal tradition, the local teacher and chronicler empow-ered the maternal blood with the continuation and transmission of the lineage.[35] Not only was the ancestral line of the Turriani pro-longed through the last daughter of Ser Alphonso, Virginia, but it was also genealogically reconstructed a generation later in the person of his granddaughter, Marietta. The continuation of the lineage through the maternal blood was also symbolically strengthened through ge-nealogical trees. Toward the end of the century, the person who drew the family tree of the Grifoni placed the name of Camilla above that of her father and followed it with the name of Camilla's son, Lorenzo Ducci. Figuratively, a woman was placed in the position to extend the trunk and prolong the lineage of the Grifoni (fig. 9.3). She also symbolically epitomized the local heritage of the new family into which she married.

During the second half of the seventeenth century, women's grow-ing power and sphere of autonomy within the family were revealed in the emerging practice of keeping the paternal surname even after a woman married.[36] In Florence a married woman only rarely used her father's surname. Usually, she joined it to that of her husband or dropped it altogether, as in the case of women married into the Gi-nori, Capponi, and Rucellai families.[37]

Poppi women successfully retained the bloodline and prolonged the memory of the maternal kinship. In particular, the use of given names revealed the inclusion of the maternal presence in the line-age. Parents often named the firstborn son after the maternal grand-father. For girls, the female derivative of either the maternal or pa-ternal grandfather's name was often used.[38] Marietta's firstborn son from her marriage with Niccolò Lapucci was named Lodovico, and

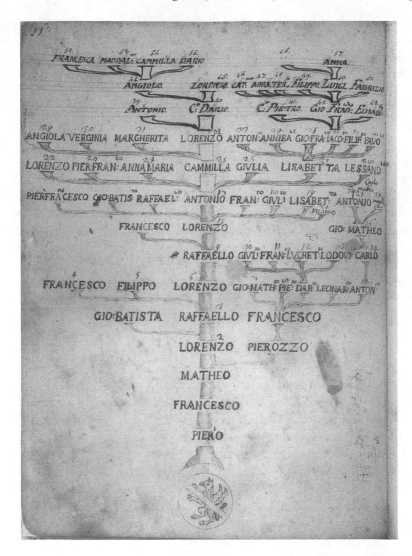

FIG. 9.3. Grifoni family tree, late seventeenth century

the given name of one of her daughters was Alfonsina, respectively the names of their maternal great-grandfather and grandfather. A few years later, Camilla Grifoni and Angelo Ducci followed a similar practice and named their only son, Lorenzo, after his maternal grandfather. If names were viewed as property, as Christiane Klapisch-Zuber argued about fifteenth-century Florence, then in Poppi the wife was represented in this possession as well as the husband. Through given names Marietta and Niccolò, and Camilla and Angelo, merged the maternal and paternal bloodlines into the persons of their sons and daughters. In the process they forged a new interpretation of the lineage which revealed a familial tradition aware of the creative force of the maternal kin. Naming children represented women's contribution to defining their identity in relation to the family and society. In exchange for preserving the stability and power of their family, women successfully imposed the memory of the maternal kinship on the lineage and contributed to the shaping of a new feminine identity among the new families who were entering the Poppi elite. By appropriating for themselves the practice of naming their children, women constructed new forms of participation as women in the public space.

Within a few years of their marriage to prominent Poppi women, men who were outsiders were invested with all the honors and privileges normally accorded to members of the Poppi elite. Citizenship was an important prerequisite for office holding. Since the late 1590s, citizenship was granted after fifteen years of residency, after ten years of marriage into a local family, or after ten years of paying taxes to the community. In any case, a formal request had to be presented to the town's council, which alone could give final approval for citizenship.[39] Angelo Ducci, who married Camilla Grifoni in 1652, was an important member of the community by the 1660s, frequently holding high public office.[40] After only six years of marriage to Suzanna Lapucci, Orazio Bassi also began to fill important civic offices as either prior or standard-bearer. Women could not legally confer the right of citizenship, but marriage with a local woman certainly facilitated the transition.

Throughout fifteenth-century Florence women were not legally allowed to conduct business transactions without the intercession of an appointed male guardian, a *mundualdus*. In Poppi a husband usually appeared as the administrator of his wife's patrimony and as her *mundualdus*. The husband had no right to sell, buy, exchange, or rent any land without the woman's consent. Thanks to his position, however, the husband exercised a role of legal guardianship, implementing a form of male domination based on gender-related inequalities.[41] It must, however, be emphasized that, at least within certain limits, women who inherited their father's patrimony were able to circumvent the gender-biased legal practice that prevented women from acting directly in business transactions. They did this by encroaching on their husbands' freedom of action. Thus, when in 1669 Orsina Dombosi, who with her sister had inherited her father's patrimony, dictated her last will, she was inverting the traditional language commonly applied to the rights and role of women: she left the usufruct of her properties to her husband, Domenico Folli, only if he remained a widower.[42]

The position of Poppi women in relation to their families' patrimonial strategies reflected the development of new forms of negotiation in the relations of power between women and men. Obviously, external events such as the economic and demographic circumstances of the time as well as the endeavors of fathers influenced family strategies of the Poppi elite and affected the position of women in society. It can be argued, however, that women themselves, by both operating within and circumventing the restraints of institutions and regulations created and controlled by their fathers and brothers, shaped the course of events and reinforced their role within the family and society.

In the long run, however, women reinforced and supported the very system that in turn undermined their position. By ensuring the preservation and transmission of elite wealth, women guaranteed the perpetuation of the power of their husbands and sons in the community. Once the stability and ascent of the Poppi elite were reasserted, conforming to a patrimonial policy common among other urban elites won women no advantage. Rather, the endeavor to complete a process of integration generated a considerable diminution of women's power. Strengthened by their consolidated status and prosperity, the men of the elite were able to negotiate a complementary relationship with central powers. Together they strengthened a decentralized political structure that promoted a decentralized system of male privilege.

As military officers, members of provincial elites exercised considerable control over local society, developed a new social solidarity with other provincial elites, and regained full authority in family politics. The redefinition of Poppi's elite families within a new regional context was reflected in a change in familial patrimonial policy in the early eighteenth century. Contrary to the preceding centuries, women were excluded from the inheritance hierarchy in favor of a more rigid patrilineal succession.

During the sixteenth century, urban elites in major Italian cities, having assured their political control, turned to primogeniture practices as a way to protect their consolidated wealth and status. The timing of this trend varied according to specific contexts and local circumstances. During the first half of the eighteenth century, the consolidation of the Poppi families and the maturation of a heightened self-image as a new regional elite were revealed in an inheritance practice that differed from the traditional one and conformed to a broader regional and Italian context. The pattern that favored female over male relatives of the same lineage was frequently replaced by a patrilineal policy of succession, and the custom of distributing the patrimony equally among all sons was often replaced by primogeniture.[43]

In 1669 Captain Jacopo Rilli left his patrimony in equal parts to all his sons and, in the event of their death, to all his daughters. In 1702 his son Giuliano Rilli changed this tradition and left all his patrimony to his two sons. The daughters were given their dowries, but, unlike his father, Giuliano never anticipated the possibility that his daughters could inherit the family patrimony. A few years later, his brother Antonio Rilli, a priest, went even further and made his nephew Jacopo, firstborn of Giuliano, his only heir. In the event of Jacopo's and his sons' death, his brother Angelo would inherit.[44] Like the Rilli and the majority of Poppi families, the Ducci and Goretti shifted their inheritance policies. Thus, in the 1740s the female line of these families was to be "forever" excluded from inheriting the family patrimony.[45]

Alongside new patrilineal strategies the old local tradition often persisted, according to which women inherited the whole family patrimony. But if in the earlier period families included daughters in their inheritance hierarchy to maintain and strengthen their position of power, now daughters were rarely mentioned by their fathers in testamentary stipulations. Even in cases in which daughters were the only surviving heir, preference in the inheritance of the family patrimony was given to male cousins, distant male relatives, and even charitable institutions. Gone also was the earlier family tradition whereby parents wanted all their children securely married. Instead, despite the demographic increase and the economic consolidation within elite families, only a few of the children married—enough to make useful and necessary marriage alliances but not too many to disperse large landed estates. Paradoxically, women were instrumental in the social ascent of their families and in the preservation of political stability prized by central powers. But the new family prosperity of local elites and the strengthened authority of central governments undermined women's future status.

Provincial elite women and men contributed to the regional integration of their families and provided stability and continuity to the growing state through their familial strategies. But for most male elites regional integration meant success, both in public and private life. For the elite men, the acquisition of positions of command in the regional army and in the peripheral administration of the state paralleled a position of domestic dominance. For female elites, regional integration meant loss of status and power and subjugation to a more patriarchal domestic unit.

Conclusion

During the seventeenth century local learned people began to cele-
brate the past of their town and gave form to a new local historical
tradition. More than two centuries after Florentine humanist writers,
the late-seventeenth-century author Giuseppe Mannucci borrowed
from earlier local chroniclers and combined the humanist tradition
with the local ecology to praise the fame of his town and stress the
legacy of his ancestors.

In his work *Le glorie del Clusentino* Mannucci celebrated the valley as a place of shepherds who provided Julius Caesar with cheese
and other dairy products. He also idealized the area as the chosen site
of persecuted Christians who had escaped from Fiesole when it came
under the pagan rule of the Roman emperors. Unclear whether the
shepherds and the Christians were connected, the author presented
them as the victims of Florentines who were identified as pagans and
animal thieves. The persecuted population, heir to a Roman and
Christian tradition, founded Poppi. On top of the hill in the middle
of the valley this Roman colony of Christian shepherds built a town
from which "aggressors and malefactors" were defeated. Mannucci,
using a metaphor elaborated by Bernardo Lapini at the beginning of
the century, compared the hill where Poppi stood to a breast (*poppa*):
"Having much benefited from the breasts of the herds, Julius Caesar
gave this land its name of 'Poppi' . . . and all its territory, from the
abundance of streams flowing through it, he named 'Casentino' from
casus [cheese]."[1]

The role of a sheltering and nursing mother attributed to Poppi by
local chroniclers provided elite families with the foundation for their
claim to historical greatness and for construing new meanings of
power and domination. From their role as builders, protectors, and

benefactors of the community the ruling families secured their legitimacy to power. No less important, by linking the past of the Casentino to a rural, imperial, and Christian heritage, the local learned men affirmed their autonomy from an urban, republican, and pagan Florentine legacy. At the same time, however, they justified domination on the basis of their participation in the regional state as supporters and sustainers of their rulers.

The mythical representation of Poppi both revealed and was influenced by the political circumstances surrounding the consolidation of the Tuscan regional state during the sixteenth century, which selected the town as the administrative center of the vicariate of the Casentino. This idealized portrayal of Poppi also represented the assertion of the collective power and prestige of local elite families. Finally, it epitomized the dual identity constructed by provincial elites as participants in both a local and a regional public life.

During the sixteenth century, in Poppi, as the centralization of the Medicean state advanced, thirty-one surname groups of families of wool manufacturers, shopkeepers, petty landowners, and notaries emerged as the Poppi ruling elite. They established a monopoly over the highest political and administrative offices in the community and concentrated the greater part of local wealth in their own hands. Furthermore, during most of the sixteenth century, the elite families of Poppi, seeking to enhance their social, political, and economic position within the community, combined endogamy with marriage alliances with provincial families from other parts of the state. The consolidation of these provincial families strengthened the political and social stability of the town.

Changes in the periphery corresponded to developments at the center. During the fifteenth century the central government strengthened its authority, enforced its control, and maintained social order by promoting the politico-administrative tradition of peripheral towns and territories. The republican government aimed at establishing new channels through which to exercise its authority by encouraging the drafting of local statutes and the elaboration of new local magistrature. During the sixteenth century, however, in light of pressures produced by broader Italian and European events, the central government began restricting the autonomy and the privileges previously granted to the periphery. Between the 1560s and 1590s, the pace toward centralization and unification of state institutions quickened as the Medicean government further strengthened its hold over the dominion. Important aspects of local administration fell under the supervision of new central institutions, leading to a more centralized and authoritarian princely system.

The development of new state structures and centralizing policies together with economic and demographic conjunctures did not encourage the social, economic, and political consolidation of provincial families. The encroachment of the central government into the affairs of the community threatened the political rights of local ruling families. Florentine intervention into the economic privileges of Poppi and, even more important, the protectionist measures of the Arte della Lana aggravated the already precarious economic situation of local shopkeepers and wool producers. Restrictive measures emanating from the textile guilds of Florence contributed to the decline of the local wool industry. Regulations aimed at controlling the production and commerce of Casentino wool began in the early part of the sixteenth century but were intensified toward the end of the century and the beginning of the seventeenth, when the Florentine wool industry suffered a drastic setback. By the 1630s the industry in Poppi had nearly disappeared. Finally, the transformation of social values attached to the notarial profession undermined the aspiration for social advancement of the lesser state functionaries who lived in provincial towns.

These circumstances, further aggravated by the plague of 1631, threatened the social status, the economic situation, and the political position of local rulers. Poppi society was transformed. It responded to these challenges with dynamic and creative resolutions that intersected and interacted with those elaborated by the central government.

Political attitudes and matrimonial alliances were revised to protect the local interests of elite families. As central authority became increasingly more pervasive throughout the state, Poppi families used to their advantage the power that was left to them. They molded new political strategies grounded on symbolic representation of power and conceived new forms of control based on exploitation of their privileged position as officeholders. In particular, by overseeing the management and distribution of public funds, the ruling families promoted their own well-being. No less important, they reinforced their social and political supremacy. Finally, having elaborated an alternative power system to that of the central government without challenging central authority, the local ruling families successfully retained control of the town.

The foundation of the power and cohesion of these families was based on a tight network of family connections and interpersonal loyalties. The endogamous policies that characterized elite marriage patterns in this period provided the Poppi families with a strong sense of cohesion, ensured their political monopoly, and guaranteed their defense of social prerogatives. Endogamy permitted those families who survived the plague to expand their holdings with those of related lineages facing extinction. Together, thus, political and matrimonial policies sustained the threatened political and social stability of the ruling families. They also guaranteed social order and political stability in the community.

The central government responded. The execution of the late-sixteenth-century reforms as well as the attainment of peace and public order did not rely solely on the ability of new institutions to incorporate society at large. They also encountered a fundamental support structure formed by municipal governments and provincial elites. As these consolidated their power by refashioning the ways of doing politics to meet centralizing constraints, the central government conceived new forms of domination. During the first part of the sixteenth century, the Florentine government restricted the privileges of the emerging local ruling class. Later in the century, however, the Medicean government fashioned its political strategies to incorporate the interests of those same ruling families.

By the beginning of the seventeenth century the elite families had undergone further transformations, reflected in the elaboration of new family policies. The Poppi ruling families abandoned their traditional activities to become large property owners and military officials of the new regional state. Town leaders who survived the plague reemerged from the crisis having all but abandoned any sort of artisan and industrial activity. Instead they concentrated their attention on property holdings that led to the impoverishment of small rural landowners. Poppi leaders also abandoned the traditional profession of notary and moved into ecclesiastical, legal, medical, and— above all—military careers in the grand-ducal state.

The militia represented the setting in which a complementary beneficial partnership between local ruling families and central powers was fulfilled. Through participation in the militia local and central rulers consolidated a system that gave them power and reinforced the perpetuation of privilege both in the local context and the regional sphere. During the second part of the seventeenth century, higher-ranking positions in the militia became available to provincial elites. A military career proved of particular value for Poppi leaders. It gave provincial elites the opportunity for local upward mobility and for new positions of leadership within the community. The military profession enabled provincial lesser elites to fulfill their aspirations of emulating the lifestyle and values of other aristocratic elites. It thus conferred on these lesser elites a new sense of nobility and helped create a Tuscany-wide social group bound by a common identity. Finally, through a military career local notables carved out a new area of power wherein they successfully combined the need to retain economic and social control within the community with the necessity of being part of the new regional entity.

If the Poppi elite benefited from the creation of the grand-ducal militia, so did the central government. Collaboration with local elites, as revealed in the formation of provincial militias, ensured order and stability throughout the state. It also contributed to strengthening a centralized structure by consolidating a decentralized organization of power.

Developments in Poppi reinforce the view that the emergence of the regional state was a much slower, more complex, and less uniform process than previously believed. Change but also continuity, transformation but also adaptation, characterized the integration of the Poppi elite into the regional state. Furthermore, if integration into the regional system meant subordination to the central government and a reshaping of traditional productive activities, it also presented the Poppi ruling class with new economic possibilities and new opportunities for social advancement.

The interaction between local rulers and central powers, between areas of central control and spheres of local autonomy, contributed to the formulation of new, fluid forms of power and domination. Together they generated a political balance that at the same time delineated and conditioned the growth of the regional state and the power relations that ensued. Together they also reinforced and legitimized local and central patterns of abuse and privilege. With the consolidation of provincial elites and military formation, gender conventions that relegated women to the dominance of men within households and society became more rigid. The consolidation of the Poppi elite grew out of the redefinition of its matrimonial and patrimonial strategies in a manner consistent with familial socioeconomic values and traditions and the changing social, political, and economic circumstances surrounding state consolidation. During the sixteenth and seventeenth centuries, an inheritance policy whereby property in the absence of direct male descendants could be transmitted to daughters in preference to nephews and male cousins prevented the decline of the Poppi elite.

This inheritance practice allowed provincial women to play a constructive role in the development of the state. It permitted Poppi women who were the last of their lines and heiresses of both the maternal and paternal sides to maintain their families' socioeconomic status. Consequently, not only were elite men able to take up careers in the grand-ducal militia, but matrimonial patterns of women also expanded from municipal endogamy to a broader provincial exogamy. Finally, control over their inheritance permitted women to fulfill a creative role in shaping a new feminine familial identity.

The ability of the Poppi elite to adapt to changing social, economic, and political circumstances and to diversify its lifestyles guaranteed more than its survival. It also allowed the elite to retain and consolidate its position in local society and integrate itself directly into the new regional state. The redefinition of Poppi elite families within a new regional context and in light of the new collective social identity was reflected in a change in familial patrimonial policy in the early eighteenth century. Contrary to the preceding centuries, women were excluded from the inheritance hierarchy in favor of a more rigid patrilineal succession. Changes in the inheritance strategies of elite families were at once products and catalysts of larger socioeconomic and political circumstances. They revealed too the success of the Poppi elite in assimilating and popularizing those aristocratic values and lifestyles that enabled them to construct a new collective regional identity.

Recent research has advanced beyond a "centrocentric" perspective by examining the provinces rather than the central government, but it has retained a "centrocentric" interpretation of regional elite formation. Leaving the municipal world, moving to the capital, and establishing a personal relationship with the central ruler have been used thus far as the interpretive parameters for successful entrance into the regional arena. However, the experience of the leading Poppi families suggests the precarious nature of such a generalization, for the regional elite was not a homogeneous group. The lesser elites who remained in the periphery contributed to the formation of regional elites as much as those who migrated to the center, but they sought to do so through different means. Lesser provincial elites emerged as regional elites by improving their social status without the necessity or the will to abandon the local terrain and by fulfilling and promoting the need of central powers to strengthen a decentralized political structure. Lesser elites were not rewarded individually for loyalty to the grand dukes. Rather, they were favored in their social aspirations as members of a new local patriciate in exchange for broadening the social basis of support for the central authority.

The practices employed by provincial families underscore the need to reconceptualize the way we understand the state. The multiformity of public and private experiences of provincial Tuscany must be incorporated as an integral part of the process of state formation. If familial strategies reveal the process and the dynamics of state building, then it is necessary to overcome the exclusive acceptance that there is a hierarchy of criteria to understanding state growth and that these criteria can lead to a dominant image of the state. The unifying role held by new institutions of the early modern state has not been disputed. Rather, the case study of Poppi has offered the opportunity to redefine the context and the participation in the process of state consolidation. By decentering and recentering the state, it has sought to challenge the traditional hierarchy in interpreting the process of state building and thus redirect the widely held assumption that institutions had a primacy over society. The impulse to state building cannot be measured simply by the ability of newly created institutions to incorporate society at large.

The case of the Poppi families points toward the inevitable interrelation between politics, the state, and gender. Clearly the history of institutions and that of human experience overlap. Many of the provincial women, men, and children, though excluded from the state's institutions and the traditional channels of politics, were not passive participants in the broader historical process. Provincial elites elaborated new ways to define their lives and forged new family strategies within certain limiting conditions. They exercised their influence within the local space and the domestic spheres and provided their own distinct input into shaping a new public terrain. Ultimately, their personal experiences helped shaped the Tuscan regional state in different and often divergent ways that varied according to provincial elites' own socioeconomic values, family traditions, and gender. The intentions of provincial elite families to preserve their socioeconomic and political hegemony combined with shifting historical circumstances. Furthermore, the collective efforts of provincial elites to redefine their identity, consolidate their local authority, and facilitate their integration into the new regional state interacted with the politics of central rulers. Intentions, circumstances, and politics, thus, merged to give shape to the new Tuscan regional system, a state, that is, which was defined along social and gender lines.

In the end, the interaction of the family with the larger society strengthened the dynamics of state consolidation. But the reverse was also true, and local families reinterpreted their interests under the influence of the state and its increasing ability to affect private life and incorporate society at large. Central and local powers developed together and strove to maintain social and political stability. The institutions of the state could be consolidated as provincial elites and central rulers acquired shared and mutual interests in the structures of the state. Provincial elites endorsed a system that was at once uniform and united precisely because they detected in those structures the means by which to expand and consolidate local interests and, foremost, defend privilege. In the process local families and central powers reelaborated new concepts of power and domination which served to shape the state.

Appendix on Sources

Most of the research for this book was conducted in Poppi and Florence. In Poppi I consulted material kept in the Archivio Vicariale (AVP) and the Biblioteca Comunale (BCP). In Florence I did research in the Archivio di Stato (ASF) and in the manuscript section of the Biblioteca Nazionale (BNF). I also consulted a few manuscripts kept in the Archivio Vescovile (AVA) and the Archivio Comunale (ACA) in Arezzo. Some of the most important serial public documents are preserved in the archives of the three towns mentioned above. What follows is a survey of some of the most significant documents I examined. They consist of impressionistic chronicles by local historians, serial public documents, notarial acts, and private family papers.

I

Chronicles written by contemporaries provide an initial comprehensive view of the town and its people. The Biblioteca Comunale di Poppi holds two chronicles written by the local notary and schoolteacher Bernardo Lapini during the first half of the seventeenth century: "Istoria o siino memorie storiche di Poppi (secolo XVII)" and "Relazione della peste in Poppi nel 1630 e memorie delle più distinte famiglie della stessa città." Another chronicle, "Descrizione delle cose più essenziali e rilevanti del Casentino con diversi ragguagli delle famiglie e persone scritto da Giuseppe di Scipione Mannucci nell'anno 1666," is preserved in the manuscript section of the Biblioteca Nazionale di Firenze.

II

Administrative serial documents such as statutes, government minutes, and tax rolls were particularly valuable in identifying people, following long-term structures, and giving meanings to the economic, social, and political reality of the town. The earlier statutory reform of Poppi (1441–59 with additions until 1625) is preserved in the Archivio di Stato di Firenze under the series Statuti Comunità Soggette. The same series also contains the statutes of the vicariate dating from 1532 to 1609. The two major statutory reforms, the "Statuti della comunità di Poppi Dentro del 1501" (with additions until 1594 and then from 1625 to 1740) and the Statuti of 1594 (with additions until 1612), are preserved in the Biblioteca Comunale di Poppi. The BCP also holds the statutory reform of the podesteria of 1572, the 1440 pact between Poppi and Florence, "Capitoli et Esentioni Intra l'Eccelsa Republica Fiorentina et il Magnifico Conte Roberto de Battifolle nella sua expulsione seguita l'anno MCCCCXXXX," and the "Statuta Criminalia Civitatis Florentia Totisque Provincia Clusentini."

Statutes were drafted by municipal councils and represented the main body of law of the community. They reveal the stages of the political development of local magistrature, the social rules according to which public life was organized, and the rights and interests of those who drafted them. Each article was approved by Florentine officials, who also provided extensive comments in case of rejection and modification. For this reason statutes also uncover the interaction between the local and the central government over matters of control and authority.

Government minutes, Deliberazioni e Partiti, are contained in the Archivio Vicariale di Poppi. I systematically examined the fourteen manuscripts between 1448 and 1733 (missing years include 1482–1506, 1557–74, 1657–67, and 1716–32). Deliberazioni record daily decisions, resolutions made, and office-holding frequency. They thus represent a unique means of understanding the pursuit of local institutions, the intentions and choices of officeholders, and the systems of social and interpersonal relations within the ruling families and among different social groups.

If statutes show a more formal and rigid perspective of the constitutional structure of the town, government minutes reveal the day-to-day administrative practice of law. When examined together, statutes and government minutes permit comparisons between intent and practice. They represent a unique source for understanding how institutions, ruling families, and the community generated a dialogue of power which defined their political discourse as it was practiced in everyday life.

The archives of Poppi, Florence, and Arezzo house the estimi, surveys of landed properties which are an exceptional source for analyzing the distribution of landed property. The Archivio Vicariale di Poppi holds the "Estimo di Poppi Dentro del 1517," "Estimo di Poppi Fuora del 1540," and "Estimo di Ragginopoli del 1598." In the Archivio di Stato di Firenze, several estimi of Poppi are kept in the series Decima Granducale (1535, 1566, and 1588). The same series also holds the estimi of the rural communes of Poppi Fuora (1590 and 1715), Fronzola (1536, 1592–93, and 1704), and Ragginopoli (1539 and 1714). Finally, the Archivio Comunale di Arezzo preserves the estimi of Poppi of 1612 and 1701.

Estimi, like all records compiled for fiscal purposes, must be examined with due caution. They list only landed property, and the evaluation of such property can be unreliable.[1] Moreover, the municipal government established the procedures for appraising and compiling the estimi. Poppi estimi, thus, differ from both the Florentine *catasto* and the *decima*, in that, instead of listing personal income, they survey landed properties with an analytical description of each cultivated piece.[2] They differ also from the urban and rural estimi of the fourteenth and fifteenth centuries, which Elio Conti examined for Florence and its countryside.[3] In this the Poppi estimi resemble the tax rolls of the pontifical states of Romagna and the Pisan estimo of 1622. In these estimi, attention is given to the amount of land owned rather than the owner's income. However, whereas the estimi of Polesine di San Giorgio studied by Franco Cazzola were based on owners' declarations subsequently elaborated by a notary, those of Imola and Pisa, like the estimi of Poppi, were based on a direct survey.[4] Once completed, the estimo was subject to approval by the Cinque Conservatori and later by the magistrate of the Nove. Despite all their limitations, estimi remain a valuable source for following the variations in the distribution of property over a long period of time. In fact, Poppi estimi were not only drawn up with the intent of making a systematic survey of landholding, but they also remained uniform in organization and descriptive method throughout the centuries under scrutiny.

Four officers were responsible for making a census of all agricultural holdings in the territory. Each owner was listed in the estimo by name and according to category of landholding and place of residence. The property itself was appraised "under the names of those who [were at the time] owners and possessors."[5] Each piece was described in terms of its location, adjoining owners, extension in *staiora*, types of cultivation, and value. In the sixteenth century rural buildings were sometimes listed but not appraised. From the 1701 estimo on, farm buildings were listed and evaluated. The inclusion of farm buildings in the overall evaluation of land coincided with an increased number of such buildings throughout the countryside following the introduction of the sharecropping system.[6]

It is difficult to establish how the value attributed to each piece of land was calculated. A letter written in 1587 by the Magistrato dei Nove to the vicar of Poppi indicated that the value was roughly based on the land's current market price.[7] Naturally, considerable doubts remain concerning these appraisals.[8] It is highly probable that a certain amount of manipulation existed, especially in regard to the wealthiest families, who, as members of the oligarchy, controlled both the production of the estimo and the distribution of the town's tax load.[9]

We know neither how the land was measured nor what system of measurement was used. According to Andrea Menzione, appraisals for descriptive estimi could be made *a occhio* or **a misura**.[10] The former, characteristic of the eighteenth century, was unreliable, and therefore estimi based on it were subject to continual revision; the latter, characteristic of the seventeenth century, was more accurate and less liable to revision. Estimi measured *a occhio* often included evaluations according to the current market price rather than the size of the holding, with the entire evaluating procedure completed by local officials instead of agricultural experts. Poppi estimi seem to embody both types of evaluation. In fact, the terminology used in describing the duties of those officials selected to revise the estimi would seem to call for an actual survey of agricultural properties. For example, in 1587 the *correttori* added a *staioro* to a piece of land which had been "improperly measured," indicating *estimi a misura*. In the 1588 estimo, moreover, the notary commented how "the officials of the estimi [had] seen and walked over all properties surveyed."[11]

By contrast, the frequency with which Poppi estimi were revised, the method of evaluating the land, and the presence of local officials would seem to place them in the category of *estimi ad occhio*. The constant need for revision of these documents can be attributed to other factors, for what varies in each successive estimi is not the size of the properties but their ownership. It may have been necessary to update the estimi in order to identify the actual owners as one generation succeeded another. Floods and changes in the type of cultivation also necessitated periodic renewal.

In the Archivio di Stato di Firenze I also consulted other serial documents. Tratte record the appointments of state officials. These registers are particularly valuable because they contain lists of lesser offices and officials which were drawn up for provincial bureaucratic positions, the date, and the place of designation. I systematically examined the records compiled between the sixteenth century and 1736 to determine who among the Poppi elite participated in the provincial bureaucracy. Mediceo del Principato contains all sorts of documents. I consulted the documents that list the names of army officers and contain various kinds of information regarding the grandducal militia. Pratica Segreta are the records of the ducal council. During the sixteenth century, this council became responsible for the supervision of most of the administration of the dominion. In this collection I examined the reports made by the secretaries of the Nove Conservatori del Dominio concerning the economic conditions of provincial towns and territory. Arte della Lana contains documents relating to the wool guild. In particular I consulted those records concerning regulations of wool production and distribution for provincial towns.

III

The third main set of documents I examined consists of notarial acts and families' account books. These more private and personal documents permit a closer look at the system of social and interpersonal relations shaped by local families. Notarial protocols are housed in the Archivio di Stato di Firenze and organized in two collections, the Notarile Antecosimiano and the Notarile Moderno. In particular I consulted all the volumes containing the testaments recorded by twenty-seven Poppi notaries between the late fifteenth and the early seventeenth centuries. Because a will was often revised and new decisions added in codicils, several copies may often exist for the same testator. Women, however, drafted fewer versions of their wills. In these documents, testators left dispositions of how to divide their properties and belongings among their heirs and the amount to be given or already given to daughters for their dowries. They also distributed gifts to charitable and religious institutions, chapels, hospitals, kin, friends, and servants.

Only a few account books by local families have been preserved in the Biblioteca Comunale di Poppi. These are "Acquisti di terre e ricordi della famiglia Grifoni, 1553–1648," "Libro della famiglia Grifoni dal 1553 al 1817," "Ricordi domestici della famiglia Grifoni (secoli XVI–XVIII)," "Ricordi domestici e cittadini della famiglia Lapucci (1560–1700)," and "Miscellanee di varie famiglie poppesi (secoli XVI–XVIII)." These documents record business and financial transactions, property assessments, copies of last wills, dowry agreements, family births, deaths, and marriages, as well as meaningful external events that affected the life of the family, such as epidemics, economic slumps, and wars.

Notarial documents and account books have provided the basis for my discussion of matrimonial and inheritance strategies. The names mentioned in the testaments and their relationship to the testator enabled me to reconstruct families' genealogies. Information derived from private family records complemented an often fragmented picture and allowed me to reconstruct the family histories presented in this book. Together, last wills and family papers reveal the decisions people took, the ties they forged with other people, the choices they made, and, lastly, the social and interpersonal system they fashioned through time. Ultimately, these two sets of documents helped me understand the network of relations which defined the domestic group and which the Poppi elite called the family.

Notes

Introduction

1. On the development of the Florentine state, see M. Becker, *Florence in Transition* (Baltimore, 1968), 2 vols., and G. Brucker, *The Civic World of Early Renaissance Florence* (Princeton, 1977).

2. On the development of the Medicean state, see E. Cochrane, *Florence in the Forgotten Centuries, 1527–1800* (Chicago, 1973); F. Diaz, *Il granducato di Toscana: I Medici* (Turin, 1976); A. D'Addario, *La formazione dello stato moderno in Toscana: Da Cosimo il vecchio a Cosimo I de' Medici* (Lecce, 1976); E. Fasano Guarini, *Lo stato mediceo di Cosimo I* (Florence, 1973); idem, "Gli statuti delle città soggette a Firenze tra '400 e '500: Riforme locali e interventi centrali," in *Statuti città territori in Italia e Germania tra Medioevo ed età moderna*, ed. G. Chittolini and D. Willoweit (Bologna, 1991), 69–124; and idem, "Considerazioni su giustizia, stato e società nel ducato di Toscana del Cinquecento," in *Florence and Venice: Comparison and Relations: Il Cinquecento* (Florence, 1980), 135–68.

3. J. Burckhardt, *The Civilization of the Renaissance in Italy* (New York, 1954); M. Weber, *The Theory of Social and Economic Organization*, ed. T. Parsons (London, 1947).

4. B. Croce, *Storia dell'età barocca in Italia* (Bari, 1929). The concept of a general crisis in Italian society has been more recently stressed by R. Romano, *Tra due crisi: L'Italia del Rinascimento* (Turin, 1971), and C. Vivanti, "Lacerazioni e contrasti," in *Storia d'Italia*, vol. 1, *I caratteri originali* (Turin, 1972), 869–948; see also P. Anderson, *Lineages of the Absolutist State* (London, 1974).

5. For a recent synthesis on this debate, see E. Fasano Guarini, "Gli stati dell'Italia centro-settentrionale tra Quattro e Cinquecento: Continuità e trasformazioni," *Società e storia* 21 (1983): 617–39.

6. A. Anzilotti, *La costituzione interna dello stato fiorentino sotto il duca Cosimo I de' Medici* (Florence, 1910); F. Chabod, *Lo stato di Milano nell'impero di Carlo V* (Milan, 1934), now in *Lo stato e la vita religiosa a Milano nell'epoca di Carlo V* (Turin, 1971), 143–84; idem, *Alle origini dello stato moderno* (Rome, 1957).

7. D. Marrara, *Studi giuridici sulla Toscana medicea* (Milan, 1965). For French absolutism, see R. Mousnier, *Les institutions de la France sous la monarchie absolute*, 2 vols. (Paris, 1974–80). The first volume of Mousnier's

work has been translated as *The Institutions of France under the Absolute Monarchy, 1598–1789: Society and State* by B. Pearce (Chicago, 1979).

8. Marrara, *Studi giuridici sulla Toscana medicea*, 33.

9. P. Goubert, *L'ancient regime*, 2 vols. (Paris, 1969–73); R. Hatton, ed., *Louis XIV and Absolutism* (London, 1976); S. Kettering, *Judicial Politics and Urban Revolt in the Seventeenth Century: The Parlement of Aix, 1629–1659* (Princeton, 1978). For England, see A. M. Coleby, *Central Government and the Localities: Hampshire, 1649–1689* (Cambridge, England, 1987), and A. J. Fletcher, *Reform in the Provinces: The Government of Stuart England* (New Haven, 1986).

10. In 1967 Marino Berengo ("Il Cinquecento," in *La storiografia italiana negli ultimi venti anni* [Milano, 1967], 490) emphasized the need to broaden the scope of research to incorporate the provinces. See also G. Chittolini, "La crisi delle libertà comunali e le origini dello stato territoriale," *Rivista storica italiana* 82 (1970): 92–120; idem, *La formazione dello stato regionale e le istituzioni del contado (secoli XIV e XV)* (Turin, 1979); idem, "Governo ducale e poteri locali," in *Gli Sforza a Milano e in Lombardia e i loro rapporti con gli stati italiani ed europei (1450–1535)* (Milan, 1982), 27–41; idem, "Stati padani, 'Stato del Rinascimento': Problemi di ricerca," in *Persistenze feudali e autonomie comunitative in stati padani fra Cinque e Settecento*, ed. G. Tocci (Bologna, 1988), 9–29; Fasano Guarini, *Lo stato mediceo*; idem, "Principe ed oligarchie nella Toscana del '500," in *Forme e tecniche del potere nella città (secoli XIV–XVII)* (Perugia, 1979–80), 105–26; idem, "Potere centrale e comunità soggette nel granducato di Cosimo I," *Rivista storica italiana* 89 (1977): 490–538; and idem, "Gli stati dell'Italia centro-settentrionale," 617–39. More recent works are J. Grubb, *Firstborn of Venice: Vicenza in the Early Renaissance State* (Baltimore, 1988), and W. J. Connell, "Clientelismo e stato territoriale: Il potere fiorentino a Pistoia nel XV secolo," *Società e storia* 53 (1991): 523–43.

11. Fasano Guarini, *Lo stato mediceo*, 49–62; see also R. B. Litchfield, *Emergence of a Bureaucracy: The Florentine Patricians, 1530–1790* (Princeton, 1986).

12. Among the most recent works on state formation in the sixteenth and seventeenth centuries, see, for Italy, J. Brown, *In the Shadow of Florence: Provincial Society in Renaissance Pescia* (Oxford, 1982); E. Fasano Guarini, ed., *Prato: Storia di una città*, vol. 2, *Un microcosmo in movimento (dal 1494 al 1815)* (Prato, 1986); O. Raggio, *Faide e parentele: Lo stato genovese visto dalla Fontanabuona* (Turin, 1990); and E. Grendi, *Il cervo e la repubblica* (Turin, 1993). For France, see W. Beik, *Absolutism and Society in Seventeenth-Century France: State Power and Provincial Aristocracy in Languedoc* (Cambridge, England, 1985), and S. Kettering, *Patrons, Brokers, and Clients in Seventeenth-Century France* (New York, 1986). For England, see W. MacCaffrey, "Place and Patronage in Elizabethan Politics," in *Eliza-*

bethan Government and Society: Essays Presented to Sir John Neale, ed.
S. T. Bindoff, J. Hurstfield, and C. H. Williams (London, 1961), 95–126, and
L. Peck, *Court Patronage and Corruption in Early Stuart England* (Boston,
1990).

13. Beik, *Absolutism and Society*. On bureaucratic elites, see Litchfield,
Emergence of a Bureaucracy, who has focused on high-ranking central officials and on Florentine patricians. On the formation of regional elites in provincial Tuscany, see M. Berengo, *Nobili e mercanti nella Lucca del Cinquecento* (Turin, 1965); Brown, *In the Shadow of Florence*; Fasano Guarini,
"Principe ed oligarchie," 105–26; L. Gai, *Centro e periferia: Pistoia nell'or-
bita fiorentina durante il '500* (Pistoia, 1980); D. Marrara, *Riseduti e nobiltà:
Profilo storico-istituzionale di un'oligarchia toscana nei secoli XVI–XVIII*
(Pisa, 1976); M. Luzzatti, "La classe dirigente di Pisa nel secolo XVI," *Archivio storico italiano* 136 (1978): 457–67; idem, "Momenti di un processo
di aristocratizzazione," in *Livorno e Pisa: Due città e un territorio nella
politica dei Medici* (Pisa, 1980), 120–22; C. Calvani, M. Falaschi, and
L. Matteoli, "Ricerche sulle magistrature e la classe dirigente di Pisa durante il principato mediceo del Cinquecento," in *Potere centrale e strutture
periferiche nella Toscana del '500*, ed. G. Spini (Florence, 1980), 77–112;
and F. Angiolini, "Il ceto dominante a Prato nell'età moderna," in Fasano
Guarini, *Prato*, 343–427. For other Italian regions, see A. Ventura, *Nobiltà e
popolo nella società veneta tra '400 e '500* (Bari, 1964); G. Borelli, *Un patriziato della terraferma veneta tra XVII e XVIII secolo: Ricerche sulla nobiltà
veronese* (Milan, 1974); and Grubb, *Firstborn of Venice*. For the Papal States,
see B. G. Zenobi, *Ceti e poteri nella Marca pontificia* (Bologna, 1976);
C. Casanova, *Comunità e governo pontificio in Romagna in età moderna*
(Bologna, 1982); R. Ago, *Carriere e clientele nella Roma barocca* (Bari, 1990);
and Laurie Nussdorfer, *Civic Politics in the Rome of Urban VIII* (Princeton,
1992).

14. See, for example, L. Atzori and I. Regoli, "Due comuni rurali del dominio fiorentino nel secolo XVI: Montopoli Val d'Arno e Castelfranco di
Sotto," in *Architettura e politica da Cosimo I a Ferdinando I*, ed. G. Spini
(Florence, 1976), 78–164; Fasano Guarini, "Principe ed oligarchie," 123–26;
Angiolini, "Il ceto dominante a Prato," 343–427; and E. Stumpo, "Le forme
del governo cittadino," in Fasano Guarini, *Prato*, 281–342. More recently
both Fasano Guarini ("Gli statuti delle città soggette," 101–24) and Chittolini ("Governo ducale e poteri locali," 27–41) have mentioned the need to
conceive of local politics as an essential component of state formation.

15. F. Angiolini, "La nobiltà 'imperfetta': Cavalieri e commende di S.
Stefano nella Toscana Moderna," *Quaderni storici* 78 (1991): 875–99;
F. Angiolini and P. Malanima, "Problemi di mobilità sociale a Firenze tra la
metà del Cinquecento e i primi decenni del Seicento," *Società e storia* 4
(1979): 17–47.

16. On the importance of the notarial profession, see L. Martines, *Lawyers and Statecraft in Renaissance Florence* (Princeton, 1968); Fasano Guarini, *Lo stato mediceo*, 43; Brown, *In the Shadow of Florence*, 178–82; Litchfield, *Emergence of a Bureaucracy*, 151; Angiolini and Malanima, "Problemi di mobilità sociale," 17–47; Angiolini, "Il ceto dominante a Prato," 382–98.

17. Beik (*Absolutism and Society*, 35), for example, underlines how in his study "none of the actors were women."

18. On the impact of sociological analysis on the study of Renaissance society, see R. F. Weissman, "Reconstructing Renaissance Sociology: The 'Chicago School' and the Study of Renaissance Society," in *Persons in Groups: Social Behavior as Identity Formation in Medieval and Renaissance Europe*, ed. R. Trexler (Binghamton, N.Y., 1985), 39–45.

19. I owe this expression to Laurie Nussdorfer (*Civic Politics*, 4), who writes that her approach "is to concentrate on what absolutism looked like 'on the ground.'" See also R. Bonney, "Absolutism: What's in the Name?" *French History* 1 (1987): 93–117.

20. T. Hareven, "The History of the Family and the Complexity of Social Change," *American Historical Review* 96 (1991): 95–124; idem, "Family History at the Crossroads," *Journal of Family History* 12 (1987): ix–xxiii. See also G. Levi, "Family and Kin—A Few Thoughts," *Journal of Family History* 15 (1990): 567–78; idem, *L'eredità immateriale: Carriera di un esorcista nel Piemonte del Seicento* (Turin, 1985), translated as *Inheriting Power: The Story of an Exorcist* (Chicago, 1988); S. Hanley, "Engendering the State: Family Formation and State Building in Early Modern France," *French Historical Studies* 1 (1989): 4–27; idem, "Family and State in Early Modern France: The Marriage Pact," in *Connecting Spheres*, ed. M. J. Boxer and J. H. Quataert (New York, 1987), 53–63; R. Rapp, E. Ross, and R. Bridenthal, "Examining Family History," *Feminist Studies* 5 (1979): 174–200; G. Benadusi, "Rethinking the State: Family Strategies and State Formation in Early Modern Tuscany," *Social History* 2 (1995): 157–78. For an earlier period, see the recent study by A. Molho, *Marriage Alliance in Late Medieval Florence* (Cambridge, Mass., 1994).

21. See, for example, the works of Christiane Klapisch-Zuber on Renaissance Florence, in which she discusses how the development of the state affected family structure; among these is "State and Family in Renaissance Society: The Florentine *Catasto* of 1427–1430," in *Women, Family, and Ritual in Renaissance Italy* (Chicago, 1985), 1–22. See also D. Herlihy and C. Klapisch-Zuber, *Les Toscans et leurs familles: Une étude du catasto florentine de 1427* (Paris, 1978); for the English translation, see *Tuscans and Their Families: A Study of the Florentine Catasto of 1427* (New Haven, 1985). For Europe in general, see the collection of essays *Family and Inheritance: Rural Society in Western Europe, 1200–1800*, ed. J. Goody, J. Thirsk,

and E. P. Thompson (Cambridge, England, 1976); L. Stone, *The Family, Sex, and Marriage in England, 1500–1800* (New York, 1979); and idem, "Family History in the 1980s: Past Achievements and Future Trends," *Journal of Interdisciplinary History* 12 (1981): 51–87.

22. For a synthesis of the literature on social history, see E. J. Hobsbawm, "From Social History to History of Society," in *Historical Studies Today*, ed. F. Gilbert and S. R. Graubard (New York, 1972), 1–26.

23. On the microhistorical method, see C. Ginzburg and C. Poni, "Il nome e il come: Scambio ineguale e mercato storiografico," *Quaderni storici* 40 (1979): 181–90, and G. Levi, "On Microhistory," in *New Perspectives on Historical Writing*, ed. P. Burke (University Park, Pa., 1992), 93–113; see also the recent discussions on microanalysis by C. Ginzburg, "Microstoria: Due o tre cose che so di lei," E. Grendi, "Ripensare la microstoria?" and J. Revel, "Microanalisi e costruzione del sociale," all in *Quaderni storici* 2 (1994): 511–75. Among some examples of the application of microhistory are the studies of C. Ginzburg, *The Cheese and the Worms* (Baltimore, 1980), and Levi, *L'eredità immateriale*; see also the collection of essays *Microhistory and the Lost People of Europe*, ed. E. Muir and G. Ruggiero (Baltimore, 1991), and E. Muir, *Mad Blood Stirring: Vendetta and Factions in Friuli during the Renaissance* (Baltimore, 1993).

24. Weissman, "Reconstructing Renaissance Sociology," 39–45.

Part I The Structures of Power

1. On the changes in the political structure of the Florentine state during the fifteenth century, see Chittolini, "Ricerche sull'ordinamento territoriale del dominio fiorentino agli inizi del secolo XV," in *La formazione dello stato regionale* (see intro., n. 10), 292–352, in particular, 303–7. For the sixteenth century, see Fasano Guarini, *Lo stato mediceo* (see intro., n. 2), and, more recently, "Gli statuti delle città soggette," 69–124, in particular, 80–81 (see intro., n. 2).

2. Diaz, *Il granducato di Toscana* (see intro., n. 2).

Chapter 1 The Local Setting

1. E. Sestan, "I Conti Guidi e il Casentino," in *Italia medievale* (Naples, 1968), 359–71. For an excellent study of the valley in the early Middle Ages, see C. J. Wickham, *The Mountains and the City: The Tuscan Apennines in the Early Middle Ages* (Oxford, 1988).

2. Wickham, *The Mountains and the City*, 198–204.

3. Sestan, "I Conti Guidi," 359–71; C. Beni, *Guida del Casentino* (Florence, 1983), 24.

4. Beni, *Guida del Casentino*, 350–51.

5. C. Guasti and A. Gherardi, *I capitoli del comune di Firenze: Inventario e regesto* (Florence, 1866–93), 597–600; Beni, *Guida del Casentino,* 250–51.

6. P. L. Lavoratti, *Il Casentino: Studio di geografia regionale* (Rome, 1964), 5–19; see also G. Barbieri, *La Toscana: Le regioni d'Italia* (Turin, 1964), 53–54, 364–66.

7. In 1776 the boundaries of the Casentino were moved to the south to include the communities of Chiusi della Verna and Castel Focognano and, later, that of Subbiano. Today the area of the Casentino is 771 square kilometers and comprises twelve communities: Stia, Pratovecchio, Montemignaio, Castel San Niccolò, and Poppi in the Alto Casentino; Bibbiena, Ortignano-Raggiolo, Chiusi della Verna, Castel Focognano, Chitignano, Talla, and Subbiano in the Basso Casentino. Lavoratti, *Il Casentino,* 14–19.

8. In 1642 the total extension of the grand-ducal territory was 13,224.60 square kilometers. Lavoratti, *Il Casentino,* 116–17; L. Del Panta, *Una traccia di storia demografica della Toscana nei secoli XVI–XVII* (Florence, 1974), 24, 60.

9. BNF, Magliabechi, II, I, 120, "Censimento dello stato fiorentino del 1552," 88. According to the census, the population of the Florentine state amounted to 590,807 inhabitants, 59,179 of whom lived in Florence and another 31,023 in the five other major cities of the state: Arezzo, Prato, Pisa, Pistoia, and Livorno. On the demographic trend in Tuscany and in Italy, see Del Panta, *Una traccia di storia demografica,* and C. M. Cipolla, "Four Centuries of Italian Demographic Development," in *Population in History,* ed. D. V. Glass and D. E. C. Eversley (Chicago, 1965), 570–87.

10. BNF, Magliabechi, II, I, 120, 88. In the middle years of the century, while the rural population of the state declined, the Casentino registered a slight increase to 21,880 inhabitants. This initial increase, however, was followed by a steady demographic downturn until 1632, when the population dropped to 12,503. Between the census of 1562 and that of 1622, while most of the dominion registered a slight increase, the population of some of the most peripheral and mountainous areas of the state declined, and in the Casentino the population dropped from 21,880 to 18,247. Among the vicariates and podesterie, those of Firenzuola and Romagna, Pieve Santo Stefano and Sestino, Borgo San Sepolcro and Anghiari all registered a fall in population. Between 1622 and 1632, the population fell by 18 percent throughout the state. In the second half of the century a steady population growth was registered in most of the rural areas of the state, and by 1642 the population of the valley had already increased to 17,196 inhabitants. In 1642, the population density of 36.8 per square kilometer was below that of the Florentine state (44.3) but in line with that of the grand-ducal territory, including the Sienese state (36.2). Del Panta, *Una traccia di storia demografica,* 34–45, 53–67.

11. C. Sodini, "Vita economica e rapporti col potere centrale di un cas-

tello di confine nell'età di Cosimo I: Casola in Lunigiana," in Spini, *Potere centrale*, 113–38 (see intro., n. 13).

12. BNF, EB, 15, 2, "Censimento dello stato fiorentino del 1632," 63.

13. ASF, Strozziane, I, 24, "Censimento dello stato fiorentino del 1642." The census of 1642 recorded 214 households and 986 people. E. Repetti, *Dizionario geografico, fisico, storico della Toscana* (Florence, 1841), 4:573.

14. BNF, Magliabechi, II, I, 120, 88; EB, 15, 2, 63; ASF, Strozziane I, 24. In 1632 the population fell to 588 households and 2,393 people.

15. Bernardo Lapini, "Istoria o siino memorie storiche di Poppi (secolo XVII)," 294, fol. 1r, BCP (hereafter cited as "Lapini, 'Istoria' ").

16. Ibid., fol. 2r.

17. Ibid.

18. Ibid., fols. 2r–3v. A fifth gate has been added and is now used to enter the town.

19. Wickham, *The Mountains and the City*, 198–200.

20. AVP, Deliberazioni e Partiti, Comunità di Poppi Dentro (hereafter cited as "Deliberazioni"), 712, 1690–1714, fols. 279v–r; ACA, "Estimo di Poppi Dentro del 1701," fol. 453r (hereafter cited as "ACA, EPD 1701").

21. ASF, Decima Granducale, 6852, "Estimo di Poppi Dentro del 1588" (hereafter cited as "ASF, DG, 6852, EPD 1588"), "Lista di botteghe del 1590," fols. 1r–21v.

22. On the social significance of the Florentine palace and its evolution from a combination of private and public space to a predominantly private residence, see R. Goldthwaite, "The Florentine Palace as Domestic Architecture," *American Historical Review* 77 (1972): 977–1012.

23. AVP, Criminale, 3984, fol. 18r.

24. G. Capponi, *Storia della repubblica fiorentina*, 2:21, in Beni, *Guida del Casentino*, 281.

25. "little streams that from the green hills . . . flow down to the Arno, making their channels cool and moist," trans. J. Sinclair (London, 1958), 373.

26. L. Alberti, *Descrizione di tutta l'Italia* (Venice, 1553), quoted in Beni, *Guida del Casentino*, 89.

27. Lapini, "Istoria," fol. 1v.

28. Bernardo Lapini, "Relazione della peste in Poppi nel 1630 e memorie delle più distinte famiglie della stessa città scritta da Bernardo di Giuliano Lapini nel XVII secolo," 160, fol. 13v, BCP (hereafter cited as "Lapini, 'Relazione della peste' "; see also G. Cherubini, "La 'civiltà' del castagno in Italia alla fine del Medioevo," *Archeologia medievale* 8 (1981): 247–80, and idem, "La società dell'Appennino settentrionale (secoli XIII–XV)," in *Signori, contadini, borghesi: Ricerche sulla società italiana del Basso Medioevo* (Florence, 1974), 121–42.

29. These banks were first built during the eighteenth century; see Lavoratti, *Il Casentino*, 72.

30. Litchfield, *Emergence of a Bureaucracy*, 105-7 (see intro., n. 11); A. Cerchiai and C. Quiriconi, "Relazioni e rapporti all'ufficio dei Capitani di Parte Guelfa," in Spini, *Architettura e politica* , 184-257 (see intro., n. 14).

31. Between 1570 and 1590, the damaged bridge on the Archiano River near Bibbiena required the office to allocate funds for its reconstruction. The bridge had a critical importance for the local markets because the traffic between Arezzo and the Lower and Upper Casentino converged there. See Cerchiai and Quiriconi, "Relazioni e rapporti," 196, 221.

32. See A. M. Galerani and B. Guidi, "Relazioni e rapporti all'ufficio dei Capitani di Parte Guelfa: Il principato di Ferdinando I," in Spini, *Architettura e politica* , 259-329.

33. In particular under Grand Duke Ferdinand I, this office spent more than four thousand scudi for the maintenance and restoration of this road. In the same period the office spent about seven thousand scudi for the restoration of the road that connected Florence with Terra del Sole, which shared with the Casentino the first tract from Florence to Pontassieve; see Galerani and Guidi, "Relazioni e rapporti," 302-3.

34. Sestan, "I Conti Guidi," 374; Guasti and Gherardi, *I capitoli del comune di Firenze*, 591.

35. Guasti and Gherardi, *I capitoli del comune di Firenze*, 599-600; BCP, "Capitoli et Esentioni Intra l'Eccelsa Republica Fiorentina et il Magnifico Conte Roberto de Battifolle nella sua expulsione sequita l'anno MCCCCXXXX," 274, fols. 43r-48r.

36. On the administrative and jurisdictional structures of the Florentine dominion from the fifteenth century until the Leopoldine reforms, see Fasano Guarini, *Lo stato mediceo*, 73-79 (see intro., n. 2).

37. On the uncertainty about the criteria that led the Medicean government to select and favor certain towns over others as centers of provincial administration, see F. Diaz, "L'articolazione del principato mediceo e la prospettiva di un raffronto," in *Florence and Milan: Comparison and Relations* (Florence, 1989), 160.

38. Giorgio Chittolini (*La formazione*, ix-x [see intro., n. 10], and "Ricerche sull'ordinamento territoriale," 293-99 [see pt. 1, n. 1]) has interpreted these developments within the context of the evolution from city-state to regional state.

39. Chittolini, "Ricerche sull'ordinamento territoriale," 309-14.

40. Territories annexed in the first phase were those of the contado that included the four vicariates of San Giovanni Valdarno, Certaldo, Scarperia, and San Miniato al Monte and the podesteria of Prato. In 1560 to these was added the capitanato of Livorno. In the mid-sixteenth century, the district was formed by fifteen captains, twelve vicars, and fifty-four podestà. Fasano Guarini, *Lo stato mediceo*, 14-15, 83-107.

41. Ibid., 40, 49; Litchfield, *Emergence of a Bureaucracy*, 112-13.

42. Fasano Guarini, *Lo stato mediceo*, 40-43; A. D'Addario, "Burocrazia,

economia e finanze dello stato fiorentino alla metà del Cinquecento," *Archivio storico italiano* 121 (1963): 362–455.

43. Chittolini, "Ricerche sull'ordinamento territoriale," 301.

44. On the origins and functions of vicariates in the Florentine territorial state, see ibid., 299–301.

45. Ibid., 301.

46. The podesterie were not always subordinate to a vicariate except in the jurisdictional field. Fasano Guarini, *Lo stato mediceo*, 38.

47. In the Romagna Fiorentina, and in Prato, Colle, and San Gimignano, the podesterie had also both criminal and civil jurisdiction; see ibid.

48. BCP, "Statuta Criminalia Civitatis Florentia Totisque Provincia Clusentini," 34, fol. IVv.

49. Fasano Guarini, *Lo stato mediceo*, 38.

50. Litchfield (*Emergence of a Bureaucracy*, 112) lists Poppi among the major administrative units of the Florentine district.

51. On the administration of justice in sixteenth-century Italian states, see Fasano Guarini, "Considerazioni su giustizia, stato e società," 135–68 (see intro., n. 2); G. Cozzi, *Repubblica di Venezia e stati italiani: Politica e giustizia dal secolo XVI al secolo XVIII* (Turin, 1982); and J. Brackett, *Criminal Justice and Crime in Late Renaissance Florence, 1537–1609* (Cambridge, England, 1992).

52. ASF, Regia Consulta, 22, Tratte, fol. 278r; Fasano Guarini, *Lo stato mediceo*, 38.

53. See Fasano Guarini, "Considerazioni su giustizia, stato e società," 137.

54. BCP, "Statuti della Podesteria di Poppi del 1572," 121, fol. 4r (hereafter cited as "BCP, SPP 1572, 121").

55. BCP, "Statuti del comune di Poppi Dentro del 1501," 277, fol. 66v (hereafter cited as "BCP, SPD 1501, 277").

56. Ibid., fols. 23v–24v; BCP, "Statuti del comune di Poppi Dentro del 1594," 273, fols. 99v–100v (hereafter cited as "BCP, SPD 1594, 273").

57. ASF, Statuti Comunità Soggette, 643, "Statuti della comunità di Poppi (1441–1625)," fol. 375r (hereafter cited as "SCS, 643, SCP").

58. BCP, SPD 1501, 277, fols. 66v, 91r.

59. ASF, Statuti Comunità Soggette, 157, "Statuti del vicariato del Casentino (1532–1609)," June 1556.

60. BCP, SPD 1501, 277, fol. 25r.

61. Quoted in S. Mannucci, *Le glorie del Clusentino* (Florence, 1687), 10.

62. H. Baron, "Imitation, Rhetoric, and Quattrocento Thought in Bruni's *Laudatio*," in *From Petrarch to Leonardo Bruni* (Chicago, 1968), 157–71.

63. Lapini, "Istoria," fol. 1r.

64. BCP, SPD 1501, 277, fols. 149r, 159r; BCP, SPD 1594, 273, fols. 21v–22r, 30v–33v.

65. Trans. C. Singleton (Princeton, 1973), 145.

66. *Motti e facezie del Pievano Arlotto*, ed. G. Farlena (Milan, 1953), 62; Cherubini, "La società dell'Appennino settentrionale," 121–23.

67. ASF, Pratica Segreta, 174, "Negozi economici delle comunità, 1556–1634," fol. 1r; Pratica Segreta, 178, fols. 5r–6r; Mediceo del Principato, f 2334, fols. 398r, 630r.

68. BCP, SPD 1501, 277, fol. 91r.

69. Giuseppe di Scipione Mannucci, "Descrizione delle cose più essenziali e rilevanti del Casentino con diversi ragguagli delle famiglie e persone scritto da Giuseppe di Scipione Mannucci nell'anno 1666," 101, BNF, Magliabechi, II, III, 359 (hereafter cited as "Mannucci, 'Descrizione' ").

70. Ibid., 100; BCP, "Ricordi domestici della famiglia Grifoni (secoli XVI–XVIII)," 401, fol. 12r (hereafter cited as "'Ricordi domestici' "); AVP, "Estimo di Poppi Dentro del 1489," V 21, fol. 53v.

71. Patterns of land distribution are discussed in Chapter 7.

72. Lapini, "Istoria," fol. 39v; Goldthwaite, "Florentine Palace as Domestic Architecture," 977–1012.

Chapter 2 The Emergence of Ruling Families

1. Chittolini, "Ricerche sull'ordinamento territoriale," 294–99, 309–11 (see pt. 1, n. 1); Fasano Guarini, *Lo stato mediceo*, 54 (see intro., n. 2).

2. SCS, 643, SCP; BCP, SPD 1501, 277, SPD 1594, 273. The riformatori met for the purpose of drawing up reforms only nine times during the sixteenth century.

3. Deliberazioni, 609, 1448–56, fol. 7v; SCS, 643, SCP, fol. 2r.

4. AVP, "Divisione Poppi Dentro e Poppi Fuora," 763, fols. 23r–v.

5. Deliberazioni, 609, 1448–56, fols. 70v–71r, 86v.

6. SCS, 643, SCP, fol. 314r; Deliberazioni, 608, 1474–81, fol. 36v.

7. SCS, 643, SCP, fols. 327r–v; Deliberazioni, 608, 1474–81, fol. 52r.

8. BCP, SPD 1501, 277, fols. 3v, 5r–6v, 9v–13v.

9. Angelo Ventura (*Nobiltà e popolo* [see intro., n. 13]) has underlined a similar development for the towns of the Venetian mainland.

10. BCP, SPD 1501, 277, fol. 12r.

11. Deliberazioni, 609, 1448–56, fols. 66r, 162v.

12. BCP, SPD 1501, 277, fols. 1r–18v.

13. Ibid., fols. 95v–96r.

14. Ibid.

15. Ibid., fols. 178v–79r. In 1633, following the plague and the consequent demographic crisis, the number of local officials was once again decreased. The general priors were eliminated, and the councilors were reduced from seven to four. At this point there were five members in the Ordinary Council and nine in the General Council.

16. Ibid., fols. 137r, 149r–v, 152r.

17. Ibid., fols. 6r–8v.

18. Ibid., fols. 9v–10v.

19. Deliberazioni, 609, 1448–56; 608, 1474–81.

20. BCP, SPD 1501, 277, fol. 13v.

21. Ibid., fol. 12r.

22. Ibid., fols. 1v–3r.

23. Ibid., fols. 51r, 79v–81r.

24. BCP, SPD 1594, 273, fols. 75r–76r.

25. For Florence, see Litchfield, *Emergence of a Bureaucracy* (see intro., n. 11), and S. Berner, "The Florentine Patriciate in the Transition from Republic to Principato," *Studies in Medieval and Renaissance History* 9 (1972): 3–15. For the Veneto, see P. Lanaro, *Un'oligarchia urbana nel Cinquecento veneto: Istituzioni, economia, società* (Turin, 1992).

26. Deliberazioni, 609, 1448–56; 608, 1574–81; 2762, 1507–11; 2271, 1511–26; 2217, 1526–39; 738, 1539–56. Specifically, 120 out of 131 positions of standard-bearer, 285 out of 346 of select prior, and 186 out of 224 of general prior. In all, 62 people divided among themselves 591 offices. The remaining 110 positions were filled by 76 people bearing no surname and therefore impossible to identify.

27. Between 1448 and 1556, twenty-seven families were standard-bearer. The twenty families holding the greatest number of public offices all sat in this office. The other seven families—the Bardi, Berlinghieri, Burchi, Mancini, Turriani, Menzani, and Montalbini—were dying out.

28. For Prato, see Angiolini, "Il ceto dominante a Prato," 358–63 (see intro., n. 13).

29. The first six families are the Mannucci, Menzani, Montalbini, Montaloni, Sociani, and Rampini. The other four are the Soldani, Tommasini, Catani, and Chiari.

30. Among the new families who became standard-bearer were the Menzani and Sociani in the first period, the Soldani and the Catani in the second.

31. Deliberazioni, 1917, 1574–92; 2216, 1593–1611; 2227, 1611–31.

32. These are the Baldacci from Anghiari and the Folli from Pisa. The Barboni were to be standard-bearer in the following period, and the Buonfanti held numerous positions but never that of standard-bearer.

33. The remaining families divided 56 positions. Of those twenty-two families who obtained the greatest number of appointments in this period, sixteen also appeared in the previous list of families with the highest frequency in office holding.

34. Between 1556 and 1632, twenty-one families were standard-bearer, of whom twenty were among those holding the majority of office. The Buondi, an ancient family, were standard-bearer, but because the family was becoming extinct, it covered few positions.

35. Such as in Pisa and Pistoia; see Calvani, Falaschi, and Matteoli, "Ricerche sulle magistrature," 71–112 (see intro., n. 13), and Fasano Guarini, "Principe ed oligarchie," 111–13 (see intro., n. 10). A narrower margin of mobility has been observed by Ventura (Nobiltà e popolo, 92–114) in the inland towns of the Venetian state.

36. Deliberazioni, 2763, 1631–45; 2842, 1646–56; 739, 1668–90; 712, 1690–1714. The standard-bearers filled 124 positions, and the remaining 493 were filled by select priors. The general priors had been eliminated from the council in 1633.

37. All three of the new families represented as standard-bearer had married into the female line of the town's ancient families whose male line was becoming extinct.

38. On the disappearance of old families and the entrance of new ones among Florentine nobles and patricians, see Litchfield, Emergence of a Bureaucracy, 139.

39. Concerning the importance of squittinio and of the riformatori, Elena Fasano Guarini ("Principe ed oligarchie," 109–10) rightly affirms how "the system seems to be characterized by a form of circulation between those who bestow positions and those who hold the most important of these: apparently, the conditions are created for the perpetuity of governing oligarchies, capable of exercising rigorous control over new entries and internal equilibrium." See also Angiolini, "Il ceto dominante a Prato," 58. For an earlier period, see J. Najemy, Corporatism and Consensus in Florentine Electoral Politics, 1280–1400 (Chapel Hill, 1982), and N. Rubinstein, The Government of Florence under the Medici (1434 to 1494) (Oxford, 1966).

40. Deliberazioni, 609, 1448–56, fol. 2r; 608, 1474–81, fol. 15v; BCP, SPD 1501, 277, fol. 2r. The tasks of the riformatori remained unchanged throughout the period in question.

41. Deliberazioni, 2271, 1511–26, fol. 6v.

42. BCP, SPD 1501, 277, fol. 60v.

43. P. Benigni, "Oligarchia cittadina e pressione fiscale: Il caso di Arezzo nei secoli XVI e XVII," in La fiscalite et ses implications sociales en Italie et en France aux XVIIe et XVIIIe siecles (Rome, 1980), 60.

44. Brown, In the Shadow of Florence, 185 (see intro., n. 12); Fasano Guarini, "Principe ed oligarchie," 114.

45. Deliberazioni, 712, 1690–1714, fols. 49v, 100v. Beginning in the mid-sixteenth century, both in Prato and in Pisa the riformatori were nominated by the grand dukes; see Angiolini, "Il ceto dominante a Prato," 356–58, 373–78; Calvani, Falaschi, and Matteoli, "Ricerche sulle magistrature," 81–82; and Fasano Guarini, "Gli statuti delle città soggette," 108–9 (see intro., n. 2).

46. BCP, SPD 1501, 277, fol. 2r.

47. Deliberazioni, 738, 1539–56, fol. 189r.

48. BCP, SPD 1501, 277, fol. 60v.

49. Deliberazioni, 2762, 1507–11; 2271, 1511–26; 2217, 1526–39; 738, 1539–56; 1917, 1574–92; 2216, 1593–1611. For 1555 only two names have been traced and three for 1579. Moreover, two of the riformatori elected in 1511 were without surname and therefore impossible to identify as part of a surname group. The missing years of the resolutions have been integrated with information from the statutes; BCP, SPD 1501, 277.

50. BCP, SPD 1501, 277, fol. 2v.

51. In 1501 there were fourteen pouches, including an extra one; see ibid., fols. 23r–v.

52. Ibid., fol. 7r.

53. On the importance of the electoral process in Florentine politics, see Najemy, *Corporatism and Consensus*.

54. For Pisa, Pistoia, and Borgo San Lorenzo, see Fasano Guarini, "Principe ed oligarchie," 107–8; for Prato, see Stumpo, "Le forme del governo cittadino," 284 (see intro., n. 14). The situation was different at Siena, where public office was hereditary. Marrara, *Riseduti e nobiltà*, 88–92 (see intro., n. 13).

55. BCP, SPD 1501, 277, fol. 18r.

56. Ibid., fol. 18v.

57. Ibid., fol. 18r.

58. Ibid., fols. 18r–v, 89r–v, 136v, 149r.

59. Only the age requirement for the Operai degli Ospedali increased, from thirty to thirty-three years of age; see BCP, SPD 1594, 273, fols. 62v, 67r, and SPD 1501, 277, fol. 18v.

60. On the phenomenon of migration of wealthy farmers to the nearby towns, see D. Herlihy, *Medieval and Renaissance Pistoia: The Social History of an Italian Town, 1200–1430* (New Haven, 1967), 184.

61. Deliberazioni, 2217, June 18, 1531, and 738, March 1553.

62. The disparity of wealth among the members of single families has also been observed for Venice by S. Chojnacki, "In Search of the Venetian Patriciate: Families and Faction in the Fourteenth Century," in *Renaissance Venice*, ed. J. R. Hale (London, 1974), 60–62.

63. Deliberazioni, 2762, 1507–11; 2271, 1511–26; 2217, 1526–39; 738, 1539–56. Bernardo held office in 1508, 1510, 1513, 1516, 1521, 1523, and 1530. Francesco held office in 1519, 1526, 1531, 1534, 1539, 1540, 1545, and 1546.

64. ASF, Notarile Antecosimiano (hereafter cited as "ASF, NA"), R 178–79: 1506–51; there are six volumes of the notarial acts of Ser Giovanni di Niccolò Rilli. Deliberazioni, 2762, 1507–11; 2271, 1511–26; 2217, 1526–39; 738, 1539–56. Ser Giovanni sat on the municipal councils in 1521, 1525, 1531, 1535, and 1545.

65. AVP, "Processo Soldani e comunità di Poppi," 763, "Lettera della co-

munità di Poppi a Sua Altezza Serenissima"; Deliberazioni, 608, 1474–81, fol. 3r.

66. Deliberazioni, 2271, 1511–26; 2217, 1526–39; 738, 1539–56; They held office in 1523, 1529, 1531, 1534 twice, 1538, 1539, 1541, 1545, 1548, 1549, 1551 twice, 1552, and 1555.

67. Deliberazioni, 2271, 1511–26, fols. 235r, 250v, 251r. 264r.

68. Deliberazioni, 2217, August 17, 1539.

69. Deliberazioni, 738, 1539–56; they held office in 1544, 1548, 1549, 1551, 1552, 1553, 1554, 1555, and 1556 twice.

70. BCP, SPD 1501, 277, fols. 158v–59r.

71. For similar cases, see Ventura, *Nobiltà e popolo*.

72. Deliberazioni, 609, 1448–56, fol. 54r.

73. Twenty-one collected volumes containing acts and legacies notarized by Ser Piero and twenty-seven by Mariano have survived. ASF, NA, C 285–87, 1537–69; ASF, Notarile Moderno (hereafter cited as "ASF, NM"), 1178–86, 1569–94, 5967–94, 1578–1629.

74. Deliberazioni, 738, 1539–56; 1917, 1574–92; Ser Piero held office in 1548, 1551, 1554, 1577, 1578, 1582, 1585, 1689, 1591, and 1592.

75. Deliberazioni, 1917, 1574–92; 2216, 1593–1611; 2227, 1611–1631; Ser Mariano filled positions in 1584, 1588, 1589, 1590, 1596, 1598, 1609, 1611, 1612, and 1623; Maestro Giovanbattista held office in 1601, 1603, 1604, 1605, 1607, 1615, 1616, 1617, 1618, 1619 twice, 1622, 1623, 1626, and 1628.

76. BCP, SPD 1501, 277, fols. 173v–74v.

77. BCP, SPD 1594, 273, fol. 68r.

78. BCP, SPD 1501, 277, fol. 149r.

79. Marrara, *Riseduti e nobiltà*, 88–92.

80. BCP, SPD 1594, 273, fols. 30r, 32v, 33v.

81. Ibid., fol. 62v.

82. Mannucci, "Descrizione," 135.

83. By 1566, Ser Mariotto was Torello Manfidi's son-in-law. ASF, Decima Granducale, 6851, "Estimo di Poppi Dentro del 1566," fol. 107r (hereafter cited as "ASF, DG, 6851, EPD 1566").

84. Deliberazioni, 2216, February 3, 1597.

85. Ibid., 1593–1611; 2227, 1611–31; 2763, 1631–45.

86. ASF, NA, F406, G. Folli, 1549–1569; NM, 40, G. Folli, 1569–1573.

87. ASF, NM, 1186, P. Catani, fols. 27r–29r. At Pescia, too, economic and professional success on the part of new families facilitated matrimonial ties with the city's patrician families; see Brown, *In the Shadow of Florence*, 190–91.

88. ASF, NM, 14530, B. Passeri, 30r–32r.

89. Ibid., 5993, M. Catani, fols. 77v–80r.

90. Deliberazioni, 1917, 1574–92.

91. Between 1584 and 1618 Girolamo filled two positions as standard-bearer, six as select prior, and two as general prior. Deliberazioni, 1917, 1574–92; 2216, 1593–1611; 2227, 1611–31.

Chapter 3 Dynamics of Power and Authority

1. Chittolini, "Ricerche sull'ordinamento territoriale," 292–352 (see pt. 1, n. 1); Fasano Guarini, "Gli statuti delle città soggette," 69–124 (see intro., n. 2); idem, "Potere centrale e comunità soggette," 490–538 (see intro., n. 10).

2. Chittolini, "Ricerche sull'ordinamento territoriale," 309–11.

3. On the paternalistic idea embodied by Cosimo, see A. M. Brown, "The Humanist Portrait of Cosimo de' Medici, 'Pater Patriae,' " *Journal of the Warburg and Courtauld Institutes* 24 (1961): 186–221.

4. SCS, 643, SCP, fol. 2r. James Grubb (*Firstborn of Venice*, 25–27 [see intro., n. 10]) has underlined a similar attitude of Vicentines toward Venice.

5. SCS, 643, SCP, fol. 2r.

6. Deliberazioni, 609, 1448–56; 608, 1474–81.

7. For Pistoia, see Connell, "Clientelismo e stato territoriale," 523–43 (see intro., n. 10). For similar interaction between Vicentines and Venice, see Grubb, *Firstborn of Venice*, 26–27.

8. Deliberazioni, 608, 1474–81, fols. 163v, 169v.

9. Ibid., fol. 199r.

10. BCP, SPD 1501, 277, fol. 53r; Chittolini, "Ricerche sull'ordinamento territoriale," 306–7.

11. Gai, *Centro e periferia*, 9–16 (see intro., n. 13).

12. BCP, SPD 1501, 277, fols. 12r, 14v.

13. Fasano Guarini, "Gli statuti delle città soggette," 102–3.

14. BCP, SPD 1501, 277, fols. 56v–57r.

15. Ibid., fols. 75v–76r, 85v.

16. Ibid., fols. 88r, 93r.

17. Ibid., fols. 99r, 112v–13r, 125r–v.

18. Ibid., fols. 90r, 93r–v.

19. Ibid., fol. 89v.

20. Ibid., fol. 93r.

21. Ibid., fol. 96r.

22. Ibid., fols. 124v–25r.

23. Ibid., fol. 126v.

24. Ibid., fols. 126v–27r. On the level of autonomy the Florentine government left to provincial communities, see Fasano Guarini, "Gli statuti delle città soggette," 81.

25. By the 1530s, however, most of these reforms were revoked, to be reestablished under the rule of Duke Cosimo. Fasano Guarini, "Potere cen-

trale e comunità soggette," 513; idem, "Gli statuti delle città soggette," 102−3; Connell, "Clientelismo e stato territoriale," 523−43.

26. Deliberazioni, 2271, 1511−26, fols. 2r, 9v, 23v, 46r, 53r, 73v, 235v; 2217, 1526−39, fols. 270r, 275v; 738, 1539−56, fol. 178r.

27. Ibid., 2762, 1507−11, fols. 10v−11v; 2271, 1511−26, fols. 56r, 132r−v, 163v, 230r, 237v; 2217, 1526−39, fols. 17r, 37v−38r, 62v, 84v. Between 1507 and 1530 the community made loans to private individuals for 5,056 lire.

28. Ibid., 2271, 1511−26, fol. 131v; 2217, 1526−39, fols. 7v, 9v, 18r, 62v, 63r−v, 93r; 738, 1539−56, fol. 213v.

29. Ibid., 2271, 1511−26, fols. 214v, 222v, 225v, 246v; 2217, 1526−39, fols. 3v, 22r−23v, 33v, 44r, 55v, 76v, 77v.

30. Fasano Guarini, "Gli statuti delle città soggette," 96, 109−16; Litchfield, *Emergence of a Bureaucracy*, 111 (see intro., n. 11).

31. Fasano Guarini, *Lo stato mediceo*, 50−53 (see intro., n. 2), and "Potere centrale e comunità soggette," 490−538.

32. Fasano Guarini, *Lo stato mediceo*, 54.

33. Fasano Guarini, "Potere centrale e comunità soggette," 514−15.

34. Fasano Guarini, *Lo stato mediceo*, 51−54.

35. In 1548, sixteen captains and podestà were nominated directly by the grand duke. In 1595, another ten were added to this number. Fasano Guarini, *Lo stato mediceo*, 40, and "Gli statuti delle città soggette," 108−9.

36. Fasano Guarini, "Considerazioni su giustizia, stato e società," 149−152 (see intro., n. 2); Litchfield, *Emergence of a Bureaucracy*, 118−20.

37. For example, Arezzo revised its statutes in 1565 and 1580. Pistoia had three statutory revisions, and numerous new drafts were made in smaller towns such as Cortona (1543), San Miniato (1546), Anghiari (1550), Empoli (1560), Montepulciano (1561), Borgo San Sepolcro (1571), and Caprese (1573). Fasano Guarini, "Gli statuti delle città soggette," 117−19; idem, *Lo stato mediceo*, 54−55; idem, "Città soggette e contadi nel dominio fiorentino tra Quattro e Cinquecento: Il caso pisano," in *Ricerche di storia moderna*, ed. M. Mirri (Pisa, 1976), 1:1−94.

38. Fasano Guarini ("Gli statuti delle città soggette," 107) underlines the example of Pistoia, where, in 1545, the Pratica Segreta supervised local administration while the local ruling families retained the management of external appearances connected with office holding.

39. Guasti and Gherardi, *I capitoli del comune di Firenze*, 599−600 (see chap. 1, n. 5).

40. BCP, "Capitoli," 274, fol. 39r. G. F. Pagnini del Ventura, *Della decima e di varie altre gravezze imposte dal commune di Firenze: Della moneta e della mercatura dei fiorentini fino al secolo XVI* (Lisbon, 1765−66), 76−77; Fasano Guarini, *Lo stato mediceo*, 15−17; E. Conti, *I catasti agrari della repubblica fiorentina* (Rome, 1966), 4, 77−78.

41. BCP, "Capitoli," 274, fol. 9r; BCP, SPD 1501, 277, fol. 101v. See also Brown, *In the Shadow of Florence*, 17 (see intro., n. 12).

42. Until the 1550s, the extension of the exemption on direct taxation was reconfirmed every twenty-five years; after this date, every five years. Deliberazioni, 608, 1474–81, fol. 54r; 2762, 1507–11, fol. 34r; BCP, SPD 1594, 273, fols. 105r–6r; "Capitoli," 274, 35–44; ASF, Senato de' 48, 10, fol. 84r; Guasti and Gherardi, *I capitoli del comune di Firenze*, 599.

43. BCP, "Capitoli," 274, 14–15; BCP, SPD 1594, 273, fol. 104v; Deliberazioni, 609, 1448–56, fol. 43r. The podesteria paid for the court of the vicar 500 lire every six months, of which Poppi paid the highest part, at 187 lire.

44. BCP, "Capitoli," 274, fols. 43r–48r. During the second half of the sixteenth century, the ruling families in Pisa also regained some former privileges; see Fasano Guarini, "Città soggette e contadi," 91–93, and Connell, "Clientelismo e stato territoriale," 523–43.

45. BCP, SPD 1501, 277, fol. 162r.

46. Ibid., fols. 173v–74v.

47. Ibid., fols. 6v–7r, 90r, 99r; SPD 1594, 273, fols. 105r–6r.

48. According to Litchfield (*Emergence of a Bureaucracy*, 114–17), the Medici elaborated special arrangements indicating a policy of privilege mostly toward the larger cities of the Florentine district.

49. Fasano Guarini, "Considerazioni su giustizia, stato e società," 135; Litchfield, *Emergence of a Bureaucracy*, 132.

50. The characteristics of the new princely state have been emphasized by Anzilotti, *La costituzione interna dello stato fiorentino* (see intro., n. 6); Marrara, *Studi giuridici sulla Toscana medicea* (see intro. n. 7); D'Addario, *La formazione dello stato moderno*, 193–245 (see intro., n. 2); Diaz, *Il granducato di Toscana*, 85–109 (see intro., n. 2); and Fasano Guarini, *Lo stato mediceo*; "Gli statuti delle città soggette," 101–24; and "Considerazioni su giustizia, stato e società," 135–68. The artistic representation of the new princely court has been analyzed by E. Borsook, "Art and Politics at the Medici Court: The Funeral of Cosimo I de' Medici," *Mitteilungen des Kunsthistorischen Institutes in Florenz* 12 (1965): 31–54.

51. On the issue of objectivity of the Medici policy toward their subjects, see Fasano Guarini, "Potere centrale e comunità soggette," 520, and "Considerazioni su giustizia, stato e società," 135–36; Diaz, *Il granducato di Toscana*, 206.

52. Litchfield, *Emergence of a Bureaucracy*, 135.

53. See Chapter 8.

54. Connell, "Clientelismo e stato territoriale," 523–43.

55. Fasano Guarini, *Lo stato mediceo*, 54–55. In the Venetian state, a larger sphere of autonomy was granted to subject cities; see Grubb, *Firstborn of Venice*, 63–66.

56. BCP, SPD 1594, 273, fols. 3r–v.

57. BCP, SPD 1501, 277, fol. 21v.

58. Ibid.

59. BCP, SPD 1594, 273, fol. 21v–22r. The chancellor and the operai were garbed like the select priors. Prescribed dress for the councilors was a simple black mantle and black hat; the *donzello* wore a green hat.

60. BCP, SPD 1594, 273, fol. 30v; Angiolini, "Il ceto dominante a Prato," 358 (see intro., n. 13). Litchfield (*Emergence of a Bureaucracy*, 151) wrote that also for Florentine new patricians, "the bureaucracy provided a means of social ascent and development of a type of *noblesse the robe.*"

61. BCP, SPD 1594, 273, fol. 30v.

62. Ibid., fol. 33v.

63. BCP, SPD 1501, 277, fol. 22r.

64. Angiolini, "Il ceto dominante a Prato," 377; Fasano Guarini, "Principe ed oligarchie," 107–9 (see intro., n. 10).

65. BCP, SPD 1501, 277, fol. 162r.

66. Ibid., fols. 164v–67v.

67. Ibid., fols. 168r, 170v. This is a reform of 1569. In 1572 the Florentine magistrates specified that the rule could not be applied in case of public or private debt involving the city of Florence and its citizens.

68. BCP, SPD 1594, 273, fols. 31v, 33v.

69. Ibid., fol. 33v; SPD 1501, 277, fol. 183v. In 1639, immunity from debt was also extended to the councilors.

70. ASF, Senato, 10, fols. 84r–v. This privilege had been granted in 1532 and reconfirmed in 1570. In Pisa, also, local officers managed the funds of charitable and religious institutions. Later in the sixteenth century, however, the offices of *governatore*, operaio, and *provveditore* of the Opere e Luoghi Pii were assigned directly by the grand duke. Similarly in Prato and Montevarchi, these officers were appointed by the central government. Calvani, Falaschi, and Matteoli, "Ricerche sulle magistrature," 86; Fasano Guarini, "Le istituzioni," in *Livorno e Pisa* (see intro., n. 13), 32, and "Potere centrale e comunità soggette," 513; Stumpo, "Le forme del governo cittadino," 290–91 (see intro., n. 14).

71. BCP, SPD 1501, 277, fols. 132v–33r, 153r.

72. Deliberazioni, 2271, 1511–26, fol. 232r; BCP, "Ricordi e memorie antiche del Monastero della Santissima Annunziata di Poppi, 1563–1661," 493, fols. 1r–5r.

73. Lapini, "Istoria," fol. 32v; Lapini, "Relazione della peste," fol. 31v.

74. AVP, "Ragioni e saldi dell'eredità di Vincenzo Amerighi, medico fisico," 1500.

75. For a general discussion on patronage as a political system in early modern Tuscany, see D. Kent, *The Rise of the Medici: Faction in Florence, 1426–1434* (Oxford, 1978); idem, "The Dynamics of Power in Cosimo de' Medici's Florence," in *Patronage, Art, and Society in Renaissance Italy*, ed.

F. W. Kent and P. Simons (Oxford, 1987), 63−77; A. Molho, "Il patronato a Firenze nella storiografia anglofona," *Ricerche storiche* 1 (1985): 5−16; S. Bertelli, "Potere e mediazione," *Archivio storico italiano* 527 (1986): 5−15; C. Klapisch-Zuber, "Parenti amici e vicini: Il territorio urbano di una famiglia mercantile nel XV secolo," *Quaderni storici* 33 (1976): 953−82; and Connell, "Clientelismo e stato territoriale," 523−43; see also S. Silverman, "Patronage as Myth," in *Patrons and Clients in Mediterranean Societies*, ed. E. Gellner and J. Waterbury (London, 1977), 7−19, and R. Weissman, "Taking Patronage Seriously," in Kent and Simons, *Patronage, Art, and Society*, 25−45.

76. In Poppi, as in Venice but unlike in Florence and Genoa, patronage had a municipal power base. For Venice, see D. Romano, *Patricians and Popolani: The Social Foundations of the Venetian Renaissance State* (Baltimore, 1987), 119−40; for Genoa, see J. Heers, *Family Clans in the Middle Ages* (New York, 1977).

77. BCP, SPD 1594, 273, fols. 37v, 43v, 44r, 67v.

78. Ibid., fols. 38r, 41r. There were three hospitals: one inside the town walls within the enclosure of Santa Maria della Misericordia and two outside the walls, the hospital of Santa Maria di Roviesine and that of San Lazzaro.

79. Ibid., fols. 40v−41v. The operai received no salary except those of the hospital, who were given one pound of pepper and two capons annually.

80. Ibid., fol. 45r.

81. Ibid., fols. 47r−v.

82. Ibid., fol. 47v.

83. Ibid.

84. Ibid.

85. Ibid., fols. 33v, 37v, 41v, 43v, 44r.

86. In particular, see Stumpo, "Le forme del governo cittadino," 286, and Fasano Guarini, "Gli statuti delle città soggette," 107.

87. On the concept of "patrimonialism," see Weber, *Theory of Social and Economic Organization*, 346−54 (see intro., n. 3). Litchfield (*Emergence of a Bureaucracy*, 157−58) noticed that although the ducal administration did not reach the extreme of France, where office was acquired by inheritance and sale, it nonetheless revealed characteristics of a patrimonial system in line with northern European monarchies.

Part II The Emergence of Local Elite Families

1. Angiolini ("Il ceto dominante a Prato," 380−90, 396−98 [see intro., n. 13]) has also stressed the lack of career advancement in the Medicean state bureaucracy. However, he sees this decline as the reason for both the migration of several of the Pratese elite and the entrance of many of these into ecclesiastical careers.

2. Litchfield, *Emergence of a Bureaucracy*, 158–66 (see intro., n. 11).

3. ASF, NA, L 93–97: 1485–1528, Giovanni Lapucci; NA, L 86: 1493–1522, Agnolo Lapucci; Deliberazioni, 2762, 1507–11, fols. 9r, 22v; 2217, 1526–39, fol. 23r.

4. BCP, "Ricordi domestici e cittadini della famiglia Lapucci (1560–1700)," 315 (hereafter cited as "'Ricordi, Lapucci'"); ASF, DG, 6851, EPD 1566; 6852, EPD 1588.

5. Deliberazioni, 609, 1448–56; 1608, 1474–81; 2762, 1507–11; 2217, 1526–39; 738, 1539–56.

6. Ibid., 1917, 1574–92; 2216, 1593–1611; 2227, 1611–31; 2763, 1631–45.

7. "Ricordi, Lapucci," fol. 3r; BCP, "Compendio o sommario di tutte le cose notabili attinenti alla nostra Badia di San Fedele," 120, fol. 35r.

8. BCP, SPD 1594, 273, fol. 44r.

Chapter 4   The Wool Industry and Its Crisis

1. On the economic instability of Europe during the decades at the end of the sixteenth century and the beginning of the seventeenth, see T. Aston, ed., *Crisis in Europe, 1560–1660* (London, 1965); G. Parker and L. M. Smith, eds., *The General Crisis of the Seventeenth Century* (London, 1978); and P. Clark, ed. *The European Crisis of the 1590s* (London, 1985).

2. See Diaz, *Il granducato di Toscana*, 342–45 (see intro., n. 2); G. Parenti, *Prime ricerche sulla rivoluzione dei prezzi a Firenze* (Florence, 1939); R. Romano, "Agricoltura e contadini nell'Italia del XV–XVI secolo," in *Tra due crisi*, 51–54 (see intro., n. 4); idem, "L'Italia nella crisi del XVII secolo," in *Tra due crisi*, 187–206; idem, "La storia economica: Dal secolo XIV al Settecento," in *Storia d'Italia*, vol. 2, *Dalla caduta dell'impero romano al secolo XVIII* (Turin, 1974), 1813–1931; M. Aymard, "La transizione dal feudalesimo al capitalismo," in *Storia d'Italia*, Annali I: *Dal feudalesimo al capitalismo* (Turin, 1978), 1131–1192; A. Ventura, "Considerazioni sull'agricoltura veneta e sull'accumulazione originaria del capitale nei secoli XVI e XVII," *Studi storici* 3–4 (1968): 674–722; and E. J. Hobsbawm, "The Crisis of the Seventeenth Century," in Aston, *Crisis in Europe*, 5–58.

3. D. Sella, *Crisis and Continuity: The Economy of Spanish Lombardy in the Seventeenth Century* (Cambridge, Mass., 1979); R. Rapp, *Industry and Economic Decline in Seventeenth-Century Venice* (Cambridge, Mass., 1976); Borelli, *Un patriziato della terraferma veneta* (see intro., n. 13); P. Malanima, *La decadenza di un'economia cittadina: L'industria di Firenze nei secoli XVI–XVIII* (Bologna, 1982); J. Brown, "The Economic 'Decline' of Tuscany: The Role of the Rural Economy," in *Florence and Milan*, 101–15 (see chap. 1, n. 37).

4. Lapini, "Istoria," fol. 41r; Deliberazioni, 738, 1539–56, fol. 56v.

5. Mannucci, "Descrizione," 110.

6. ASF, DG, 6852, EPD 1588, "Botteghe," fols. 2r, 3v.

7. Mannucci, "Descrizione," 112.

8. ASF, DG, 6852, EPD 1588, "Botteghe," fol. 2r; Mannucci, "Descrizione," 110.

9. It was a distance of about three hundred meters. Lapini, "Istoria," fol. 39v.

10. Ibid.

11. R. Goldthwaite (*Wealth and the Demand for Art in Italy, 1300–1600* [Baltimore, 1993], 190–92) traced the development of private palaces in Florence from the beginning of Cosimo's rule in the 1430s and in Venice from the closure of the nobility in the fourteenth century. He emphasized that the timing for the development of domestic architecture varied according to specific local contexts.

12. Lapini, "Istoria," fol. 39v; ACA, "Estimo di Poppi Dentro del 1612," fol. 143r (hereafter cited as "ACA, EPD 1612"). On the increasing tendency of urban elites to avoid craft and trade activities, see C. Donati, *L'idea di nobiltà in Italia, secoli XIV–XVIII* (Bari, 1988), 279–84.

13. Lapini, "Istoria," fol. 39v; ASF, NM, 1186, P. Catani, fols. 46v–48v.

14. Mannucci, "Descrizione," 112; Lapini, "Istoria," fol. 39r.

15. Lapini, "Istoria," fols. 39v, 40v.

16. Lapini, "Relazione della peste," fol. 22r.

17. Ibid.; ASF, NM, 5994, M. Catani, fols. 127r–28v.

18. Lapini, "Istoria," fol. 41r; ASF, DG, 6852, EPD 1588, "Botteghe," fol. 3v.

19. Lapini, "Istoria," fols. 40v–41r.

20. Ibid., fol. 39v.

21. Ibid.

22. Deliberazioni, 2216, 1593–1611, May 1599, 97v; ASF, DG, 6852, EPD 1588, "Botteghe," fol. 2r.

23. ACA, EPD 1612, fol. 146r.

24. I have not found any notarial acts in his name and therefore do not know if he ever practiced in the profession. Lapini, "Istoria," fols. 40r–v; Mannucci, "Descrizione," 137; ASF, NM, 10586, S. Mannucci, 116r–17v.

25. ASF, NM, 10586, S. Mannucci, Testament 1632, fols. 116r–17r; Mannucci, "Descrizione," 137; Lapini, "Istoria," fol. 87v.

26. Lapini, "Istoria," fol. 41r.

27. ASF, NM, 5994, M. Catani, fols. 127r–28v.

28. Lapini, "Istoria," fol. 41r.

29. ASF, DG, 6852, EPD 1588, "Botteghe," fol. 3v.

30. Lapini, "Relazione della peste," fol. 22r.

31. Goldthwaite, *Wealth and the Demand for Art in Italy*, 183–255.

32. ASF, DG, 6852, EPD 1588, "Botteghe," fol. 1r.

33. Ibid., fols. 1r–21v; ACA, EPD 1612. Data concerning variations in the number of shops are taken from annotations written at a later date in the margins of the original list of 1590 and in Deliberazioni, 2216, 1593–1611, fols. 41r–v, 97v, 137r.

34. For the activity of the leather industry in the fourteenth and fifteenth centuries, see F. Melis, "Momenti dell'economia del Casentino nei secoli XIV e XV," in *Catalogo della mostra su armi antiche (secoli XIV–XV)* (Poppi, 1967).

35. For a reference to dye works and tanning in town, see BCP, SPD 1501, 277, fol. 160r.

36. Brown, *In the Shadow of Florence*, 106–7 (see intro., n. 12).

37. Possibly some of the shops generically described as "shops," particularly those already rented out in 1590, were, at least formerly, involved in some phase of wool production.

38. ASF, Conventi Soppressi, 224, 89, fol. 13r.

39. Lapini, "Istoria," fol. 12v; Lapini, "Relazione della peste," fols. 13r–v.

40. Malanima, *La decadenza di un'economia cittadina*, 289–305; C. M. Cipolla, "The Decline of Italy: The Case of a Fully Matured Economy," *Economic History Review* 5 (1952): 178–87.

41. Judith Brown ("Economic 'Decline' of Tuscany," 111–12) has also observed how the Florentine guilds through protectionist measures limited rural production during the sixteenth century. See also P. Malanima, "Le attività industriali," in Fasano Guarini, *Prato*, 218–19 (see intro., n. 12).

42. L. Cantini, *Legislazione toscana raccolta ed illustrata* (Florence, 1800–1808), 93.

43. ASF, Arte della Lana, 15, fols. 54r–55v. Other outlying towns in the countryside and district of Florence enjoyed similar privileges; see Atzori and Regoli, "Due comuni rurali," 104–5 (see intro., n. 14).

44. ASF, Arte della Lana, 15, fols. 12r–v.

45. Ibid., fols. 54r–55r. In Prato, too, as in other cities under Florentine domination, the wool industry was characterized by the production of low-grade textiles destined for local markets. Malanima, "Le attività industriali," 225–27, and *La decadenza di un'economia cittadina*, 49, 59–60, 89.

46. ASF, Arte della Lana, 15, fol. 4r.

47. Ibid., fol. 79v. The Prato and Impruneta fairs absorbed the greater part of the cloth produced throughout the state; Malanima, "Le attività industriali," 226, and *La decadenza di un'economia cittadina*, 59.

48. ASF, Arte della Lana, 15, fols. 79r–81r; Malanima, "Le attività industriali," 226–27.

49. The industry of Prato, unlike that in other minor towns of the territory, was the object of privileged treatment. For example, in 1586 the central government allowed Prato producers to increase the value of the wool they

produced from three lire ten soldi *a braccio* to four lire ten soldi *a braccio* and to sell it freely throughout the regional markets. In 1562 a similar request came from Empoli. Malanima, "Le attività industriali," 226–27.

50. ASF, Arte della Lana, 15, fols. 58r–v. Counterfeiting was carried on in other towns; see, for example, for Montopoli in the vicariate of San Miniato, Atzori and Regoli, "Due comuni rurali," 106.

51. ASF, Arte della Lana, 15, fols. 59r–v, 60r–v, 92r–93r; proclamations concerning this procedure were repeated in 1604 and 1618, indicating that cases of counterfeit continued to occur. The same order was issued to the producers of Montopoli; Atzori and Regoli, "Due comuni rurali," 105–6.

52. BCP, "Capitoli," 274, fol. 40r.

53. According to Malanima (*La decadenza di un'economia cittadina*, 154), the collapse of the Florentine wool industry at the end of the sixteenth century and the beginning of the seventeenth was due principally to the high cost of labor and of raw materials.

54. ASF, Arte della Lana, 15, fols. 131, 62v–63v.

55. ASF, Pratica Segreta, 178, fols. 224r–29v.

56. R. Romano, "Produzione di beni non agricoli in Italia tra Medioevo e Rinascimento," in *Tra due crisi*, 82–83. For the relationship between the agricultural and industrial sectors, see E. Labrousse, *Esquisse du mouvement des prix et des revenues en France au XVIIIe siecle* (Paris, 1933).

57. Romano, "L'Italia nella crisi del XVII secolo," 189; Del Panta, *Una traccia di storia demografica*, 34–38 (see chap. 1, n. 8).

58. As throughout Italy, the agricultural crisis preceded the industrial; Romano, "L'Italia nella crisi del XVII secolo," 191–204.

59. BCP, SPD 1501, 277, fols. 88r–v.

60. Deliberazioni, 2217, 1526–39, fols. 76v–77v; BCP, SPD 1594, 273, fol. 5v. Between 1522 and 1528 Tuscany, like the rest of Italy, was beset by a series of famines and epidemics including plague. Without ever having disappeared altogether, contagious disease broke out again in August 1530 and reached its peak in the spring of the following year; see A. Corradi, *Annali delle epidemie occorse in Italia dalle prime memorie fino al 1850* (1865–94; Bologna, 1974), 1:391–460.

61. Deliberazioni, 2217, 1526–39, fols. 8v–9r, 11r.

62. As a result of the widespread famine of 1539–40 and that of 1554, made more acute by the upheavals caused by the war against Siena, Cosimo I was forced to import grain from Naples and Sicily to provide for the large number of poor in the state. Even in years of normal grain harvests, Tuscany was not self-sufficient, and the situation became extremely serious in times of famine. B. Licata, "Grano e carestie in Toscana ai tempi di Ferdinando I dei Medici," in Spini, *Architettura e politica*, 336 (see intro., n. 14).

63. The Magistrato dell'Abbondanza had the task of controlling the production and commerce of cereals in the state and, in case of famine, of sup-

plying the capital's storehouses with imported grain. From the time of Cosimo I, Tuscany consumed more grain than it could produce, owing to population growth coupled with numerous famines and bad harvests in 1537, 1554, 1579–80, 1590–91, and the first decades of the seventeenth century; see Diaz, *Il granducato di Toscana,* 131, and Licata, "Grano e carestie in Toscana," 330–419.

64. Deliberazioni, 2217, 1526–39, fol. 193r.

65. Ibid., 738, 1539–56, fols. 9v, 10r–v, 13v.

66. Ibid., fols. 30r, 57v, 63v, 144r, 160v, 189v.

67. Ibid., fols. 56r, 160r; the Lapucci, Lapini, Grifoni, and Battistoni, among others, were listed as lenders.

68. Romano, "Agricoltura e contadini nell'Italia," 51–68; N. S. Davidson, "Northern Italy in the 1590s," in Clark, *European Crisis of the 1590s,* 157–76.

69. The famine of 1590–91 was widespread and touched all the Mediterranean area. Diaz, *Il granducato di Toscana,* 327–34.

70. Prices began to rise at the midpoint and peaked at the end of the sixteenth century. Licata, "Grano e carestie in Toscana," 337–38; G. Parenti, "Prezzi e salari a Firenze dal 1520 al 1620," in *I prezzi in Europa dal XIII secolo a oggi,* ed. R. Romano (Turin, 1967), 210.

71. Licata, "Grano e carestie in Toscana," 336, 343–44.

72. Proclamations aimed at regulating the sale of cereals had been issued by Cosimo I since the middle of the sixteenth century. Diaz, *Il granducato di Toscana,* 130–32; Licata, "Grano e carestie in Toscana," 345.

73. The other areas were the Mugello Valley, the mountains of Pistoia, the lower Valdarno, Campiglia, and the Maremma di Volterra. Licata, "Grano e carestie in Toscana," 346–48.

74. Ibid., 357.

75. Ibid., 368.

76. Ibid., 349, 350–51.

77. BCP, SPD 1594, 273, fols. 49r–v.

78. AVP, Deliberazioni e Partiti, Podesteria di Poppi, 504 (hereafter cited as "Deliberazioni, 504, PP"), 1598–1632, fols. 74v, 76v; Cherubini, "La 'civiltà' del castagno in Italia," 247–80 (see chap. 1, n. 28).

79. Deliberazioni, 504, PP, 1598–1632, fols. 74v, 76v, 77r; Davidson, "Northern Italy in the 1590s," 157–76.

80. On the economic crisis of the 1620s, see R. Romano, "Tra XVI e XVII secolo: Una crisi economica, 1619–1622," *Rivista storica italiana* 74 (1962): 480–531, and F. Braudel, *The Mediterranean and the Mediterranean World in the Age of Philip II* (London, 1973). For a recent review of the literature on the relative decline of Italian cities, see J. Brown, "Prosperity and Hard Times in Renaissance Italy?" *Renaissance Quarterly* 42 (1989): 761–80, in particular 774–80.

81. In 1625 the local government had not yet succeeded in repaying the debt, nor, for that matter, had the majority of communities in the dominion; failures to repay the debt were reported in Deliberazioni, 504, PP, 1598–1632, July 1622, July 1623, December 1624, September 1625; ASF, Pratica Segreta, 174, fol. 1r.

82. ASF, Pratica Segreta, 174, fol. 1v.

83. Ibid., fol. 1r.

84. Ibid., fol. 1v.

85. On the plague, see C. M. Cipolla, *Fighting the Plague in Seventeenth-Century Italy* (Madison, Wis., 1981); P. Preto, *Epidemia, paura e politica nell'Italia moderna* (Bari, 1987); and L. Del Panta, *Le epidemie nella storia demografica italiana, secoli XIV–XIX* (Turin, 1980).

86. Corradi, *Annali delle epidemie*, 2:61. For studies on the regional impact of the plague, see R. Galluzzi, *Istoria del granducato di Toscana sotto il governo della casa Medici* (Florence, 1781), 3:450–51; C. M. Cipolla, *Cristofano e la peste: Un caso di storia del sistema sanitario in Toscana nell'età di Galileo* (Bologna, 1976), 7–14; and idem, *Chi ruppe i rastrelli a Monte Lupo?* (Bologna, 1977). On Venice, see P. Preto, *Peste e società a Venezia, 1576* (Vicenza, 1978).

87. Del Panta, *Le epidemie*, 158–62.

88. On the organization of health measures taken in time of plague, see C. M. Cipolla, *Public Health and Medical Profession in the Renaissance* (New York, 1976); idem, *Cristofano e la peste*; idem, *Chi ruppe i rastrelli a Monte Lupo?*; and idem, *I pidocchi e il granduca: Crisi economica e problemi sanitari nella Firenze del '600* (Bologna, 1979).

89. BCP, "Vacchetta dei casi del colera a Poppi, 1631–1633," 239, fols. 2r–6v (hereafter cited as "'Vacchetta'"). In July the elected officials were Feliciano Sociani, Alamanno Soldani, Giovanfrancesco Rilli, Jacopo Crudeli, Lodovico Lapucci, Bartolomeo Martini, Scipione Mannucci, and Bartolomeo Sociani.

90. Ibid., fol. 39r.

91. One of the first communities to be hit by the plague was Corsignano in the commune of Poppi Fuora; see ibid., fols. 7r–9r.

92. Ibid., fols. 9r–10r.

93. Ibid., fols. 9r–11v; L. A. Muratori, *Del governo della peste e delle maniere di guardarsene* (Turin, 1721), 8; Cipolla, *Cristofano e la peste*, 20–23, 83, 95, and *Chi ruppe i rastrelli a Monte Lupo?*, 23–24.

94. "Vacchetta," fol. 12r.

95. Ibid., fol. 14r; the school was closed on June 2.

96. Ibid., fol. 18r. The plague was transmitted by rats carrying fleas. According to Del Panta (*Le epidemie*, 37, 78–79), cases of entire families being stricken were common in that the presence of even one infected person could indicate a sizable number of infected rats within the house itself. Not

all those bitten died; the mortality rate of bubonic plague was between 60 and 85 percent.

97. "Vacchetta," fol. 35r.

98. Ibid. In contemporary chronicles, the *lazaretti* are described as lacking in hygiene and as being "rotten and miserable ghettos." Lapini, "Relazione della peste," fol. 9v; Muratori, *Del governo*, 22; Cipolla, *Cristofano e la peste*, 16–19.

99. Bubonic plague spread mainly during the hot and humid summer months. On the seasonal pattern of the plague, see Del Panta, *Le epidemie*, 48–54.

100. "Vacchetta," fols. 50v, 55v; on September 15 one of the three undertakers was let go, even though suspicion of contagion continued until the end of December.

101. Ibid., fol. 53r.

102. Ibid., fols. 54r–56v.

103. Del Panta, *Le epidemie*, 158–63; Brown, *In the Shadow of Florence*, 56–57.

104. "Vacchetta," fols. 55v–56r.

105. On the social impact of the plague, see Corradi, *Annali delle epidemie*, 119–20; Cipolla, *Cristofano e la peste*, 81–82; F. Braudel, *Capitalismo e civiltà materiale (secoli XV–XVIII)* (Turin, 1977), 53–54; and Del Panta, *Le epidemie*, 84–85.

106. "Vacchetta," fol. 10r.

107. Ibid., fols. 12r–27r.

108. These were the Cascesi, Niccoletti, Catani, Pauolozzi, Fatucchi, Rastrellini, and Fontanini families.

109. These were the Battistoni and Beccai families.

110. In Tuscany, one of the last serious epidemics was that of typhoid fever in 1648–49. For example, Antonio Grifoni and his son, Lorenzo, died of typhoid fever in 1648. BCP, "Acquisti di terre e ricordi della famiglia Grifoni, 1553–1648," 410, fol. 89r (hereafter cited as "'Acquisti di terre' "); Del Panta, *Le epidemie*, 163–66.

111. These were the Rilli, Soldani, Martini, Sociani, Tommasini, Crudeli, Mannucci, and Buonfanti from Poppi; the Baldacci and Folli transferred to town toward the middle of the sixteenth century.

Chapter 5 Bureaucrats and Notaries

1. Fasano Guarini, *Lo stato mediceo*, 43 (see intro., n. 2); Brown, *In the Shadow of Florence*, 178–82 (see intro., n. 12); Litchfield, *Emergence of a Bureaucracy*, 151 (see intro., n. 11); Angiolini, "Il ceto dominante a Prato," 343–427 (see intro., n. 13); Angiolini and Malanima, "Problemi di mobilità sociale a Firenze," 17–47 (see intro., n. 15).

2. According to Elena Fasano Guarini (*Lo stato mediceo*, 43), throughout the sixteenth century, Tuscan notaries "were leading figures who, in the exercise of both public and private functions, found the means of social advancement." Judith Brown (*In the Shadow of Florence*, 178–82) also remarked that thanks to their training in the law and the notarial arts as well as practice in the local administration, Pesciatine elite families "found themselves thrust into prominent positions in the Grand Duchy of Tuscany."

3. In Prato, too, the doctorate was considered important. In fact, between 1543 and 1765, 218 Pratesi graduated from Pisa; see Angiolini, "Il ceto dominante a Prato," 391–92; for Pescia, see Brown, *In the Shadow of Florence*, 178–79.

4. When Count Fabrizio Rilli died in 1825, he donated the family library, comprising about nine thousand volumes and two hundred manuscripts, to Poppi, declaring his intention "of procuring a source of culture, of civility and of education to residents of the town"; see A. Brezzi, *La biblioteca "Rilliana" di Poppi: Passato e presente di una biblioteca* (Poppi, 1985), 11–13. For private legacies to young Pratesi, see Angiolini, "Il ceto dominante a Prato," 393–95.

5. Deliberazioni, 609, 1448–56, fol. 3v; BCP, SPD 1501, 277, fol. 90r.

6. BCP, SPD 1594, 273, fol. 79v.

7. Lapini, "Istoria," fol. 33r.

8. BCP, SPD 1501, 277, fol. 91r. In 1572, representatives of the rural communes had no say in the drafting of the reform of the podesteria statutes. This was written by only one person, Piero Mariani, a notary from Poppi. BCP, SPP 1572, 121, fol. 2r.

9. BCP, SPD 1594, 273, fol. 46r; Lapini, "Relazione della peste," fol. 31r.

10. On the important role of notaries, see Martines, *Lawyers and Statecraft* (see intro., n. 16).

11. Litchfield, *Emergence of a Bureaucracy*, 110–25; Ago, *Carriere e clientele* (see intro., n. 13); V. I. Comparato, *Uffici e società a Napoli (1600–1647)* (Florence, 1974).

12. The increase occurred among the lesser officials, such as notaries, chancellors, and minor judges who accompanied the vicars, podestà, and captains as staff in the provincial towns. In 1736, according to Litchfield (*Emergence of a Bureaucracy*, 123), the relationship between population and civil servants was one bureaucrat for each 450 inhabitants. See also Fasano Guarini, *Lo stato mediceo*, 83–113.

13. Litchfield, *Emergence of a Bureaucracy*, 150.

14. For Prato, see Angiolini, "Il ceto dominante a Prato," 385–88; for Pescia, see Brown, *In the Shadow of Florence*, 178–80.

15. Mannucci, "Descrizione," 105.

16. Deliberazioni, 609, 1448–56. I have not traced Ser Francesco's no-

tarial acts. However, both the title of "ser" and the position of chancellor, which he held without interruption from May 1455 until March 1457, attest to his profession of notary. ASF, NA, L 93–97, L 86.

17. Deliberazioni, 2762, 1507–11, fol. 22v; ASF, DG, 6851, EPD 1566; ASF, NM, 5967, M. Catani, fol. 57r. In February 1508, the council listed Ser Giovanni as "notary from Poppi residing in Florence." Ties with the town remained close, since at the middle of the sixteenth century Ser Giovanni's son still possessed land at Poppi and, later, a granddaughter of his married Giuseppe Rastrellini of Poppi.

18. ASF, NA, L 86; Deliberazioni, 2762, 1507–11, fols. 9r, 22r. Ser Agnolo was active as a notary from 1493 until 1522 and has left seven volumes of acts attesting to this activity. Between 1512 and 1519 Ser Agnolo was prior three times and standard-bearer twice in the local government. However, it is probable that Ser Agnolo also occupied posts in the state bureaucracy from time to time. In fact, in November 1507, as in February 1508, the minutes of the town council list him as *"assente"* and *"in officio."* See Chapter 7 for a picture of the Lapucci's economic situation.

19. Deliberazioni, 738, 1539–56, fol. 177r. The magistracy of the Otto di Guardia e Balia was in charge of keeping public order and had jurisdiction over criminal justice; see Litchfield, *Emergence of a Bureaucracy,* 68; on the Otto di Guardia, see Brackett, *Criminal Justice and Crime* (see chap. 1, n. 51).

20. Deliberazioni, 738, 1539–56, fols. 74r, 89v, 149v; 2227, 1611–31, fol. 23r. Again at the beginning of 1544, in August 1545, and in January 1550, Ser Francesco was listed by the council as *"assente"* and *"in officio."*

21. The other son of Giovanbattista was Vincenzo, who did not follow a professional career.

22. ASF, Nove Conservatori, 3350, Suppliche, fol. 656r.

23. Ibid.

24. Ser Francesco's register of notarial acts consists of only two written pages. The remainder of the book is blank. The few notarial acts registered date from the last month of 1580 to the first of 1581. ASF, NM, 6213, 1580–81.

25. ASF, DG, 6852, EPD 1588; 6873, "Estimo di Poppi Fuora del 1590" (hereafter cited as "ASF, DG, 6873, EPF 1590"); 6857, "Estimo di Fronzola del 1592–93" (hereafter cited as "ASF, DG, 6857, EF 1592–93"); AVP, "Estimo di Ragginopoli del 1598," 1421 (hereafter cited as "AVP, ER 1598, 1421").

26. Deliberazioni, 2227, 1611–31.

27. ASP, Università, Seconda Serie D, II, 4, "Dottorati 1610–1635," fol. 11r.

28. Mannucci, "Descrizione," 52, 105.

29. AVP, "Estimo di Poppi Fuora del 1616," 1298, fols. 371r–72v.

30. J. Brown, "The Patriciate of Pescia in the Fifteenth Century," in *I ceti dirigenti nella Toscana del Quattrocento* (Firenze, 1987), 279–87.

31. In Florence, during the seventeenth century, the number of lawyers remained stationary, and the number of degrees in the legal profession granted by Tuscan universities declined; see Litchfield, *Emergence of a Bureaucracy*, 159, 164.

32. ASF, Bandi e Ordini, Appendice, 37, fol. 100r.

33. Ibid., fols. 70v, 100r.

34. Brown, "Patriciate of Pescia," 279–87.

35. Brown, *In the Shadow of Florence*, 180–81.

36. Angiolini, "Il ceto dominante a Prato," 387.

37. In the seventeenth century, the honor of Florentine citizenship and the title of nobility were conferred upon the Rilli. By then, however, the family was residing in Florence, even though it retained closed ties with Poppi.

38. Litchfield, *Emergence of a Bureaucracy*, 190–200. For trends of salaries in the Milanese state, see Chabod, "Usi e abusi nell'amministrazione dello stato di Milano a mezzo il '500," in *Studi in onore di Giuseppe Volpe* (Florence, 1958), 95–191.

39. In Florence, from the 1430s notaries were not allowed to participate in the *signoria*; see Martines, *Lawyers and Statecraft*, 49–51. On the changing status of notaries in the sixteenth and seventeenth centuries, see Litchfield, *Emergence of a Bureaucracy*, 147, 158–66.

40. Martines, *Lawyers and Statecraft*, 34.

41. Ibid., 34–40.

42. Litchfield, *Emergence of a Bureaucracy*, 164–66.

43. Ibid., 77–83, 91–92.

44. Ibid., 165–66.

45. Deliberazioni, 2227, 1611–31; 2763, 1631–45; 2842, 1646–56.

46. ASF, NM, 20727–32.

47. Deliberazioni, 2842, 1646–56; ASF, Tratte, 608, 1642–54, fols. 207v, 208v, 209r; Tratte, 609, 1654–64; Tratte, 610, 1664–74, fol. 194r.

48. In 1472 Lorenzo il Magnifico declared the University of Pisa, founded in 1338, the new center of education for young Florentines. In 1543, after years of stagnation, the university was reopened by Cosimo de' Medici, who made it the grand duchy's official university. In fact, for young Tuscans desiring state recognition of their diplomas, study at the University of Pisa was obligatory. D. Marrara, *L'Università di Pisa come università statale nel granducato mediceo* (Milan, 1965).

49. Litchfield, *Emergence of a Bureaucracy*, 166.

50. AVP, "Ragioni," 1500; ASP, Università, Seconda Serie D, II, 4, "Dottorati," 1610–1635; Serie D, II, 5, "Dottorati," 1636–1682. I have not been able to locate any names from Poppi in the lists of those who graduated from Pisa prior to the seventeenth century.

51. Franco Angiolini ("Il ceto dominante a Prato," 380–90, 396–98) has also stressed the lack of career advancement in the Medicean state bureaucracy. He sees this decline as the reason for both the migration of several of the Pratese elite and the entrance of many of these into ecclesiastical careers.

52. In 1570 the wool beater's shop was mentioned by Pierantonio in his "Ricordi." By 1590 the shop was rented. "Ricordi, Lapucci," fol. 3r; AVP, "Estimo di Poppi Dentro del 1590," V 24, fol. 73r (hereafter cited as "AVP, EPD 1590, V 24").

53. On the declining participation of patricians in the peripheral bureaucracy of the state, see Litchfield, *Emergence of a Bureaucracy*, 146.

54. Mannucci, "Descrizione," 135; ASF, NM, 19238–39, F. Baldacci, 1664–1701.

55. ASF, Tratte, 610, 1664–74, fols. 203r–6r; Tratte, 611, 1674–84, fols. 205r–10v; Tratte, 612, 1684–93, fols. 180v–83r; Tratte, 613, 1693–1701, fols. 182r–84r.

56. Federigo filled four posts as standard-bearer and three as prior. Deliberazioni, 739, 1668–90; 712, 1690–1714; ASF, Tratte, 613, 1693–1701, fols. 182r–84r.

57. Deliberazioni, 2763, 1631–45, fol. 177r. For similar behaviors among the Pratese elite, see Angiolini, "Il ceto dominante a Prato," 378.

58. G. Chittolini, "L'onore dell'ufficiale," in *Florence and Milan*, 101–33 (see chap. 1, n. 37).

59. Elena Fasano Guarini ("Principe ed oligarchie," 123–26 [see intro., n. 10]) has emphasized the need to analyze the formation of regional elites by placing them within the context of the state. However, she has also stressed the importance of professional careers in the state bureaucracy and the departure from the local world as the necessary prerequisites for the "gradual expansion, beyond the urban confines, of regional areas in which some members of the local elite could find new possibilities. The decline of the communes' oligarchies gives rise to a regional ruling class."

60. ASF, Mediceo del Principato, v 2332, "Ruolo delle Bande del Duca di Firenze estratto da tutte le bande de' soldati, 1547," fol. 272r. Between 1530 and 1556, Raffaello was prior eight times and standard-bearer three times. Deliberazioni, 2217, 1526–39; 738, 1539–56.

61. Mannucci, "Descrizione," 100. Mannucci wrote that Annibale went to Rome *"con gli affitti et arte del campo."* Rome represented the destination preferred even by young Pratese in search of fortune, particularly in ecclesiastical careers. According to Angiolini, the reason for this choice was in the limited possibility of reaching the summit of public office in Tuscany, reserved as this was only to Florentine citizens or others upon whom citizenship had been conferred; see Angiolini, "Il ceto dominante a Prato," 380–90, 396–98.

62. Mannucci, "Descrizione," 99.

63. Ibid., 99-100, 137; Deliberazioni, 2216, 1593-1611, fol. 121v; 2842, August 1, 1655.

64. ASF, Decima Granducale, 6860, "Estimo di Fronzola del 1709" (hereafter cited as "ASF, DG, 6860, EF 1709"); Decima Granducale, 6867-68, "Estimo di Ragginopoli del 1714" (hereafter cited as "ASF, DG, 6867-68, ER 1714"); Decima Granducale, 6874-75, "Estimo di Poppi Fuora del 1715" (hereafter cited as "ASF, DG, 6874-75, EPF 1715"); ACA, EPD 1701, fol. 453r.

65. Antonio was first a lecturer at Pisa and then a lawyer in Florence; Annibale, also a lawyer, chose to reside in Rome; Giovanbattista, doctor of theology, was canon of San Lorenzo at Rome; Filippo was *ministro di deposteria* and gentleman-in-waiting of Cosimo III; and Jacopo, lawyer and lecturer at Florence, married the Florentine patrician Caterina, daughter of Averano Simonetti and Aldobrandina Uguccioni. There were similar cases in Prato. See Angiolini, "Il ceto dominante a Prato," 390.

66. ACA, EPD 1701, fol. 453r; Litchfield lists the Rilli-Orsini among the new patricians appearing in Florence after 1530 and awarded a title of nobility in the eighteenth century. In fact, Jacopo's two sons were a count and a knight. Toward the middle of the eighteenth century, both were still listed in Poppi's estimi as property owners; Litchfield, *Emergence of a Bureaucracy*, 379.

Chapter 6 Strategies of Matrimony

1. On the importance of marriage alliances to preserve status and wealth in Italy, see L. Fabbri, *Alleanza matrimoniale e patriziato nella Firenze del '400: Studio sulla famiglia Strozzi* (Florence, 1991); R. B. Litchfield, "Demographic Characteristics of Florentine Patrician Families, Sixteenth to Nineteenth Centuries," *Journal of Economic History* 29 (1969): 191-205; R. Merzario, *Il paese stretto: Strategie matrimoniali nella diocesi di Cuomo, secoli XVI-XVII* (Turin, 1981); G. Motta, *Strategie familiari e alleanze matrimoniali in Sicilia nell'età della transizione, secoli XVI-XVII* (Florence, 1983); T. Astarita, *The Continuity of Feudal Power: The Caracciolo of Brienza in Spanish Naples* (Cambridge, England, 1992); and D. Zanetti, *La demografia del patriziato milanese* (Pavia, 1972); in Europe, see P. Bourdieu, "Marriage Strategies as Strategies of Social Reproduction," in *Family and Society*, ed. R. Forster and O. Ranum (Baltimore, 1976), 117-44. For a later period, see R. Forster, *Merchants, Landlords, Magistrates: The Dupont Family in Eighteenth-Century France* (Baltimore, 1980).

2. Herlihy and Klapisch-Zuber, *Tuscans and Their Families* (see intro., n. 21); D. Herlihy, "Mapping Households in Medieval Italy," *Catholic Historical Review* 58 (1972): 1-24; J. Kirshner and A. Molho, "The Dowry Fund and the Marriage Market in Early Quattrocento Florence," *Journal of Modern*

History 50 (1978): 403–19; Brown, *In the Shadow of Florence,* 32–44 (see intro., n. 12); J. Hajnal, "European Marriage Patterns in Perspective," in Glass and Eversley, *Population in History,* 101–43 (see chap. 1, n. 9).

3. In 1547 Romana di Francesco Sociani married Torello Lapucci, bringing him a dowry of 380 scudi. Of Torello's second marriage to Caterina Gaetani, mention is made in Pierantonio Lapucci's memoirs. ASF, NA, C 285, P. Catani, fol. 48v.

4. "Ricordi, Lapucci," fol. 15v.

5. Deliberazioni, 738, 1539–56, fol. 177r.

6. "Ricordi, Lapucci," fol. 15v.

7. ASF, NM, 10827, Bernardo Lapini, fol. 15r.

8. ASF, NA, M 249, Ser Vectorio di Biagio di Matteo Martini, 1497–1518; M 231, Ser Biagio di Agniolo di Ser Vectorio Martini, 1547–1570.

9. In the early years of the sixteenth century, Ser Vectorio Martini was often absent *"in ufficio"* and therefore unable to occupy certain civic positions for which his name had been drawn. Deliberazioni, 2762, February 1508, May 1510.

10. ASF, NM, 1186, P. Catani, fols. 37r–42r.

11. "Ricordi, Lapucci," fols. 1v, 5v–6r.

12. See Chapter 7.

13. "Ricordi, Lapucci," fol. 5v.

14. Ibid., fol. 6v.

15. Raul Merzario (*Il paese stretto,* 19–20) in his work on the diocese of Cuomo has also underlined the large number of marriages between fourth-degree relatives. As an explanation, he cites both economic considerations and a desire to consolidate family interconnections that were dying out.

16. "Ricordi, Lapucci," fol. 6v–8r.

17. Ibid., fol. 13v–15r.

18. Mannucci, "Descrizione," 112.

19. Ibid., 110; Lapini, "Istoria," fols. 39r–v.

20. ASF, NM, 1186, P. Catani, Testament 1584, fols. 46v–48v.

21. ASF, NA, C 285, P. Catani, fols. 9r, 97r; ASF, NM, 5992, M. Catani, fols. 104v–9v.

22. ASF, NM, 5992, M. Catani, 104v–9v. Ser Santi was a notary from 1563 to 1593. Their only son, Jacopo, died prematurely in 1597 without issue. ASF, NA, B 2737, S. Buondi, 1563–68; ASF, NM, 4527–29, S. Buondi, 1572–93; "Ricordi, Lapucci," fol. 18r.

23. ASF, NM, 1186, P. Catani, fols. 66r–68r; 14530, B. Passeri, fols. 33r–34v; Marietta was wedded to Egidio di Bernardino Rilli and Leonida to Francesco di Domenico Lapini.

24. Ibid., 11178, G. Chimentelli, fols. 5r–6r.

25. Mannucci, "Descrizione," 110; ASF, NM, 1186, P. Catani, 1591, fols. 37r–42r; 11178, G. Chimentelli, fols. 5r–6r; ASF, Mediceo del Principato, f 2334, fols. 630r–31r.

26. Litchfield, "Demographic Characteristics," 197–98; for a similar pattern of endogamy together with a limitation of the number of marriages, see S. Cohn and O. Di Simplicio, "Alcuni aspetti della politica matrimoniale della nobiltà senese, 1560–1700 circa," in *Forme e tecniche del potere nella città* , 314 (see intro., n. 10).

27. In Pescia, too, the first regional matrimonial exchanges involved local men and women from other towns, whereas daughters of Pescia's nobility continued to marry local men. As in Poppi, financial considerations were the basis of endogamous marriage for Pescia's women. Brown, *In the Shadow of Florence,* 187–88.

28. Throughout the modern era the general population trend was that of a greater number of women than men. D. E. C. Eversley, "Population, Economy, and Society," in Glass and Eversley, *Population in History,* 39; S. Peller, "Birth and Death among Europe's Ruling Families since 1500," in Glass and Eversley, *Population in History,* 94.

29. "Ricordi, Lapucci," fol. 10v.

30. Ibid., fols. 13v–14r.

31. Ibid., fol. 13r.

32. Ibid., fol. 15r. This is not the first case in which a portion of the dowry was paid in land. This is in contrast with the Florentine custom, whereby a woman never received real estate from her family. C. Klapisch-Zuber, "The Griselda Complex: Dowry and Marriage Gifts in the Quattrocento," in *Women, Family, and Ritual* (see intro., n. 21), 213–24.

33. On the phenomenon of preferential patterns in matrimonial exchanges and on the cyclical movement of dowries, see Motta, *Strategie familiari;* G. Delille, "Classi sociali e scambi matrimoniali nel salernitano," *Quaderni storici* 33 (1976): 983–97; idem, *Famiglia e proprietà nel regno di Napoli* (Turin, 1988); and Merzario, *Il paese stretto,* 64–84.

34. On the rise in the real value of dowries among Italian elites between the sixteenth and the seventeenth centuries, see Litchfield, "Demographic Characteristics," 203, and *Emergence of a Bureaucracy,* 43; R. Malanima, *I Riccardi di Firenze: Una famiglia e un patrimonio nella Toscana dei Medici* (Florence, 1977), 92; and Brown, *In the Shadow of Florence,* 42 n. Diane Hughes ("From Brideprice to Dowry in Mediterranean Europe," *Journal of Family History* 3 [1978]: 262–96) revised the notion that laws of "supply and demand" were the sole considerations behind the increase of dowries. Rather, the increase of dowries was connected to the women's possibility of inheriting the paternal estate. The evidence collected in my documents confirms the observation by Diane Hughes. See section IV in this chapter and Chapter 9.

35. "Ricordi, Lapucci," fol. 20v.

36. ASF, NM, 5967, M. Catani, fol. 81v; 5994, M. Catani, fols. 11v–14r; 10586, S. Mannucci, fols. 81r–v; "Ricordi, Lapucci," fol. 20v; Lapini, "Istoria," fol. 48r; AVP, EPD 1590, V 24, fols. 164r–v.

37. "Ricordi, Lapucci," fols. 22v, 31v, 32v; ASF, NM, 10586, S. Mannucci, fols. 86v–87v. Lucrezia and Torello had at least two sons, Pierantonio, who died at birth in 1620, and another Pierantonio, born in 1621, who died in infancy. AVA, Battesimi San Marco, 87, 1600–1660.

38. ASF, NM, 5994, M. Catani, fols. 11v–14v.

39. "Ricordi, Lapucci," fols. 32v, 33r.

40. Ibid., fol. 26r.

41. Ibid., fol. 29r; ASF, NM, 10586, S. Mannucci, fols. 111v–12r; 5992, M. Catani, fols. 104v–9v.

42. ASF, NM, 19170, G. Barboni, fols. 16r–17r; "Ricordi, Lapucci," fols. 28r–v, 39r.

43. We have little information about the Dombosi family and know only that by 1627 a sister, Orsina, was married to Domenico Folli, a druggist from Poppi, and that Maestro Francesco died of plague in Poppi in 1631. ASF, NM, 19170, G. Barboni, Testament 1669, fols. 16r–17r; "Ricordi, Lapucci," fols. 28r–v, 32r–v.

44. AVA, Battesimi San Marco, 87, 1600–1660.

45. ASF, NM, 10829, B. Lapini, Testament 1625, fols. 43r–44r.

46. AVA, Matrimoni San Marco, 87, February 11, 1618, fol. 4r; ASF, NM, 10829, B. Lapini, fols. 49r–50r.

47. "Ricordi, Lapucci," fols. 26r–v. From 1630 on we have no record of this branch of the Martini, who, at least in the male line, probably died out during the plague. Vectorio and Giovanbiagio di Octavio were the last to hold local office, Vectorio as standard-bearer in August 1630 and Giovanbiagio as general prior in August 1631. Deliberazioni, 2227, 1611–31.

48. Anthony Molho ("'Tamquam vere mortua': Le professioni religiose femminili nella Firenze del tardo Medioevo," Società e storia 43 [1989]: 1–44), using evidence from the Monte delle Doti of Florence, observed a marked increase of young girls entering the convent during the 1530s. For sixteenth- and seventeenth-century Florentine patricians, see Litchfield, "Demographic Characteristics," 203. For the Veneto, see J. C. Davis, The Decline of the Venetian Nobility as a Ruling Class (Baltimore, 1962).

49. "Ricordi, Lapucci," fols. 19r–20r, 23r.

50. Molho, "'Tamquam vere mortua,'" 15–17.

51. "Ricordi, Lapucci," fols. 22r–v. Merzario, too, emphasizes the excessive importance that has customarily been attributed to paternal authority in the matter of matrimonial choice. Instead, he proposes "the hypothesis of the existence of a matrimonial system based on values which transcend individuals but in which they can identify themselves because they represent the common denominator of social relationships" (Il paese stretto, 5).

52. "Ricordi, Lapucci," fols. 19v–20r, 23r.

53. Ibid., fol. 19v.

54. Brown, In the Shadow of Florence, 37–38.

55. This position contrasts with that presented by D. Herlihy ("Some Psychological and Social Roots of Violence in the Tuscan Cities," in *Violence and Civil Disorder in Italian Cities, 1200–1500*, ed. L. Martines [Berkeley, 1972], 129–54) on fifteenth-century Tuscany. According to Herlihy, the decline of marriageable men and the increase in dowries led a number of women to marry below their social scale.

56. "Vacchetta." On the demographic crisis of noble European and Italian families, see Litchfield, "Demographic Characteristics," 191–205; Cohn and Di Simplicio, "Alcuni aspetti," 315, 321–24; Davis, *Decline of the Venetian Nobility*, 137; and Angiolini, "Il ceto dominante a Prato," 366 (see intro., n. 13). For England, see L. Stone, *The Crisis of the Aristocracy* (Oxford, 1965).

57. Mannucci, "Descrizione," 110; ASF, NM, 10586, S. Mannucci, Testament 1632, fols. 116r–17v; Lapini, "Istoria," fols. 40r–v.

58. ASF, NM, 10586, S. Mannucci, Testament 1630, fols. 94r–95r.

59. Dianora Ulivi had brought her husband's family a dowry of almost one thousand scudi and, later, an estate in Romagna. ASF, NM, 5994, M. Catani, Testament 1613, fols. 127r–28r; Lapini, "Istoria," fol. 41r; "Vacchetta," fol. 42r.

60. ASF, NM, 5994, M. Catani, Testament 1613, fols. 127r–28r.

61. The other half went to her sister, Ginevra, wife of Torello Crudeli; "Acquisti di terre," fol. 63v.

62. "Vacchetta," fol. 42r; Lapini, "Relazione della peste," fol. 22r.

63. Niccolò had at least ten children, six daughters and four sons. ASF, NM, 15822, Filippo Barboni, fols. 9r–10r; AVA, Battesimi San Marco, 87, 1570–1782.

64. AVA, Matrimoni San Marco, 87, 1614–1720, April 25, 1633, February 5, 1646. Agnoletta and Pietro Scorsoni resided in Poppi, where their children were born. AVA, Battesimi San Marco, 87, 1634.

65. This phenomenon has been observed for Tuscan elites by Brown, *In the Shadow of Florence*, 40–41; R. Goldthwaite, *Private Wealth in Renaissance Florence: A Study of Four Families* (Princeton, 1968), 171–72; and D. Kent, *Household and Lineage in Renaissance Florence: The Family Life of the Capponi, Ginori, and Rucellai* (Princeton, 1977), 136–40.

66. "Ricordi, Lapucci," fols. 3r, 6r. For about five years, until 1574, Pierantonio Lapucci, his wife, Antonia, children, mother, and mother-in-law lived under the same roof. In fifteenth-century Florence, as in Prato and Pistoia, the cohabitation of a husband's and wife's families was an exceptional situation; see C. Klapisch-Zuber, "Demographic Decline and Household Structure: The Example of Prato, Late Fourteenth to Late Fifteenth Centuries," in *Women, Family, and Ritual* (see intro., n. 21), 31–32, and also Kent, *Household and Lineage*, 35.

67. "Ricordi, Lapucci," fols. 2v–3r.

68. Ibid.

69. Ibid., fols. 21v–22r. In Renaissance Florence, too, brothers were obliged to provide support and a dowry for their sisters should their father die. Kent, *Household and Lineage*, 30.

70. Kent, *Household and Lineage*, 135–37; Goldthwaite, *Private Wealth*, 271–72; Brown, *In the Shadow of Florence*, 41. For Siena, see Cohn and Di Simplicio, "Alcuni aspetti," 324.

71. In Poppi, a widow with minor children was assured the usufruct of all her husband's possessions and the right to administer them. Therefore, a widow who chose not to remarry continued to live independently with her children in her husband's home. Upon reaching maturity, the children had to guarantee their mother an income and allow her, should she so desire, separate rooms in the house. Often when there were no children, the widow returned to her father's home. Also in Renaissance Florence an upper-class widow was assured an income if she agreed to leave her dowry with her husband's family. Nevertheless, unlike in Poppi, the fifteenth-century Florentine widow had less independence from both her husband's family and her father's; see C. Klapisch-Zuber, "The 'Cruel Mother': Maternity, Widowhood, and Dowry in Florence in the Fourteenth and Fifteenth Centuries," in *Women, Family, and Ritual*, 121–22. For seventeenth-century Florence, see G. Calvi, *Il contratto morale: Madri e figli nella Toscana moderna* (Bari, 1994).

72. Upon her husband's death, Caterina Gaetani decided to return to Florence, probably to live with her brother, Luigi. Caterina and Luigi exploited Torello's estate without paying much attention to the administration of the land. In fact, when both died of plague in 1631, Lodovico, Pierantonio's grandson and Torello's heir, complained bitterly of the damage that the Gaetani's indifference had caused the livestock, lumber, and borders of his uncle's farms. "Ricordi, Lapucci," fols. 33r–v.

73. Ibid., fol. 15v; ASF, NM, 5992, M. Catani, fols. 104v–9v.

74. ASF, NM, 10586, S. Mannucci, fols. 86r–87r.

75. Kent (*Household and Lineage*, 146) has found one instance, in 1488, when Adovardo di Carlo Bencivenni's only daughter was preferred over distant relatives in the agnatic group. According to Klapisch-Zuber ("Griselda Complex," 216), a Florentine woman, at most, upon the death of her brothers and nephews, could inherit one-fourth of the estate; the remainder went to the agnatic group. See also Brown, *In the Shadow of Florence*, 37, and S. Cohn, *Death and Property in Siena, 1205–1800* (Baltimore, 1988).

More recently J. Kirshner ("Materials for a Gilded Cage: Non-Dotal Assets in Florence, 1300–1500," in *The Family in Italy from Antiquity to the Present*, ed. D. I. Kertzer and R. P. Saller [New Haven, 1991], 201–7), on the basis of A. Wrigley's and J. Goody's findings that 20 percent of the European population had only daughters and no sons, has pointed out that Florentine women inherited their families' property when no male heirs survived; what varied, however, were the legal rights allowed to married daughters over their families' patrimonial property. T. Kuehn ("Some Ambiguities of Female Inheritance Ideology in the Renaissance," in *Law, Family, and Women: Towards a Legal Anthropology of Renaissance Italy* [Chicago, 1991], 238–57) has further emphasized the need to take into consideration the varieties of negotiations involved in women's rights to inheritance. For a discussion on the broader implications of women inheriting their families' patrimony, see S. Chojnacki, "Patrician Women in Early Renaissance Venice," *Studies in the Renaissance* 21 (1974): 176–203, and J. Goody, "Inheritance, Property, and Women: Some Comparative Considerations," in Goody, Thirsk, and Thompson, *Family and Inheritance*, 10–36 (see intro., n. 21); for eighteenth-century England, see E. P. Thompson, "The Grid of Inheritance: A Comment," in Goody, Thirsk, and Thompson, *Family and Inheritance*, 328–60. See also A. Wrigley, "Fertility Strategies for the Individual and the Group," in *Historical Studies of Changing Fertility*, ed. C. Tilly (Princeton, 1978), 135–54.

76. Brown, *In the Shadow of Florence*, 37–38, 41–42, 190–91; Angiolini, "Il ceto dominante a Prato," 366. For the fifteenth century, see Klapisch-Zuber, "'Cruel Mother,'" 117, and "The Name 'Remade': The Transmission of Given Names in Florence in the Fourteenth and Fifteenth Century," in *Women, Family, and Ritual*, 284.

77. BCP, SPD 1594, 273, fol. 69r. In Florence, father-in-law and son-in-law were never considered relatives to whom it was denied contemporary holding of public office; see Kent, *Household and Lineage*, 69, 169. See also Herlihy, "Mapping Households in Medieval Italy," 1–24.

78. On variations on the definitions of lineage and agnation, see Kuehn, "Some Ambiguities of Female Inheritance," 246–57. J. P. Cooper ("Patterns of Inheritance and Settlement by Great Landowners from the Fifteenth to the Eighteenth Centuries," in Goody, Thirsk, and Thompson, *Family and Inheritance*, 296), by studying Castillian upper-class families, noticed that if preference was given to daughters "over collateral males in inheritance," the meaning of the lineage narrowed.

79. ASF, NM, 10829, B. Lapini, Testament 1625, fol. 39r; Camilla's Testament 1636, fols. 57v–58r. Pietro Teri, father of the two sisters, was a knight of Santo Stefano from Salutio, who had married Margherita Sestini from Bibbiena, where he lived.

80. Ibid., 5994, M. Catani, fols. 82v–93r.

81. Ibid., 10586, S. Mannucci, fols. 76r–77r.

82. Ibid., 10829, B. Lapini, fols. 56v–57r; 10586, S. Mannucci, fols. 104v–5v.

83. The farms of Petra, Castelluccio, Bacciano, la Chiesina, Valdasciame, Frullame, le Casenove, and la Sova; see ibid., 15815, F. Barboni, Testament 1642, fols. 110r–11r.

Part III The Consolidation of a Regional Elite

1. See, for example, M. Barbagli's *Sotto lo stesso tetto: Mutamenti della famiglia in Italia dal XV al XX secolo* (Bologna, 1984), in which the discussion on the early modern period is limited to a few pages. The recent overview on the Italian family by Kertzer and Saller (*Family in Italy* [see chap. 6, n. 75]) continues to reflect a fundamental void for the sixteenth and seventeenth centuries. See also F. Benigno, "The Southern Italian Family in the Early Modern Period: A Discussion of Coresidential Patterns," *Continuity and Change* 4 (1989): 165–94; Delille, *Famiglia e proprietà* (see chap. 6, n. 33) and "Classi sociali e scambi matrimoniali" (see chap. 6, n. 33); O. Raggio, "La politica della parentela: Conflitti locali e commissari in Liguria orientale (secc. XVI–XVII)," *Quaderni storici* 21 (1986): 721–58; Motta, *Strategie familiari* (see chap. 6, n. 1); Merzario, *Il paese stretto* (see chap. 6, n. 1); and Calvi, *Il contratto morale* (see chap. 6, n. 71).

Chapter 7 Patterns of Landownership

1. ASF, DG, 6852, EPD 1588, fol. 159r; Deliberazioni, 608, March 28, 1477, fol. 68v.

2. BCP, SPD 1501, 277, fols. 48r–49r.

3. Deliberazioni, 2762, 1507–11, fol. 15v.

4. AVP, "Estimo di Poppi Dentro del 1517," V 22 (hereafter cited as "AVP, EPD 1517, V 22"); ASF, Decima Granducale, 6850, "Estimo di Poppi Dentro del 1535" (hereafter cited as "ASF, DG, 6850, EPD 1535"); DG, 6851, EPD 1566; 6852, EPD 1588; ACA, EPD 1612; ACA, EPD 1701.

5. BCP, SPD 1501, 277, fols. 47v–48r

6. A. Menzione, "Agricoltura e proprietà fondiaria," in Fasano Guarini, *Prato*, 134 (see intro., n. 12); E. Conti, *La formazione della struttura agraria moderna nel contado fiorentino* (Rome, 1965), vol. 3, sec. 2, 411. In Pisa property holding by Florentine patricians emerged during the second half of the sixteenth century; see P. Malanima, "La proprietà fiorentina e la diffusione della mezzadria nel contado pisano nei secoli XV e XVI," in *Contadini e proprietari nella Toscana moderna* (Florence, 1979), 1:345–76. For the fifteenth century, see G. Cherubini, "La proprietà fondiaria in Italia nei secoli XV e XVI nella storiografia italiana," *Società e storia* 1 (1978): 24.

7. Brown, *In the Shadow of Florence*, 207–10 (see intro., n. 12).

8. In 1516 Pope Leo X had allowed the taxation of ecclesiastical property acquired from that moment on. Conti, *I catasti agrari*, 170–71 (see chap. 3, n. 40).

9. ASF, Miscellanea Medicea, 224, "Censimento dello stato fiorentino del 1562," fol. 179; ASF, DG, 6851, EPD 1566.

10. BNF, EB, 15, 2, fol. 63; ACA, EPD 1612.

11. Because the population of Poppi in 1632 was smaller than it would have been in 1612 because of the plague of 1631, the reader should assume a 30 percent population decline.

12. ASF, Strozziane, I, 24, Censimento.

13. For the 1745 census, see Repetti, *Dizionario geografico*, 4:573 (see chap. 1, n. 13).

14. ACA, EPD 1701.

15. The same phenomenon of a diminished number of proprietors in respect to a demographic increase occurred in Pescia between 1427 and 1535. Brown, *In the Shadow of Florence*, 100.

16. Conti, *La formazione*, vol. 3, sec. 2, 411; Menzione, "Agricoltura e proprietà fondiaria," 134.

17. "Ricordi, Lapucci," 27; ASF, NM, 5992, M. Catani, fols. 104v–9v.

18. ASF, NM, 10586, S. Mannucci, Testament 1632, fols. 116r–171r; Mannucci, "Descrizione," 137; Lapini, "Istoria," fol. 87v.

19. On the increase of legacies to civic and religious institutions in time of plague, see Herlihy, *Medieval and Renaissance Pistoia*, 190 (see chap. 2, n. 60). See also Cohn, *Death and Property in Siena* (see chap. 6, n. 75).

20. AVP, EPD 1517, V 22; ACA, EPD 1701.

21. B. H. Sliker Van Bath, *The Agrarian History of Western Europe* (London, 1963); Brown, *In the Shadow of Florence*, 62.

22. Herlihy and Klapisch-Zuber, *Tuscans and Their Families*, 103–4 (see intro., n. 21); see also Herlihy, *Medieval and Renaissance Pistoia*, 183.

23. Conti has traced this same trend for other communes in the Florentine countryside between 1427 and 1498; see *La formazione*, vol. 3, sec. 2. For a similar trend in Pescia, see Brown, *In the Shadow of Florence*, 103.

24. C. Rotelli, *La distribuzione della proprietà terriera e delle colture a Imola nel XVII e XVIII secolo* (Milan, 1967), 39–41; F. Cazzola, *La proprietà terriera nel polesine di San Giorgio di Ferrara nel secolo XVI* (Milan, 1970), 39–41.

25. This trend has also been observed in the rest of Italy and Europe in general. For the Venetian state, see B. Pullan, *Rich and Poor in Renaissance Venice: The Social Foundations of a Catholic State* (Oxford, 1971), 159.

26. In Prato the concentration of landownership was more noticeable in the mid-fifteenth and mid-seventeenth centuries than in the Cinquecento. In the zone of Imola, concentration began in the seventeenth century, and small landowners were still the majority in the preceding century. Angiolini, "Il ceto dominante a Prato," 349 (see intro., n. 13); Rotelli, *La distribuzione della proprietà*, 28, 110–13. On land concentration in Pescia and Pistoia, see Brown, *In the Shadow of Florence*, 100–104, and Herlihy, *Medieval and Renaissance Pistoia*, 180–92.

27. B. Pullan, *Crisis and Change in the Venetian Economy in the Sixteenth and Seventeenth Centuries* (London, 1968), 16–19.

28. In the same period in Prato the number of wealthy families remained largely unvaried, and the amount of their wealth increased. Angiolini, "Il ceto dominante a Prato," 348–51.

29. Unfortunately, we have little information concerning the wool beater's (*battilana*) shop. From Pierantonio's "Ricordi" we know that the furnishings of the shop were divided between the two brothers, Pierantonio and Torello, on their father's death in 1570. The shop itself, however, was left to Pierantonio. Subsequently, in the estimo of 1588, the shop was listed as rented. "Ricordi, Lapucci," fols. 2v–3r; ASF, DG, 6852, EPD 1588, "Botteghe," fol. 5r.

30. ASF, DG, 6850, EPD 1535; AVP, "Estimo di Poppi Fuora del 1540," 1462 (hereafter cited as "AVP, EPF 1540, 1462").

31. ASF, DG, 6851, EPD 1566.

32. Ibid., 6852, EPD 1588; 6857, EF 1592–93; 6873, EPF 1590; AVP, ER 1598, 1421.

33. ASF, DG, 6850, EPD 1535.

34. At this date there is no mention of the damage, so Jacopo had either sold the land or repaired the riverbanks; see ibid., 6851, EPD 1566.

35. "Ricordi, Lapucci," fols. 2v–3r.

36. Ibid., fol. 3r.

37. ASF, DG, 6850, EPD 1535, fols. 17r–v, 29r–v; 6851, EPD 1566, fols. 90r–91v.

38. ASF, Decima Granducale, 6855, "Estimo di Fronzola del 1536 (hereafter cited as "ASF, DG, 6855, EF 1536"); 6857, EF 1592–93.

39. "Ricordi, Lapucci," fols. 5v–6r.

40. Ibid., fol. 1v.

41. Ibid., fols. 2v–3r.

42. In 1571 when the statutes of the podesteria of Poppi were revised, a special index was created for this type of agreement, whose principal purpose was to eliminate recourse to usurers. According to the terms of these pacts, the creditor had to agree to resell the land to its original owner (and his debtor) within five years for a price equal to that of the original debt. BCP, SPP 1572, 121, fols. 27v–28r; "Ricordi, Lapucci," fols. 3v–4v.

43. *Opere* were units of measurement based on the amount of time necessary to work a certain field. These were used in the case of vineyards. Elio Conti (*I catasti agrari*, 143) has calculated that sixteen *opere* were the equivalent of a vineyard of one hectare or five *staiora*.

44. "Ricordi, Lapucci," fols. 3v–4r.

45. Through a study of the 1427 *catasto*, David Herlihy and Christiane Klapisch-Zuber (*Tuscans and Their Families*, 96–97) noticed that Florentines owned almost two-thirds of the state's rural wealth. For Venetian patricians, see Pullan, *Crisis and Change*.

46. The communes constituting the podesteria of Poppi were the follow-

ing: Poppi Dentro and its surroundings, Poppi Fuora, Fronzola, Ragginopoli and Lierna, Riosecco and Lucciano, and Quota. Citizens of Poppi do not appear in the estimi of Quota and Lierna. In the communes of Riosecco and Lucciano, four families from Poppi appear in the 1529 estimo: Pauolozzi with seventeen hectares, Cascesi with ten, Rilli with eight, and Soldani with four. However, in 1547 there remained of these only the Cascesi with less than one hectare and the Soldani with a little more than one hectare. ASF, Decima Granducale, 6878 bis, "Estimo di Riosecco del 1529"; AVP, 1419, "Estimo di Quota del 1520"; 1177, "Estimo di Quota del 1554"; 921, "Estimo di Quota del 1579"; 1181, "Estimo di Quota del 1647"; 1179, "Estimo di Lierna del 1493"; 1178, "Estimo di Lierna del 1539"; 1318, "Estimo di Riosecco del 1547."

47. Fasano Guarini ("Un microcosmo in movimento," in *Prato*, 857–58) has traced the lack of an aristocratization among Prato's ruling class to the lack of domination of the latter over Prato's contado, owing in part to the prevalence of Florentine and ecclesiastical proprietors in the countryside. See also Herlihy, *Medieval and Renaissance Pistoia*, 190.

48. ASF, DG, 6855, EF 1536; 6857, EF 1592–93; 6860, EF 1709; 6861, "Estimo di Ragginopoli del 1539"; 6867–68, ER 1714; 6873, EPF 1590; 6874–75, EPF 1715; AVP, ER 1598, 1421; AVP, EPF 1540, 1462.

49. BCP, "Libro della famiglia Grifoni dal 1553 al 1817," 402, fol. 2r (hereafter cited as "'Libro, Grifoni' ").

50. Ibid., fols. 2r–v.

51. In the preceding years, Ser Raffaello had bought from Piero Fontanini other fields belonging to the farm: April 4, 1563, less than a hectare of tillable land valued at 400 lire; October 30, 1564, half of a hectare at 100 lire; November 11, 1564, 0.6 hectare of cultivated and wooded land at 150 lire; October 5, 1565, land valued at 700 lire. La Fonte farm was approximately between 12 and 14 hectares in all; see ibid., fols. 4r, 5r, 5v, 10r.

52. Ibid., fols. 1v–22v.

53. Ibid., fols. 3v, 4r.

54. Ibid., fols. 4v, 7r.

55. Ibid., fol. 13v.

56. Ibid.

57. Ibid., fol. 16v.

58. Agnolo's brother, Andrea, also became indebted to Grifoni for at least three parcels of land which he, too, was unable to repurchase; see Ibid., fols. 14r, 15v, 16r, 17v, 20v, 21v.

59. Ibid., fols. 1v–22v.

60. Ibid., fols. 40v–41r, 46r–v.

61. Ibid., fol. 28r. Licata, "Grano e carestie in Toscana," 330–419 (see chap. 4, n. 62).

62. "Libro, Grifoni," fol. 47r.

63. AVP, ER 1598, 1421.

64. Deliberazioni, 738, 1539–56.

65. The Turriani were part of the ruling families, although in this period the male line, nearing extinction, had not occupied enough public offices to be included among the leaders mentioned in Chapter 2. On the importance of the numerical composition of the patrician families of Venice, see Chojnacki, "In Search of the Venetian Patriciate," 55 (see chap. 2, n. 62).

66. On the phenomenon of concentration of the most fertile lands of the contado in the hands of the wealthiest citizens, see Herlihy, *Medieval and Renaissance Pistoia*, 190.

67. This has also been discussed for fifteenth-century Pistoia elites by Herlihy; see ibid.

68. Also for Prato, Franco Angiolini ("Il ceto dominante a Prato," 347–55) has shown a lack of correspondence between wealth and political predominance. According to Angiolini, in the case of newcomers whose fortunes were tied to an expanding textile industry and who had absorbed a large part of the landed wealth formerly belonging to Prato's old families, entry into the ranks of the leading circle was forbidden. However, unlike in Prato, in Poppi marriage into older Poppi families provided entrance into the ruling elite. On the impoverishment of the Venetian nobility between the sixteenth and the eighteenth centuries, see Davis, *Decline of the Venetian Nobility* (see chap. 6, n. 48).

Chapter 8 The Army

1. J. R. Hale, *War and Society in Renaissance Europe, 1450–1620* (Baltimore, 1986), 116–18, 130–36; see also W. Barberis, *Le armi del principe: La tradizione militare sabauda* (Turin, 1988), 171, and idem, "Continuità aristocratica e tradizione militare nel Piemonte sabaudo," *Società e storia* 4 (1981): 529–92. Only in the second half of the eighteenth century could many non-nobles be numbered in the officers corps of the Savoia in Piedmont; see S. Loriga, "L'identità militare come aspirazione sociale: Nobili di provincia e nobili di corte nel Piemonte della seconda metà del Settecento," *Quaderni storici* 74 (1990): 445. In France the army became a means to social mobility only after the French Revolution, when merit became the element for entrance into the army; see S. Finer, "State- and Nation-Building in Europe: The Role of the Military," in *The Formation of National States in Western Europe*, ed. C. Tilly (Princeton, 1975), 151.

2. R. Puddu, "Istituzioni militari, società e stato tra Medioevo e Rinascimento," *Rivista storica italiana* 87 (1975): 749–69; Finer, "State- and Nation-Building," 84–163; Hale, *War and Society*, 130–36; A. Corvisier, *Armies and Societies in Europe, 1494–1789* (Bloomington, 1979); P. Pieri, *Il Rinascimento e la crisi militare italiana* (Turin, 1952); G. Parker, *The Army*

of *Flanders and the Spanish Road, 1567–1659: The Logistics of Spanish Victory and Defeat in the Low Countries Wars* (Cambridge, England, 1972). One of the best recent books on the social history of the war is M. Gutmann, *War and Rural Life in the Early Modern Low Country* (Princeton, 1980), on the impact of war on civilians and everyday life.

3. For a brief discussion of this profession's popularity in some communities of the Tuscan state, see Atzori and Regoli, "Due comuni rurali," 137–38 (see intro., n. 14), and Angiolini, "Il ceto dominante a Prato," 387–88 (see intro., n. 13).

4. ASF, Miscellanea Medicea, 33, no. 2, fol. 2r. On the problem of brigandage in Tuscany, see A. Vanzulli, "Il banditismo," in Spini, *Architettura e politica*, 421–60 (see intro., n. 14).

5. On the political crisis of the seventeenth century, see Parker and Smith, *General Crisis* (see chap. 4, n. 1); Anderson, *Lineages of the Absolutist State* (see intro., n. 4); Beik, *Absolutism and Society* (see intro., n. 12). For a general European overview on the development of state relief systems, see B. Pullan, "The Roles of the State and the Town in the General Crisis of the 1590s," in Clark, *European Crisis of the 1590s*, 285–300 (see chap. 4, n. 1).

6. For Florence, see S. Berner, "Florentine Society in the Late Sixteenth and Early Seventeenth Centuries," *Studies in the Renaissance* 18 (1971): 203–46.

7. Fasano Guarini, "Considerazioni su giustizia, stato e società," 154–55 (see intro. n. 2).

8. On the relationship between state building and military structures, see Finer, "State- and Nation-Building," 84–163; Puddu, "Istituzioni militari, società e stato," 749–69; and Corvisier, *Armies and Societies in Europe*.

9. On the military organization of the Medicean state, see J. Ferretti, "L'organizzazione militare in Toscana durante il governo di Alessandro e Cosimo I de' Medici," *Rivista storica degli archivi toscani* 1 (1929): 248–75; 2 (1930): 58–80; F. Angiolini, "Politica, società e organizzazione militare nel principato mediceo: A proposito di una 'Memoria' di Cosimo I," *Società e storia* 31 (1986): 1–51; Marrara, *Studi giuridici sulla Toscana medicea*, 52–53 (see intro., n. 7); and Pieri, *Il Rinascimento*.

10. Ferretti, "L'organizzazione militare in Toscana," 1:251–52; 2:64–69.

11. ASF, Mediceo del Principato, f 2334, fols. 408r–9r.

12. Ibid., f 2356, I, fols. 9r–v; f 2353, III, fol. 27r.

13. Ibid., f 2334, fols. 408r–9r; f 2356, I, fols. 9r–v; f 2353, III, fol. 27r; v 2360a, fols. 194v–98r.

14. Pieri, *Il Rinascimento*, 438–40.

15. Deliberazioni, 609, 1448–56, fols. 16v–17r. For a similar behavior in Piedmont, see Barberis, "Continuità aristocratica," 558.

16. Ferretti, "L'organizzazione militare in Toscana," 1:254–56, 265–66; ASF, Consulta, 27, fols. 141r–v.

17. Ferretti, "L'organizzazione militare in Toscana," 2:74–77.

18. ASF, Mediceo del Principato, 187, "Lettera di Cosimo al Commissario Albizi, 5 aprile 1548," in Ferretti, "L'organizzazione militare in Toscana," 1:62.

19. The military units of Borgo San Sepolcro, Montepulciano, and Pontassieve were described in similar terms. ASF, Mediceo del Principato, f 2334, fols. 388v, 398r, 399r, 402r, 403v.

20. Ibid., fol. 459v.

21. Ibid., fols. 630r–31r.

22. Ibid., f 2353, III, fol. 87v.

23. In 1643, at the beginning of his career, Jacopo had been elected sergeant in the Banda del Casentino at Poppi; see ibid., 2354, fol. 128v; Mannucci, "Descrizione," 99, 100.

24. ASF, Mediceo del Principato, 2354, fol. 128v; Mannucci, "Descrizione," 99, 100.

25. J. C. Davis (Decline of the Venetian Nobility, 66–67 [see chap. 6, n. 48]) has stressed the importance of ecclesiastical careers among Venetian nobles in preserving the family patrimony.

26. ASF, Mediceo del Principato, 2354, III, fol. 37r; Lapini, "Istoria," fol. 61v. Lodovico's brother, Pierfrancesco, won an Amerighi scholarship to Pisa, graduated in theology, and in 1648 became parish priest of Fronzola. AVP, Ragioni, 1500, I, fol. 123r; II, fols. 7r, 16r, 17v, 21v, 24v, 27v; "Ricordi, Lapucci," fol. 36v.

27. AVP, "Estimo di Poppi Fuora del 1655," 1485, fol. 306r (hereafter cited as "AVP, EPF 1655, 1485").

28. Among these the Frenchman Andre Tiraqueau, who in 1566 wrote Commentarii de nobilitate et iure primogeniorum; the dialogue of Il gentilhuomo, written by the Venetian Girolamo Muzio, edited in 1564; and the Trattato della nobiltà by the Tuscan Lorenzo Ducci, edited in 1603, all cited in Marrara, Riseduti e nobiltà, 5–58 (see intro., n. 13). See also Donati, L'idea di nobiltà in Italia (see chap. 4, n. 12).

29. There was a similar trend in Siena; see Marrara, Riseduti e nobiltà, 56–58, 111–12.

30. Mannucci, Le glorie del Clusentino, 159 (see chap. 1, n. 61).

31. Lapini, "Istoria," fols. 12v–13r.

32. Deliberazioni, 609, 1448–56, fol. 31v.

33. Ibid. Carlo went to Florence as ambassador for the government of Poppi at least three times between April 1450 and May 1451; he was elected standard-bearer on September 22, 1450, and was riformatore in February 1451 and 1455.

34. ASF, NA, N 82, C. Niccoletti, 1464–1529.

35. Deliberazioni, 738, 1539–56, fol. 56v.

36. Lapini, "Istoria," fol. 42r; ASF, DG, 6852, EPD 1588.

37. Lapini, "Istoria," fol. 42r; "Ricordi domestici," fol. 49.

38. ASF, Mediceo del Principato, f 2353, III, fol. 87v; 2354, I, fol. 35v; Lapini, "Istoria," fol. 13r.

39. ASF, NM, 5994, M. Catani, Luchino Niccoletti's testament, 1607, fols. 82v–93r.

40. Lapini, "Istoria," fol. 32v.

41. According to Ferretti ("L'organizzazione militare in Toscana," 1:253; 2:65–67), the captain of the military districts were recruited locally. This is true for Poppi only after the middle of the seventeenth century.

42. ASF, Mediceo del Principato, v 2360a, fols. 194v–98r.

43. During the late seventeenth century a similar trend characterized the civic bureaucracy. Vicars were reconfirmed in their positions for up to four years. Litchfield, *Emergence of a Bureaucracy*, 117 (see intro., n. 11); Angiolini, "Il ceto dominante a Prato," 379.

44. "Ricordi domestici," fols. 19v–20r.

45. Ibid., fol. 4r; ASF, Mediceo del Principato, f 2360 a, fols. 196v–97r.

46. Deliberazioni, 739, 1668–90; 712, 1690–1714; 1122, 1733–53, fol. 191v.

47. Hale, *War and Society*, 168–70.

Chapter 9   Strategies of Patrimony

1. Mannucci, *Le glorie del Clusentino*, 158 (see chap. 1, n. 61).

2. ASF, NM, 10829, B. Lapini, fols. 51v–52v.

3. "Libro, Grifoni," fol. 26v; "Acquisti di terre," fols. 66r–84r.

4. "Ricordi domestici," fols. 11r, 52r; "Libro, Grifoni," fols. 50v, 52r; "Acquisti di terre," fol. 59v. Lisabetta Grifoni took religious orders with the name of Sour Laudamina. ASF, NM, 10586, S. Mannucci, Codicillo 1630, fols. 91r–v.

5. The plague took a heavy toll in the Grifoni family. On June 30, 1631, Antonio wrote in his account book that he was the sole survivor "of the Grifoni's *casa* together with a seven-month-old son named Lorenzo and a two-year-old daughter named Lessandra." Following the plague, Antonio was the sole remaining heir to the Grifoni fortune. "Libro, Grifoni," fol. 51r; "Acquisti di terre," fols. 87r–89r; ASF, NM, 10586, S. Mannucci, Giulio Grifoni's testament, 1631, fols. 102v–4v.

6. "Ricordi domestici," fols. 10v–11v.

7. We have no indication that the Soldani from Montevarchi and Poppi were related. In a will of 1666, Giulia's mother, Margherita Niccoletti Grifoni, left to her daughter the usufruct of a parcel of land, "for such time that she [would] not live with her husband since she was . . . separated from him with good reason and [did] not live with him." ASF, NM, 15822, F. Barboni, fols. 88v–89v.

8. "Ricordi domestici," fols. 10v–11v; Mannucci, "Descrizione," 99. Concerning emigrants who returned to their towns of origin to marry, see Merzario, *Il paese stretto*, 130 (see chap. 6, n. 1).

9. Camilla was given by her mother a dowry of fifteen hundred scudi in addition to more than one-quarter of the paternal patrimony, which amounted to four thousand scudi. The remainder, excluding the family home where the mother was living, was divided between the mother and the other two sisters. "Ricordi domestici," fols. 61v–62v.

10. ASF, NM, 15822, F. Barboni, fols. 64v–65v; 19171, G. Barboni, 46v–54r; ACA, EPD 1701, fols. 90v, 92v.

11. Angiolini, "Il ceto dominante a Prato," 401 (see intro., n. 13).

12. In Pescia, matrimonial alliances extended to a regional level from the beginning of the sixteenth century. Brown, *In the Shadow of Florence*, 187 (see intro., n. 12).

13. "Ricordi, Lapucci," fols. 41v, 43r.

14. Ibid., fols. 38v, 47r–v.

15. AVP, EPF 1655, 1485, fol. 306r; ASF, NM, 19171, G. F. Barboni, fols. 24v–25v.

16. Kent, *Household and Lineage*, 142 (see chap. 6, n. 65).

17. "Ricordi, Lapucci," fols. 48r–v. By this date, therefore, the other branch of the Lapucci was also extinct, at least in the male line. The sole survivor was, in fact, Virginia di Giovanbattista, widow of Bernardino di Stefano de Rossi.

18. Ibid., 48v–49r.

19. ASF, NM, 15822, F. Barboni, fols. 65v–67v; Tratte, 611, 1674-84; 612, 1684-93; "Ricordi, Lapucci," fols. 44r–47r.

20. Deliberazioni, 739, 1668–90; 712, 1690–1714; 1122, 1733–53; the Bassi-Lapucci family died out in the eighteenth century, and its estate was divided among the Opera degli Ospedali, Francesco Soldani, and the Berterini family, with whom the last Bassi had probably intermarried. ACA, EPD 1701, fol. 104r.

21. On the attractiveness of heiresses as marriage partners in early modern Europe, see Goody, "Inheritance, Property, and Women," 10–36 (see chap. 6, n. 75).

22. "Ricordi domestici," fols. 19v–20r. These were the professional choices undertaken at the beginning of the century, by Lorenzo's uncles on his mother's side: Giulio embarked upon an ecclesiastical career, and after having lived in Rome for some time, he returned to Poppi as prior of the parish of San Lorenzo; Filippo, who had graduated in law from Pisa, dedicated himself to his studies in Poppi. Antonio, the only one to marry and the last male descendant of the Grifoni family, became a lieutenant in the militia. Mannucci, "Descrizione," 101, 103; "Libro, Grifoni," fol. 53r; Lapini, "Relazione della peste," fol. 16r; AVP, Ragioni, 1500.

23. BCP, "Miscellanee di varie famiglie poppesi (secoli XVI–XVIII)," 409.

Margherita married Lieutenant Alessio and Lorenzo married Maddalena, both offspring of Lieutenant Francesco Maria Goretti. Angela married Doctor Cesare Goretti, son of Captain Matteo.

24. "Ricordi domestici," fol. 90r.

25. Ibid., fol. 78r; Maria Maddalena Goretti brought her husband a dowry of two thousand scudi, and an equal amount was given her brother by Margherita Ducci.

26. Ibid., fol. 43v; Pellegrina Vannucci was the daughter of Cosimo Vannucci from Arezzo and Alfonsina Lapucci from Poppi. Giuliano was the great-grandson of Jacopa Niccoletti, sister of Lorenzo Ducci's grandmother.

27. Camilla, daughter of Alamanno Soldani, Maria Maddalena's great-grandmother, was a cousin on her mother's side of Margherita Niccoletti Grifoni, Dario Ducci's great-great-grandmother.

28. AVA, Matrimoni San Marco, 87, fol. 72v. Giovanbattista Zabagli was the son of Bonifazio, brother of Teodora Zabagli, who was Jacopo Rilli's wife. BCP, "Entrate e uscite degli eredi di Jacopo Rilli, 1672," 407, fol. 3v; "Ricordi domestici," fols. 91r, 92r.

29. Klapisch-Zuber, "'Cruel Mother,'" 117–31 (see chap. 6, n. 71), "Griselda Complex," 213–24 (see chap. 6, n. 32), and "Name 'Remade,'" 283–309 (see chap. 6, n. 76).

30. See in particular the articles on reconstructing genealogies in *Quaderni storici* 86 (1994).

31. Calvi, *Il contratto morale* (see chap. 6, n. 71), and idem, "Maddalena Nerli and Cosimo Tornabuoni: A Couple's Narrative of Family History in Early Modern Florence," *Renaissance Quarterly* 45 (1992): 312–39.

32. Astarita, *Continuity of Feudal Power*, 175–201 (see chap. 6, n. 1).

33. Marietta was named sole heiress of the Battistoni patrimony with the obligation to provide her only surviving sister, Suor Deodata, with an annual income of twenty-one lire. ASF, NM, 5967, M. Catani, fol. 81v; 5994, M. Catani, fols. 11v–14r; 10586, S. Mannucci, fols. 81r–v.

34. Lapini, "Istoria," fol. 46r.

35. G. Pomata, "Legami di sangue, legami di seme: Consaguinetà e agnazione nel diritto romano," *Quaderni storici* 86 (1994): 299–334.

36. For similar cases, see Ago, *Carriere e clientele*, 37–38 (see intro., n. 13).

37. Kent, *Household and Lineage*, 36–37.

38. Klapisch-Zuber, "Name 'Remade,'" 306. On the use of given names, see also Kent, *Household and Lineage*, 36–37.

39. BCP, SPD 1594, 273, fol. 68.

40. Deliberazioni, 739, 1668–90; 712, 1690–1714.

41. On the issue of the *mundualdo* and on the lack of legal rights for a woman to act in business transactions in fifteenth-century Florence, see T. Kuehn, "'Cum Consensu Mundualdi': Legal Guardianship of Women in

Quattrocento Florence," in *Law, Family, and Women*, 212–37 (see chap. 6, n. 75).

42. ASF, NM, 19170, G. Barboni, fol. 16v; "a patto che non pigli nuova moglie ma stando vedovo." On the inversion of gender hierarchy, see N. Zemon Davis, "Women on Top," in *Society and Culture in Early Modern France* (Stanford, 1975), 124–51.

43. For similar trends among European upper classes during the seventeenth and eighteenth centuries, see J. Thirsk, "The European Debate on Customs of Inheritance, 1500–1700," in Goody, Thirsk, and Thompson, *Family and Inheritance*, 177–91 (see intro., n. 21).

44. ASF, NM, 19170, G. F. Barboni, fols. 21r–28v; 19171, G. F. Barboni, fols. 25r–v, 86v–88r.

45. "Libro, Grifoni," fols. 62r–71v.

Conclusion

1. Mannucci, *Le glorie del Clusentino*, 8–9 (see chap. 1, n. 61).

Appendix on Sources

1. For a discussion of the limits and methodological problems concerning fiscal records, see Conti, *I catasti agrari*, 8–9 (see chap. 3, n. 40), and Brown, *In the Shadow of Florence*, 205–10 (see intro. n. 12).

2. Pagnini del Ventura, *Della decima e di varie altre gravezze*, 76–77 (see chap. 3, n. 40).

3. Conti, *I catasti agrari*, 131–97. For an analysis and description of the 1427 catasto, see Herlihy and Klapisch-Zuber, *Tuscans and Their Families* (see intro., n. 21).

4. C. Rotelli, *L'economia agraria di Chieri attraverso i catasti dei secoli XIV–XVI* (Milan, 1967), and idem, *La distribuzione della proprietà*, 23–26 (see chap. 7, n. 24); Cazzola, *La proprietà terriera nel polesine di San Giorgio*, 25–28 (see chap. 7, n. 24); A. Menzione, "Storia dell'agricoltura e utilizzazione delle fonti catastali: L'estimo pisano del 1622," in Mirri, *Ricerche di storia moderna*, 125–42 (see chap. 3, n. 37).

5. BCP, SPD 1501, 277, fols. 47v–48r.

6. Rotelli, *La distribuzione della proprietà*, 21–22.

7. ASF, DG, 6852, EPD 1588.

8. See Levi, *L'eredità immateriale*, 83–121 (see intro., n. 23).

9. David Herlihy (*Medieval and Renaissance Pistoia*, 181 [see chap. 2, n. 60]) has also underlined the difficulty in tracing the exact mechanism that regulated land appraisal. See also Rotelli, *La distribuzione della proprietà*, 42.

10. Menzione, "Storia dell'agricoltura," 134–35.

11. ASF, DG, 6852, EPD 1588, fol. 159r.

Index